BACK FROM
TOBRUK

Related Titles from Potomac Books

Broadcasts from the Blitz: How Edward R. Murrow Helped Lead America into War
—Philip Seib

Beyond the Killing Fields: War Writings
—Sydney Schanberg

From Axis Victories to the Turn of the Tide: World War II, 1939–1943
—Alan Levine

BACK FROM
TOBRUK

CROSWELL BOWEN

EDITED BY
BETSY CONNOR BOWEN

Potomac Books
Washington, D.C.

Library of Congress Cataloging-in-Publication Data
Bowen, Croswell, 1905–
　　Back from Tobruk / Croswell Bowen ; edited by Betsy Connor Bowen. — 1st ed.
　　　p. cm.
　　ISBN 978-1-59797-985-6 (hardcover : alk. paper)
　　ISBN 978-1-59797-986-3 (electronic)
　　1. World War, 1939–1945—Africa, North. 2. World War, 1939–1945—Personal narratives, American. 3. American Field Service. 4. World War, 1939–1945—Medical care. I. Bowen, Betsy. II. Title.
　　D766.82.B69 2013
　　940.54753—dc23
2012031570

Printed in the United States of America on acid-free paper that meets the American National Standards Institute Z39-48 Standard.

Potomac Books
22841 Quicksilver Drive
Dulles, Virginia 20166

First Edition

10 9 8 7 6 5 4 3 2 1

To my brother,

Capt. William Dougherty Bowen, U.S. Army,

and to the memory of the men of the American Field Service

who gave their lives in North Africa and the Middle East

while helping sick and wounded soldiers

In my case, the effort of those years [in the Middle East] . . . quitted me of my English self, and let me look at the West and its conventions with new eyes: they destroyed it all for me . . . with a resultant feeling of intense loneliness in life, and a contempt, not for other men, but for all they do.

—T. E. Lawrence, *Seven Pillars of Wisdom*

CONTENTS

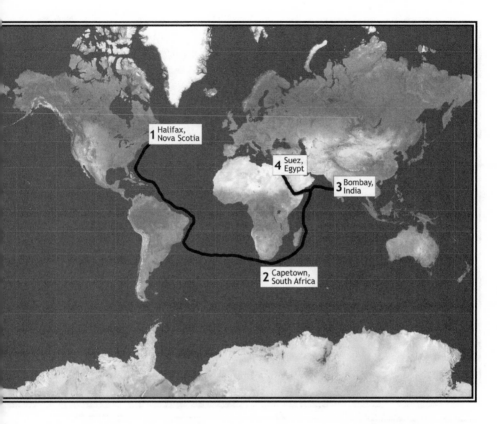

Bowen's AFS unit began its journey to the Libyan front aboard the *Warwick Castle* out of Halifax, Nova Scotia, with stays in Capetown, South Africa, and in Bombay, India, taking a zig-zag course to avoid submarine attacks, finally reaching Suez, Egypt, aboard HMS *Talma*. (Source image is from NASA's Earth Observatory "Blue Marble" series and adapted by Chad Blevins)

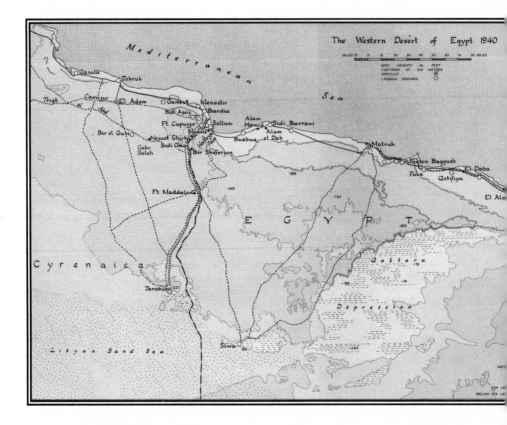

This line of coastal towns along the Mediterranean, as well as the vast inland deserts of Egypt to the east and Libya to the west, was, beginning in 1940, the site of WWII operations. Italian troops first pushed east to Sidi Barrani; then Wavell pushed west. As the war intensified, seesaw retreats and advances followed until the Allies finally accepted surrender in Tunisia in May 1943. For Bowen, many were stops along the way in June 1942 as he headed west toward Tobruk and then east toward Cairo as a medical evacuee. (Map provided by the Probert Encyclopaedia)

FOREWORD

Croswell Bowen began writing and taking photographs for *Back from Tobruk* while en route with his unit of American Field Service volunteer ambulance drivers to serve alongside the British Eighth Army in North Africa in 1941, before the United States entered the war. He finished the book in 1943 in his Manhattan apartment. Its message had taken shape not on the front lines of battle, as he had expected it might, but rather in the field dressing stations and hospital ships among the wounded and dying of "war's reverse supply lines."

The North Africa Campaign Bowen joined would be remembered as a "war without hate." Although the fighting was bitter, it was not so much so as World War II fighting would later become. There were few civilians in the Western Desert, so there were few civilian casualties. The Allies respected the German commander in chief Erwin Rommel. Rommel respected the Geneva Convention. Both sides went to the aid of each other's wounded and were evacuated side by side in the same stretcher lines, Bowen among them.

It was a strange fate for Bowen, a Catholic pacifist at heart, to enter this unique campaign. Maybe he would have reached different conclusions returning from another war, but on his voyage home, he found himself united in shared suffering even with his former battlefield enemies. He thought of the simple nobility, profound suffering, and deep humanity of the men he had encountered on his journey. He had seen the sick and wounded from all over the globe treat each other with respect and compassion. "Here, perhaps, lies the hope of the world of tomorrow," he wrote.

Steaming past the Statue of Liberty back into New York Harbor, he gave voice to his new pride in America's conceptions of freedom and respect for the dignity of man: "The enemy is in us, not in others. It is selfishness, money-lust, ignorance, unkindness and anger. . . . The answer, too, is in us. It lies in the simple truths that men of good will live by, the good that is in all of us." He concluded, "When the great leaders sit down at the peace table," they might take a lesson from those men.

The country Bowen returned to did not have peace in mind. Women were saving bacon fat in jars to create glycerin for explosives. They were saying tearful good-byes to husbands and sons. Men were coping with rationed gas and automobile tires and parting from mothers, sweethearts, and wives. Children were gathering milkweed pods for parachute silk. The airwaves were dense with patriotic speeches.

Bowen tried to get *Back from Tobruk* published. His publicist's material pictured him with a camera slung around his neck and a tin helmet on his head as if he were at that very moment under fire. The jacket copy read, "Out of the scorching hell of the Libyan desert and the fortress of Tobruk, Croswell Bowen, ace photo-reporter, brings back to the American people a magnificent eye-witness account of the savage warfare being waged across the trackless Libyan wastes for the crucial prize of Suez."

If savage warfare and trackless Libyan wastes had attracted readers, the book would not have delivered them. Bowen wanted to promote peacemaking in a country that was hungry for victory. He advocated world federation when patriotism was at a fever pitch. Despite the breadth of experience he packed into his memoir, it would go largely unread for some sixty-five years. The times were not right. The rejection letters were unequivocal. No publisher bought the book.

Bowen did succeed in publishing some of his photographs in *Look* ("War in Africa," December 1942) and *Town & Country* ("The Angel and the Rats of Tobruk," January 1943). To earn money to have his lame leg treated, he sold a piece to *Esquire*, based on his interviews with Australian field engineers on how land mines and booby traps are set. They published it as "Soldiers Learn the Hard Way" (September 13, 1943). Sequences from the memoir and more photographs appeared as "Camera Over the Desert: A Photo Report" in a small Bronxville, New York, magazine, the *Villager* (March 1944).

Nobody would have thought less of Bowen for abandoning his reporting assignments after he became a war casualty. But paradoxically, suffering the bombs of Tobruk gave him the courage to bear witness to the suffering of others. He documented the brutality of war and the resilience of the human spirit. The writing is direct, clean, and economical. It does not draw attention to itself. He simply tells you what he sees.

War was the crucible that turned Croswell Bowen into a storyteller. Perhaps that is why he never really put aside this book. In the manuscript are the penciled suggestions of a friend he'd asked to read it in the last decade of his life. He kept on thinking it could be better. He kept on wanting to get it out there. But his war book remained unpublished, growing moldy and insect-eaten in a leaky barn and the negatives stuck together by humidity.

Croswell Bowen was my father. The young journalist in these pages is unmistakably the man I knew growing up. He had a genius for listening and an effortless, abundant curiosity. Those were the gifts that made him a crackerjack reporter. Then too, as always, he was a great stretcher of limits, out there on the thin edge taunting the "stuffed shirts" and the "brass hats" who would have kept him from stepping over the line. When he sailed out of Halifax for war, he had signed on as a volunteer to document for publicity purposes the American Field Service's humanitarian operations in the Middle East and North Africa (together referred to in my father's account as simply "the Middle East"). Onto that, he had piggybacked a freelance assignment with *Collier's* to send photographs and stories from the front—real-life tales the folks back home would be hungry for. Submitting work on the same subject to two different publications simultaneously is a common survival skill in a profession not known for paying generously. But the security-minded British became suspicious of his *Collier's* assignment, suspecting that under American Field Service (AFS) cover *Collier's* was sneaking him in as a rogue player who might send back photographs and stories that had not gone through military censorship. The director of army press relations for the British told him that his photography should be confined to AFS operations.

But my father kept on going about things just as he always had, only a bit more quietly. He probably began to think of the material he would have delivered to *Collier's* as a photo-essay he would publish, along with his diary, after the war. Things worked for a while, but eventually the impulse to throw himself at a story got the better of him. He interviewed a group of escaped prisoners from Crete before military intelligence reached them. His protestations that, even if he had sent back the story, no self-respecting newspaper at home would publish it probably fell on deaf ears. He had even aroused the concern of his commanding officer, who suggested he take a desk job in Cairo.

By then, though, seriously shaken by the direct bombing of his encampment and hobbling about on a leg weakened for unknown reasons, he had begun to question his own commitment to taking pictures when men's lives were at stake. As a Catholic he could not ignore the commandment "Thou shalt not kill." That is why he had joined the non-combatant American Field Service in the first place. But were his pictures really helping his country? In what would be the last few days of his work in the Western Desert, under orders from his commanding officer, my father took photographs of American Field Service operations near Tobruk. He climbed a structure to shoot the loading of troops onto the hospital ship *Londonhovery Castle* in Tobruk Harbor from above, but fell on his weak leg. "My Rolleiflex was not hurt," he said. His condition grew worse until he could hardly walk at all. When it became clear he was seriously ill, a British medical officer ordered him to take sick leave. There the pictures stop. The diary takes over. My father was no longer able to shoot pictures. His war was finished. One can only imagine his vigilance as he lay unable to walk, placed on a stretcher and transported away from the front in hospital trains, ships, and ambulances, anesthetized with strong narcotics, anxious lest his photographs be separated from him.

Now the real story of my father's war begins. Struggling with pain and the loss of not only his ability to walk but also to take pictures, observing and somehow keeping notes on the men around him as well as himself, he falls into several simple but deeply moving conversations.

I think the best chapter is the one in which he and a seriously wounded German soldier, sharing the same ambulance, speak stretcher-to-stretcher about their lives, their hopes, and their pain. Otto is simply another young man in a very tough spot, with the same hopes, dreams, and fears as the Tommies. Bowen feels no hatred for him, only compassion. By the time the ambulance journey is over and the Allies and their prisoners have to separate, the two sides are trading hearty jibes about the other's rations. Incidents such as this were not uncommon in the North Africa campaign.

And so his odyssey, which began as a young man's romantic adventure, now leads him through a chamber of horrors of what war does to the human psyche. A brilliant British Army psychiatrist, Maj. Alexander Kennedy,* comes to his bedside in the Fifteenth Scottish General Hospital in Cairo to tell him that the trouble with his leg was not "bomb neurosis," as it first had been diagnosed. Maybe, Bowen hoped, the doctor would also find a way to heal his fellow patient, one he would come to know as the "mad despatch rider," a youth driven into psychosis by failing to deliver a message he believed would have saved his company. Maybe the world would begin to add wounded souls, not just dead bodies, to the price of war. Is the human cost worth it? "The more I see of war, the less I think of the whole business," he said.

Sensitivity to the trauma of war remained with my father for the rest of his life. He could find common ground with just about anyone, and he did, but it was not the journalist pals he'd made in Cairo, but the experience among the sick and wounded that was on his mind as he traveled home. Intuiting an Allied victory, he hoped that America would rise to the challenge of creating a world without war, a world where men could live as brothers.

Yet my father's feelings about war were even more complex. He loved his faith, but he also loved his country. He never lost the simple, quiet pride in what he had done. He despaired over the Vietnam War and joined its veterans in protest against it, but when they threw their medals at the Capitol steps, he went over and picked them up. He himself had

---

* Alexander Kennedy (1909–1960) went on to a distinguished career in civilian life, eventually becoming professor of psychological medicine at Edinburgh University. As reported by Dominic Streatfeild in *Brainwash: The Secret History of Mind Control* (Picador, 2008), Kennedy delivered a paper before the Royal Institution in 1960 on the application of wartime techniques to peacetime psychiatry entitled "The Scientific Lessons of Interrogation," in which he discussed the application of wartime techniques to peacetime treatment of psychiatric illness. Kennedy referred to work he had done on the use of sensory deprivation in interrogation while stationed at the Combined Services Detailed Interrogation Centre (CSDIC) in Cairo. This precipitated a BBC investigative report that ignited a "brainwashing scandal" in the House of Commons, eliciting a denial from British prime minister Harold Macmillan. Kennedy died three months later.

received an Africa Star and a War Medal, which he kept in his cuff links box. He put the Vietnam vets' medals there also. Once he opened that box and showed them to me. "I would not have done that," he said.

After centuries of being whipped by wind, the curves and angles of a rock become clearer. It hasn't been centuries, only a lifetime of distance on the subject of this book, but surely that's got to be worth something. I think *Back from Tobruk* is about something more important than what the country he came home to wanted to hear. I think it is about something more radical than my father himself may have been fully ready to acknowledge. It's about how one man goes to war seeking romantic adventure and comes back home with his eyes opened. The costs of even a just war are overwhelming. War is nothing more than the greatest of all insults to the dignity of man. Croswell Bowen cherished that dignity.

My father's accomplishments as a writer continue to expand in my mind. Growing up, I had become aware of his books and articles as he was writing them. But his war adventure happened before I was born. He never talked much about it. To read this book after all those years is staggering. He didn't speak about the war, but he sure had written about it.

There is a special immortality that storytellers can achieve. Long after we laid him to rest in the earth of a Connecticut hillside, his larger-than-life spirit will fill the quiet room where I write. My hope is that by making his North Africa adventure available and illustrating it with both his photographs and those of others found in the Library of Congress and the archives of the American Field Service, that quiet room will fill up with photographers whose cameras bore witness to that same campaign. That room would not be quiet for long. My father loved throwing parties, and he would have especially loved that one.

As he did covering all his stories, my father kept copious handwritten notes in spiral-bound reporters' notebooks on just about everything he heard, saw, felt, and thought. He carefully wrote down the lyrics of the Tommies' songs as they echoed in his head. He was overjoyed when the reel-to-reel tape recorder came out and immediately began using one for interviews, but it was too late to capture the British Eighth in song. He wrote of setting up a typewriter in a dark, flea-infested dugout outside Tobruk, single-spacing to conserve paper. When he returned home to his West Twelfth Street apartment in New York and began to work on the book full time, a typist retyped his drafts.

Growing up, my sisters and I knew there was a "war book," but for a long time we had seen only half of it, bound in a tattered black-leather clip binder. Where was the other half? We'd come upon his prints and negatives while playing in the barn, but nobody quite understood they were meant to be part of the war book.

Before his death in 1971, my father made plans to donate his papers to his two schools, Choate Rosemary Hall, a New England boarding school, and Yale University. After he died, my sister Lucey put those plans into motion. Choate took his war book, and it stayed there until I visited the library in 2006 and the curator gave physical possession back to his estate.

That was the manuscript I used. Its condition varied. Sometimes there was only a first or second carbon copy; sometimes there was clear type-script. Optical character recognition (OCR) gave results that were at best usable and at worst gibberish. Voice-to-text software took over when the OCR results were bad. Then my all-too-human brain pulled the results into line with the original. How gratified my father would be to know that his words, written at a time when a twin-lens Rolleiflex camera shooting on black and white film, notebook, and pencil were "the newest and old-est instruments for recording impressions," survived into an era when high-resolution full color images can be instantly sent around the world.

Very little content editing was necessary. Where it was, it was usually because a later editor, or perhaps my father himself, excised passages that I felt should have stayed in. In a very few cases there were instances where it appears he may have discarded passages due to political conditions at the time. Possibly because it seemed too pacifist for a wartime audience, he softened the conclusion of his encounter with the wounded German soldier Otto. I retained the original. I also decided to retain the spelling of certain words, some British and others by now archaic, as reflective of his era.

The fruits of the generosity and support of my husband, Bob, and my two sisters, Lucey and Molly, are throughout these pages. Without my husband's steadfast encouragement, intelligence, and enthusiasm for the task, I could not have taken it on. My sister Lucey made sure that the manuscript of *Back from Tobruk* found safekeeping in a library during a time when it might well have been lost. My sister Molly's tender and complex feelings for our father made delving into this part of his life with her an adventure.

Lois Ault of the Wayne Historical Society gave me her time and encouragement in the project's early stages, when it especially mattered. The dedication of Eleanora Golobic and Nicole Milano, American Field Service archivists, to preserving the history they have been entrusted with set my course right several times. The staff of the Library of Congress helped me locate photographs. I was fortunate to find in Robert Astle and Hillel Black professional support I truly needed. Both made valuable editing suggestions and helped turn a family heirloom into a published book. Thanks also to the team at Potomac Books: Elizabeth Demers, Liz Norris, Don McKeon, Kathryn Owens, Kathleen Dyson, and Laura Briggs. Finally, without the curiosity of my nephew Bowen Ames to learn more about his grandfather, my rediscovery of this material would not have come about.

BETSY CONNOR BOWEN
WAYNE, MAINE
2012

PREFACE

Taking documentary photographs is my work. It is the reason I went to the war. It has long been a strong conviction of mine that a modern reporter should simultaneously make use of the camera and the notebook. They are the newest and oldest instruments for recording impressions.

In my photographs and reporting, I try to be objective and impersonal. Those are the aims of a good journalist.

In my diary, I have allowed myself to be subjective. This, I felt, was justifiable on the grounds that, just as my Super-XX film is used to record light impressions of men and scenes, so my mind and notebook could be used to record observations, spoken words, and emotions. Furthermore, I went to war as one kind of person and came back as another. Everything seems different now. Why? Setting down the narrative of my own experience might provide the answer. I am an average American with a conventional upbringing, education, and a reasonable share of prejudices. Anyone could have felt, seen, smelled, and observed the same or similar things about this war.

The pronoun "I" is employed freely in recording an impression or emotion that was essentially me. The pronoun "you" is for an impression that anyone might feel.

The purpose of recording in detail what soldiers said and did on the days leading up to the attack and fall of Tobruk is not an attempt to reveal the inside news story of the event, or to present a journalistic scoop. This stretch of days at that particular North African battlefront offers a reasonably good case history for a war experience. The Allied forces had tasted victory in the desert and were about to taste terrible defeat. Still later, of course, they were to achieve the complete conquest of North Africa.

What took place at Tobruk has happened many times, is happening, and will happen again in this war. Journalistically and historically, the significance of the fall of Tobruk, I contend, is that it was the turning point in the morale of the British officer class. It galvanized them into the point of view of attack or be lost. This contention, I hasten to add, is not based on any inside knowledge of military strategy or power politics but on an ephemeral impression or hunch.

The diary is not presented in precisely the form I wrote it on location. My notebooks ran into several hundred thousand words. I copied down the sentences of many hundreds of soldiers, officers, and civilians in twelve countries on this forty-thousand-mile journey. Much of what I copied down proved unimportant. Much that I did not write down seemed important when I returned and remembered. Occasionally, actual names have been changed to fictitious ones to avoid embarrassing those I quoted. I have telescoped time here and there to facilitate the narrative. But, aside from this, the diary is a true, sincere, and honest attempt on the part of one American to record an actual war experience.

INTRODUCTION

A barren, barely inhabited strip of desert along the North African coast stretching from Tunisia to Egypt became the stage for the first major battles of World War II. Hitler wanted to capture the Suez Canal. Mussolini pursued his dream to re-create the Roman Empire. Beginning in 1940, the British and their allies sent their divisions to the region. And so, the battles began.

Before the war, Tobruk was a small city in northeastern Libya with the best deep-water port in North Africa. By the end of the war it would be rubble, its harbor so filled with sunken hulls that ships could not enter it. The city had been captured by the British on January 22, 1941, before America entered the war, but beginning in March 1942 Gen. Erwin Rommel's Afrika Korps and Italian divisions drove the Allies back to the Egyptian border, leaving Tobruk isolated and under siege.

The American Field Service was founded in 1914 after the outbreak of World War I, when young Americans living in Paris volunteered as ambulance drivers at the American Hospital of Paris. It merged into the U.S. Army upon America's entry into the war in 1917 but was reactivated as an ambulance unit in 1939 at the start of World War II.

Croswell Bowen left New York City in November of 1941 with the first AFS unit to go to North Africa and the Middle East. News of Pearl Harbor came to his unit aboard ship. Tobruk had held against Rommel's siege because of the "Rats of Tobruk," the determined Allied troops, dug in there. As Bowen's AFS unit was nearing the region, the Allies lifted the siege and went on to push the Axis forces west of Tobruk, to the "Gazala line," which ran from Gazala south for some fifty miles and was heavily fortified with mines. But by the spring of 1942, Rommel was expected to take the offensive and attempt to break through the line. Bowen was in Cairo when he heard about American-supplied tanks (operated by Commonwealth forces) pouring into the desert and felt hope surge that the Allies might keep the Axis on the run.

In June of 1942, at the midpoint of this narrative, Bowen's AFS unit arrives on the outskirts of Tobruk, just as Rommel is beginning his campaign to recapture it. He did, and with that the Allies felt the first sting of defeat.

Then, at El Alamein in October and November of 1942, the Allies, with Lt. Gen. Bernard L. Montgomery commanding the Eighth Army, stopped Rommel and put him back on the defensive. They would celebrate their first major victory together when Montgomery took Tripoli in January of 1943. After that, the mood of the war seemed to shift. "Before El Alamein we never had a victory," Winston Churchill said. "After El Alamein we never had a defeat."

1 OFF TO THE WARS

TRAIN LEAVING GRAND CENTRAL STATION, NEW YORK CITY, NOVEMBER 6, 1941

Our departure is a military secret.

Wives, mothers, and sweethearts, however, are saying good-bye in the murky light of an underground platform in Grand Central Station. As the train starts up, one woman's face fixes itself firmly in my mind. Tears have washed away her powder. Her lips are full, almost pouty. Her eyes are wide and glassy. Her body is taut in a rigid numbness. She looks as if she ought to cry but either can't or won't. Her face is the symbol of all women who see their lovers off to war. She is the wife of the commanding officer of the unit. I am glad I am unmarried and alone.

There are a hundred of us. We are members of the first unit of the American Field Service to serve with the British in the Middle East. The men are volunteer ambulance drivers who have paid $200 of their own money for their uniforms and kit. They receive no pay. America is not yet in the war but they are eager "to get into it." From their conversations you judge most of them are not only running into something, but running away from something. One man's wife has just divorced him.

Another is a college instructor who loathes the work. Several are drunken failures. Others are conscientious objectors or self-styled "idealists." There is an ex-marine who says, "I got that hatred in me. All service men got it. You got to go where there's killin'." Many are college boys bored with experiencing life vicariously from textbooks and novels. One of them states flatly that he's going because he read A Farewell to Arms.

The train emerges from the darkness of the underground tunnel and the tenement houses flashing past my window intensify my awareness of time. Ever since I can remember, looking out of the window of a moving train has given me the sensation of seeing time pass. For example, my train is crossing a bridge; ahead is a forest. I know that in a minute or two, I will be passing the forest. Looking ahead at the forest, I try to project myself into time and space as to what I will feel and think when I am actually passing the forest. Then the forest is going by and all I think is that the moment when I was on the bridge is gone forever. I feel sad and lost.

Now on this train I feel the same way. Why am I going on this venture into dangerous time? I'm going to take pictures of the war.

I think over some of the silly photographic assignments I've covered: pictures of half drunken couples holding hands at nightclubs, fashion shows, stuffy banquets, rowdy cocktail parties, interiors of ridiculously expensive apartments, pretty girls, and legs, legs, legs. I remember huge piles of pictures I've seen on the desk of great photo magazines; hundreds and hundreds of eleven-by-fourteens of girls with their legs showing or half dressed. The editors pour over these pictures, studying and sorting them. They are forever searching and searching for that sublime picture of a pair of legs, or thighs, or breasts, which, because of some unusual pose or peculiarity of the female body, produces agonizing promise or quivering excitement.

The camera is, to me, a wonderful and magic instrument for recording life, for preserving forever moments out of swiftly passing time. But its magic, and the talents of those who use it skillfully, is being increasingly perverted. I am glad to be going on an assignment into which I can honestly and wholeheartedly sink my teeth.

I am being allowed to cover a war as a photographer and writer. It is the fulfillment of something I wanted more than anything—to be a war correspondent—the dream of everyone who has ever worked as a newspaper reporter. Thinking about it, I realize how easily it was arranged. I went to the American Field Service and said I had no money but I'd like to go along and take pictures of the work of the Field Service. They looked me over and checked on me and said I could go.

Then I went to see Charles Colebaugh, managing editor of *Collier's*, and said, "I am going to the Middle East to take pictures but I need money." He assigned Bill Chessman, *Collier's* Art Editor, to look over the peacetime picture stories I'd done. At the end of a week they agreed to advance me a sum of money, an expense account, and full credentials as a representative of *Collier's*. It was more than enough to purchase my uniforms, kit, and a large supply of photographic materials and equipment. So now I am a war photographer representing one of the most powerful magazines in America. I am on top of the world.

But I also know I am going for many other reasons. I am curious about war, about what it's really like. As a little boy I can remember my dreams were filled with men going over the top of the trenches and being tangled in barbed wire. I can remember a dream that often recurred. I am assigned with ten other soldiers to shoot a spy or a traitor. Invariably, in the dream, I shoot at something near the man I am supposed to shoot at. But I never know if my bullet hit him and I am worried about this as I wake up.

I am going because I want to be a romantic character, to be a glamorous figure like a war correspondent. Perhaps, too, it is because unconsciously I want to do something astounding, something that will astound the people who knew me back home in Toledo, Ohio when I was a little boy. I am also fully aware that I am going because I want to shake myself out of the rut of my life. For ten years I have lived in New York since leaving college. During that time I have held newspaper jobs, done magazine articles, held advertising jobs, been fired repeatedly, and fallen in and out of love as the seasons changed. All I am proud of is a book I did, a prose-photograph study of the Hudson River. I also know that if I don't go into the war now, I'll be drafted into it, perhaps doing some job I won't like at all.

Finally, I am going because I've always wanted to see and know the lands of the Middle East. I will see with my own eyes the holy land where Jesus walked, Crusader castles, Arabs, the Sphinx, the pyramids, and war in the Libyan Desert. In my teens, the writings of Lawrence of Arabia had made a deep impression on me. Yes, it is a wonderful adventure to be going on.

We are called into one car for a meeting and double up on seats and stand in the aisle. A suave Britisher, whose clothes and face suggest Anthony Eden, addresses us. He is Maj. Rex Benson, Military Attaché at the Embassy in Washington.

"I want to wish you Godspeed and safe crossing," he says. "You are going on this mission to preserve what you are leaving. Britain is grateful for this self-sacrificing act you are making. There is a bit of business, as there always is. Do not be without your Red Cross brassard and your identification card. The best of luck. Safe crossing and a happy return."

The train stops briefly at New Haven where I went to college and rushes through Wallingford where I went to prep school. I imagine the boys coming off the field from football practice. Did I learn anything on the playing fields of Choate? I remember a line our Headmaster always put into his sermons: "Oh to be in England now that April's there." I still have that awe of England.

It is dark when the train pulls into South Station in Boston. We are in civilian clothes but it is evident that we are moving as a group. My luggage is a problem. There are a duffle bag and sleeping bag, two large suitcases, a small one, and two cases of 144 flash bulbs, two heavy boxes of photographic chemicals and films. I carry my cameras with me in a neat leather bag. In a canvas musette bag, I carry toilet articles, pajamas, and a clean shirt. Buses take us to the Hotel Manger, where AFS men from the last war give us a dinner. We rush to catch the train at North Station, which is next to the hotel, and as we pass through the gate a sign tells us where we are going—Halifax.

The men talk and drink well into the night. They are as excited as children on their way to the circus. Morning finds the train speeding through the bleak Canadian countryside. The stations at which we stop are filled with Canadian soldiers. They are going home, or returning from, leave. I see one soldier and a girl, both carrying ice skates. Many of the soldiers are members of Canadian branches of Scotch regiments and wear khaki Tam o'Shanters with red flowers or plaid overseas caps. Some wear kilts. At one station, the boys manage to buy several cases of Canadian ale. It helps to while away the long day on the train.

HALIFAX

Shortly after midnight the train enters the outskirts of Halifax. Shades are ordered pulled down for the blackout. It is our first serious sign of war. A Canadian officer from a Scotch Highland regiment greets us.

"We'll give you the best we got, men," he says. "This is the army and got to get used to it. I know because I was in the last show. You'll get two blankets and a mattress. Bear with us." One senses weariness in him. His name is Major André, the same name as the charming British spy famous for being hanged during the Revolution.

Our billets are in the Embarkation Building, in a large warehouse filled with double-decker iron beds. The next morning we are allowed to visit the town. It is filled with naval officers and men from the Allied forces. We do some last-minute shopping for toiletries like razor blades and toothpaste. From dinner on we are confined to barracks to await sailing orders.

The Embarkation Building is filled with a variety of Allied soldiers and sailors. There are, for example, eight men from the crew of a cargo ship torpedoed en route to Africa. The entire crew of eighty was rescued from their lifeboats and most of them have returned to England. These eight are detained because they witnessed a bar-room brawl in which a soldier was stabbed to death. While we are talking over their adventure, one of them puts on pajamas. A witty Limey sailor looks over at the man and says, "Oh ho, pee-jamas, blimey, if he ain't a gentleman. Come on sweetie, let's go to bed together."

The sailor shows me a collection of food he's taking home to England, tins of butter and jam, ham, and egg powder. He seems intent on explaining his philosophy. "I'm a typical Englishman, I am. I am a Cockney and happy as a lark. Nobody's better'n me. The King 'es no better'n me. He can only sit on one chair, sleep on one bed, eat on one plate. Roosevelt 'es no better'n me. 'Es got worries. I got one of the sweetest women in the world for a wife." He hears one of the other sailors saying, "To win this war we got to exterminate the bastards."

"How you going to exterminate the Germans, man," my Limey says, "It's the trade unions in Germany that's going to win the war for us, you blinkin' Scotchman. They're workingmen in Germany, and workingmen in France and workingmen in Russia. Me, I'm a workingman. It's the workingman what's going to win the war." Their talk confuses me. I walk over to an open door of the warehouse overlooking a British troop transport just arrived from England.

Although the ship, the *Warwick Castle*, is in almost complete darkness, it is alive with troops being slowly disembarked. Small bands of troops are waiting on the decks of the ship. Some are moving single file up and down hatches along the decks, going fore or aft. From two gangplanks the ship is disgorging the troops. Each soldier carries a duffle bag, a canvas covered helmet, a Bren gun, or an officer's suitcase or trunk. Here and there we hear the crisp call of a command. A group comes to attention and begins to file off the ship. The soldiers don't seem like human beings but rather like grotesque gnomes and giants doing strange things in the darkness. From the afterdeck come the sounds of Tommies' voices. The words are sung slowly to a simple melody and ring out clearly in the night. Then from another part of the ship comes another song. Both tell of a soldier's joy upon returning to civilian life.

Then a group of Americans, men from our unit, answer the song that the Tommies are singing with "Sewanee River," "East Side, West Side," "Let Me Call You Sweetheart," and "Down By the Old Mill Stream."

The activity on the troop transport ends slowly like an old clock running down. Lone Tommies begin returning aboard ship to fetch heavy boxes of ammunition, machine guns, and antiaircraft guns encased in wooden boxes. The singing gets softer and less frequent. The drizzling rain stops, and the black sky becomes grey before the rising moon.

At four o'clock comes the order for American Field Service men to go aboard. Our ship is big and gray and being rapidly loaded with soldiers and all the miscellaneous paraphernalia an army carries. There are boxes of medical supplies, metal boxes of money, hymn books, dominoes, phonograph machines, typewriters, band instruments, order blanks, extra uniforms, blankets, rifles, guns, camouflage netting, bicycles, and portable kitchens. At the gangway we are given a ticket with the cabin number marked on it. At the end of the gangplank are an officer and some military police (MP) of the United States Navy. We are aboard an American troop transport commanded by the U.S. Navy. It is taking British soldiers to the Middle East. Who says America is not in the war?

When I reach my cabin I find that it is a first class meant for two, but eighteen other men are assigned to it. The metal bunks fill up the room and are in tiers four high.

We awake the next morning to find the Tommies are still coming aboard. Our luggage has become scattered around with the Tommies' kit. My boxes of flash bulbs are being used as stools to sit on. The Tommies are curious as to what flash bulbs are for (the name is printed on the cases), whereupon I get a nickname that persists throughout the war: "Flash" Bowen.

Our unit is very much the center of attention on the ship first, because we are Americans and second, because we know we're headed for Cairo. The Tommies and their officers don't know where they're going. Our destination gives them a pretty good idea. The entire day and the next night troops are still coming aboard. None of the officers or men is allowed to go ashore. Once embarked, everyone must stay aboard.

The next morning is cold and wet. Our ship is released from her dock moorings and tugs pull her into position. The engines throb violently as she moves into the main stream of Halifax Harbor. A nearby steamer blinks signals like a Broadway billboard. There is little swell or choppiness, although the wind is high, because the water is surfaced with oil. A few guards, some Canadian embarkation officers, and Bill Wallace of the AFS stand on the dock waving good-bye. Tug whistles and ship whistles sound through the morning mist.

Inside the ship, the breakfast mess lines wind through the intestines of the hull like tapeworms. In the passageways of the officers quarters the "batmen," or officers' personal servants, sit on the floor quietly polishing brass and sewing on buttons for their masters. On the forecastle, the snappily dressed British officers watch the activity of the departure, pointing things out to each other with their swagger sticks—but with restraint. They have visited a great "Dominion of the British Empire" without setting foot on its shores. Officers of the U.S. Navy go about their duties and commands with seriousness. They are puzzled and worried about carrying British troops to war. "Either we're in it or not," one of them says, "but orders are orders. Let's hope we get it over with soon." The Yankee sailors (most of the crew actually comes from around Boston) work on the ship's lines, swearing loudly and throwing themselves with abandon into their work as if they were showing the British officers how it's done.

The ship pauses for a moment after the tugs push her into the main channel and then hurry away. It is as if she were reflecting for a moment before taking her direction.

I think of the lines of A. E. Houseman,

A single redcoat turns his head.
He turns and looks at me. . . .
What thoughts at heart have you and I
We cannot stop to tell;
But dead or living, drunk or dry,
Soldier, I wish you well.

Then the ship moves slowly down the channel to the sea. We pass the steel net stretched across the channel to keep submarines out of Halifax Harbor. "An Englishman dove his submarine under the net in the harbor at Ostend and played havoc with Jerry shipping," a British officer at the rail, says. "Brave fellow, he was. I saw him come ashore at Valetta and there were great cheers for him."

As we move out to sea, big U.S. Navy ships come into view through the heavy mist. There is the *Ranger*, an aircraft carrier, looking like a modern table sticking out of the water and two heavy cruisers with their blue-grey guns scarcely visible, like match sticks. A dozen submarine destroyers hover about. Every few minutes, two airplanes circle overhead. Hopping off the carrier, they look like mosquitoes gliding along the deck, then dropping off sharply only to soar immediately into the air. When they land they look like flies alighting on sticky paper. The three troop transports and three cargo ships making the journey line up two abreast. The airplane carrier is ahead to the starboard. The heavy cruisers are on both sides of the troop ships. The destroyers form lanes still further away so that they are four abreast. They make lanes that extend beyond both the horizon to the stern and the bow. A gentle tossing of the ships tells us we are well out to sea. The blue-grey Navy planes patrol the great rectangular area made by the convoy as it begins the long voyage to war.

Going to war these days, I decide, is like leaving on a world cruise without the confetti and the ship's orchestra.

CONVOY OFF NEW ENGLAND

One of the ship's painters, Czar Babcock from Fall River, Massachusetts, is also an amateur navigator and tells me we are off the New England coast. "I figger along about Maine," he says. I think of a vacation I had once at Squirrel Island just off Boothbay Harbor; of a Maine fisherman who took me at dawn well out to sea in his motor launch to haul up his lobster pots. I'm with a girl with flowing golden hair and a *dirndl* who beat me at tennis and took my heart with her to Boston when it was all over.

Czar is known among his mates as a "seagoin' lawyer" because of his fast meaningless talk. He's been in the U.S. Navy ever since he was a kid. One of his favorite topics of conversation concerns his invention of an invisible ship, a new secret weapon to win the war. The principle of the invention, which he claims to have patented, is that this ship vibrates so fast it can't be seen. By way of demonstrating, he snaps a springy piece of metal, and points out that you can't see the arc in which it vibrates.

On the subject of the British, Czar's views have not remained static. When the Tommies came aboard they were "limey bastards." "Why the hell is the U.S. Navy bein' used to take the British Army to their war?" he says. "Why don't they use their own Navy . . . they're supposed to have such an all-powered Navy."

The first change in Czar's attitude and that of his mates comes about as a result of the ship's PX refusing to take English money. The Tommies are without cigarettes, candy, soap, or any of the other personal needs of soldiers. Cigarettes are six cents at the PX; Hershey bars are two for a nickel. The American sailors find themselves in the role of "Lady Bountifuls." I watch Czar and his mates passing out cigarettes to a group of Tommies. In each case the Tommy refuses even though he's dying for a smoke. When pressed further he accepts two or three cigarettes and says, "Thanks teddy much, that's teddibly nice of you." The Yankee sailors wince at the accents. They think it's something they put on.

"Them Tommies ain't got nothin," Czar reflects, "not even pride. Why the stuff they take off their officers, the way they speak to 'em, washing their clothes, waitin' on 'em at table. I hope you notice in the U.S. Navy no white man waits on table in no officer's mess."

While the exchange system is being set up, the passing out of cigarettes and candy by the U.S. crew assumes wholesale proportions. The Tommies gorge themselves on candy. "Sweets are rationed in England, you know," they point out. Some of the crew is highly amused with introducing the Tommies to gum chewing. Finally, Yankee swapping enters in. A pack of cigarettes fetches the cap or regimental badge the Tommy wears. Two packs bring a large pocketknife issued to soldiers in the artillery. The British officers find it necessary to issue an order stating that troops disposing of their cap badges or army-issue materials will be placed on a charge. Meanwhile a large number of the crew is sporting belts ringed with the insignia of ancient and honorable English regiments, many of which fought against America in the Revolution.

Czar's next change in attitude is the result of his being given a crew of ten Tommies to help him with his painting chores. "They're nice guys when you get to know 'em," he says. "They're willin' to work. And they're grateful when you do anything for 'em."

Czar's attitude toward the British officers remains unchanged, however. You feel sure he'd take a poke at one of them at the drop of a hat. "They're stuck up and they put on airs," he says. "Who the hell do they think they are? We licked 'em in the Revolution, didn't we? We're paying for the war, aren't we? For my money I'd sink the lot of 'em."

Czar and his mates are meeting a pretty good cross section of England on this voyage. The troops are part of the Eighteenth Division of British Territorials, numbering about twenty-five thousand troops. The bulk of them are conscripts, bookkeepers, coal miners, bus drivers, carpenters, and many who've been unemployed for years. There is a sprinkling of regular army noncoms and officers running through each regiment. As defenders of the Empire, they sailed from Hull two weeks ago on three British troop ships and were met two hundred miles later by an escort of the U.S. Navy. At Halifax, they were marched aboard our U.S. Navy troop transports and now we're off on the long voyage to the Middle East around the Cape.

CONVOY OFF NEW YORK

We are about off New York City now and it's dark and rainy, and there are heavy swells. I've had dinner and it's a quarter past eight. The theater crowds are milling along Broadway and Times Square. A few couples are still lingering over too many martinis. It will be an exciting winter in New York and I won't be there, the first winter I won't be there in ten years. Ferryboats are taking those who've worked late to their New Jersey homes.

Some of the rewrite men on the morning papers are just coming into work. The tickers are hammering in the news from all over the world at the offices of the big press associations. There's a fire in the garment district and a suicide on upper Park Avenue. The tabloids are just coming off the press. There's a war on. The Axis claims . . . an official British communiqué today stated . . . Rome radio says. Beside the city is the Hudson, Thomas Wolfe's dark and secret river, full of strange time, flowing forever in darkness to the sea.

This ship is overcrowded and it smells bad. It was a very fancy ship once. It was the pride of the U.S. lines and was called the *America*. When it became a troop transport in 1940, it was renamed USS *West Point*. Mrs. Eleanor Roosevelt christened her at Newport News. It was built for the North Atlantic run and carries twelve hundred passengers comfortably. On this voyage, which will take three months, it carries almost six thousand troops. Overcrowding is made all the worse by the fact that officers, commanding the troops, occupy the first-class staterooms under virtually normal conditions. These five hundred officers eat in the big cocktail lounge and are served special food. One of the Tommies sums up the attitude of most of them: "Officers, of course, gets the best of everything."

There are three hundred Tommies living in the ship's library, five hundred in the main living room. Against the background of landscape murals, metal frescoes, and expensive woodwork you see duffel bags, rifles and bayonets, tin hats, sun helmets, and naked Tommies lying in tiers of metal bunks. They are talking, reading, smoking (against regulations), or sleeping.

Far down in the ship's hold next to the oil-burning boilers, in "Hell's Kitchen," the overcrowding is most noticeable. It is steaming hot and noisy. Steel bunks are six and eight feet high. The air reeks of sweaty human bodies. "It's so crowded down here," one Tommy says jokingly, "we have to breathe in and out together by number." He's not far from the truth, the way it looks to me.

What would happen in Hell's Kitchen if we were hit by a torpedo or shell? Of course, there are supposed to be elaborate lifeboat drills. There are warning bells for "battle stations" or "abandon ship" drills. You are supposed to carry your kapok life preserver with you at all times. You are supposed to form in certain lines, up this hatchway or down that hall, and wait on a certain deck. I figure the men in Hell's Kitchen, however, are licked before they start. Submarines prefer to hit the boilers. Immediately after a submarine is sighted, the watertight doors close automatically. To be saved, the eight hundred men in this boiler hold would have to climb up a narrow ladder and go out through the hatch one at a time. If each man took thirty seconds to get out, six hours and forty minutes would be required for all of them to reach deck. This, of course, is based on the assumption that the explosion is elsewhere in the ship and the men do not panic.

CONVOY THROUGH THE CARIBBEAN SEA

The sun is going down slowly and the sky is broken. Shafts of light shoot upward from the horizon fanwise. Now and then the sun bursts forth from the clouds, lighting up the side of the transport ahead of us. It changes from dull grey to shiny blue-grey in an instant. One of the Tommies has brought his accordion up on deck and is joined by two others with a violin and a mouth organ. Other Tommies gather around and sing.

As I get more and more acquainted with the Tommies aboard, I think of my brother Bill, who has been a private in the U.S. Army for a year, and his fellow American soldiers down at Fort Dix. Both Bill and the common British soldier are civilians turned soldier either under compulsion or by choice; both speak English. Here any similarity ends as far as I can see now. Where Bill and his pals at Fort Dix have a sense of adventure about their life in the army, the Tommy has a deep sadness surfaced with whimsicality. American soldiers give an impression of being boastful. ("Any American can lick a German with one hand tied behind his back.") Whereas the Tommy appears extremely modest and well-mannered. He wouldn't think of hooting at a pretty blond. Officers, to the American private, are either "good guys" or "heels," no better or worse than anyone else, they're just in a different branch of the army business. To the Tommy, an officer is something from another world. He is chosen from a different class of people. One speaks to him as a butler speaks to his master, "Beggin' your pardon, Sir. No Sir. Yes Sir. If I may venture to say so, Sir," with heels together, palms flat against the thighs, the body rigidly at attention, shoulders back, chin out, and eyes staring straight ahead.

British officers are smartly turned out, with highly polished brass buttons, pips on their shoulders, and Sam Browne belts with mahogany lusters. Their social charm is apt to be overwhelming when they want it to be. Things are either black or white, no grays. It's done or it simply isn't done. Listen to Capt. Duncan Campbell of the Royal Signals on the subject of "our men":

> "In dealing with one's men the main thing is you look out for their creature comforts—their food, a place to sleep."

> "Our men are going to war with blood lust, that's the thing. They've seen their wives and families and children blitzed and bombed. They want revenge."

> "Certainly, my men grumble. It doesn't bother me. There is a saying in the British Army that all goes well when the men grumble but look out when the grumbling stops."

CONVOY APPROACHING THE WEST INDIES

The British officers aboard are a little hurt because there has been virtually no social intermingling with the officers of the U.S. Navy. Members of the British Army have a profound respect for their country's Royal Navy. There is an expression in the British Army invariably used when anything goes wrong, "Thank Christ for the Navy." The British officers are prepared to carry over some of this respect to members of the American Navy.

But the U.S. Navy officers are keeping relations "strictly business." They feel considerable irritation at being used to carry the British through danger zones to "their war." Then, too, many of them are Naval

Reserve officers and go about their work with great deliberateness. The British officers have a studied casualness, on the other hand. Many of the naval officers are from small towns and have a provincial distrust of foreigners.

The British officers have invited the Americans to come into their mess but the Americans shyly refuse. They have not invited the British to their mess nor entertained them either officially or unofficially. I ask one naval officer why this condition exists and his only explanation is that there is nothing in Navy regulations providing for this kind of a situation.

There is no saluting between the British and American officers.

One gob, patrolling the deck, finds a Britisher smoking during the blackout. It is not quite dark but the "darken ship" signal has sounded and the officer feels his cigarette no more visible than the ship itself is in the twilight. The gob knocks the cigarette from the officer's hand and says he's got a good notion to lock the officer up. He doesn't, but the incident adds to the gulf.

There are numerous meetings attended by both British and American officer personnel. They concern ways of speeding up the mess line, abandon ship drills, fire drills, air raid drills, cleaning details, entertainment for the troops, equitable distribution of supplies, preparing American food rations for the Tommy's palate, and so on. Little is accomplished. The British officers tell me it's the Navy's fault; the Navy officers say they can't get along with the British. So far there has not been one emergency drill.

Every day the troops get orders in a mimeographed bulletin signed by the OC Ship (officer commanding Army personnel aboard the ship). When the Navy's orders concern anything that might have to do with the troops, they are included in the daily Ship's orders. Today an order comes through to the British from the U. S. Navy regarding whistling. It marks the high point of Anglo-American relations aboard the *West Point*. All Navies, of course, consider whistling aboard ship extremely unlucky.

Landlubbers that we of the AFS unit are, we have whistled to our heart's content. The wording of the order, issued by the *West Point*'s Executive Officer, a Commander, is as follows:

> As you are aware, the practice of whistling is not condoned aboard ship. It is considered impractical to ask troop personnel to change their habits in this respect, but an effort should be made to discontinue the practice in the vicinity of office spaces and living quarters of ship's personnel. Complaints received from both officers and crew have confirmed the personal observation that this practice is both distracting and annoying.

TRINIDAD

Hot breezes sweep our decks. We are seeing our first land in ten days— green mountains that lose their peaks in a low-hanging mist. The mountains look like small lumps of earth covered with green moss. We sail so close we can see tiny caves worn by the water. A boy from Idaho with the AFS, leaning over the railing, says, "How beautiful it is here. I shall bring my girl here for our honeymoon after the war and wander these mountains."

It is almost noon and we are approaching Trinidad. The band has come up on deck and is playing "After the Ball," "Ta-rara Boom-de-de-ay," and "The Poets and Peasants." Horizontal bars of colored lights stretch across the coastline. The five other ships in the convoy are in a straight line ahead of us. Everybody moves to the side of the ship looking on the land.

As we enter the harbor at Trinidad, a tramp ship flying a Venezuelan flag sails out. Venezuela is neutral. How easily word of our whereabouts could be flashed to the German Embassy at Caracas.

A group of sailors tries to sneak a pet goat aboard ship but is discovered. Later, after the ship has sailed, I hear a discussion of the incident in the ship's fitters shop. We are drinking coffee and eating toast. Being in a room full of Americans assuages my homesickness. "Sailors," says "Chips" Taylor, one of the ship's carpenters from Kansas City, "are a funny bunch of people. Seems like they're always fooling around with some kind of animal or other."

"I remember a fellow out in China Station. Loved China more than he did the good old USA," elaborates Chips. "He had a monkey with him on his destroyer. Name of that monkey was Chatter or Gibber or something to do with talk. He loved that monkey so much that he got him enrolled in the U.S. Navy. Chatter had a regular enlistment card. He even had a record card showing how many times he'd been put on report, how many deck court-martials he'd had, and how many summary court-martials, and how many general court-martials, by gum. When this fellow would go ashore, Chatter would get a liberty pass. At inspections he'd get in line just like he was one of the sailors."

"Say, Yank," says Sledge Shimkin, one of the ship's fitters from Wilmington, Delaware, "have another cup of coffee. That's an American drink. You've been drinkin' too much of this Limey tea. It's bad for you." I accept his offer, perhaps too eagerly.

"Well, as I was saying," continues Chips, "around 1936 I was sent out to China on a naval transport ship. We was to bring home all sailors and marines who'd been out there more than four years. This China Station sailor felt terrible. He didn't want to go back because on our troop ship there was a strict rule, 'No animals allowed.' Well, this fellow was fixin' so he wouldn't have to go back. But we got to like him, and he liked us and our ship, so he decided he'd just bring Chatter back to the good old USA. The next night he got a little under the weather and went to his old ship, the destroyer, and got Chatter. He fussed over Chatter's uniform and talked to him considerable."

"He walks up the gangway of our ship with Chatter and we all was watchin'. Well, who should happen to be standing around on deck but the

Skipper himself, one of the toughest officers in the whole U.S. Navy. But that don't stop Chatter and this fellow. They just walk right up to the Skipper and Chatter puts down his little duffle bag, salutes the Captain, and then hands over his papers. We was all waitin' for the old man to blow up. He don't say anything for a minute or two and then busts out with the biggest smile any of us had ever seen on any officer, let alone the Skipper."

"Anyway Chatter got to the USA and then last I heard he was a mascot down in Norfolk."

"Hells bells," says Sledge, "remember that battlewagon that sailed out of Seattle with a girl as a mascot—that is until the officers discovered she was aboard. They didn't dare put her in the ship's prison and she stayed in sick bay until they hit the next port. A lot of sailors lost their ratings on account of that."

"Yes," Chips said, "there was an airplane courier who had a poodle dog as a mascot. Then some of the sailors have birds and cats as mascots. I just guess sailors are funny people."

SOUTH OF THE EQUATOR

For six days the convoy zigzags southward, keeping close to the shores of Brazil, then, somewhere off Rio de Janeiro, heads directly into the rising sun. This, we are sure, indicates we are moving toward the southern tip of the continent of Africa.

Toward midnight on December 7, I am listening to the talk of three British sentries in a hallway just off the hurricane deck. Two members of the U.S. Navy gun crew are inside catching a quick smoke. A petty officer, on patrol, comes by and bawls out the sailors.

"Aw gee," one of the sailors replies, "have a heart. It's raining out there. We just came inside for a minute because we can't smoke in the blackout. You'd do the same thing. Be a human bein.'"

"Then get on back to your posts. I got my orders. You got yours," the petty officer says and walks away.

"We'd be put on a charge," one of the sentries says, "if we talked back like that in the British Army."

The conversation continues along on the same subject. The sentry, like many of the British Tommies aboard, has had a bee put in his bonnet when he sees the easy manner Americans have with each other. They can't quite get over the way Americans speak right up to their officers.

Suddenly, our conversation is interrupted by a South Carolina colored boy from the officers' mess who comes running from below four steps at a time. He is so terribly excited I stop him and ask, "What's the matter?"

"Leave me be, man," he says, "I want to get to that gun crew. We are in it. I want to let those boys know so they'll look out for any Jap ships."

Later, I find out that the mess boy overheard news of Pearl Harbor ahead of the rest of us while he was serving coffee to the ship's radio officers.

The news is eventually announced in the movies to the British officers. They rise and cheer. "We're Allies now," says David, a British officer in charge of Military Police aboard the ship and my friend. "You'll feel differently about everything now that you're in it too." He's right. I don't feel quite so aloof and objective about the war.

The next morning, a mimeographed typewritten copy of the news is distributed. Somehow seeing news this important distributed this way, and not in bold headlines as I imagine the New York newspapers are handling it, makes it lack conviction. Here is what it said:

U.S.S. *WEST POINT*
WAR EXTRA
December 8, 1941
NOTE: PLEASE DO NOT TELEPHONE OR VISIT
RADIO ROOM. LATEST INFORMATION WILL BE
DISSEMINATED BY BULLETINS AND PUBLIC

ADDRESS AS SOON AS RECEIVED
HAWAII ATTACKED BY JAPANESE

The United States has placed war plans in effect against Japan following air attacks on Pearl Harbor at 7:30 a.m., Honolulu time (8:30 p.m. local time), Sunday, December 7, 1941. The White House announced that President Roosevelt was quickly assembling all facts, etc.

One of the Navy officers tells me that the Captain of the ship had a special sealed envelope marked: OPEN ONLY IN CASE WAR IS DECLARED. I wonder if his hand trembled much when he broke open the seals.

THIRTY-FIVE HUNDRED MILES FROM CAPE TOWN

Four of the best friends I've made aboard this ship are British officers. They have a nice roomy cabin in the First Class section and make me more than welcome any time I turn up. We sit around and talk, play pontoon, the English equivalent for black jack, and keep an English phonograph going with American foxtrots. They are much amused at my running around talking to the Tommies and making notes on what I hear. They refuse to believe anything I tell them I've heard except what they want to believe.

Their curiosity about America is insatiable. American movies have given them the idea that in the United States (1) everything is in a continual mad, frantic rush (movies about New York); (2) you see gangsters machine-gunning each other every day on the streets of our cities (George Raft movies); (3) Hollywood movie stars are as fascinating and interesting as the roles they play. I like to feel I've gotten over to them that there are serious aspects of my country and the life of my people, not conveyed by Hollywood.

On the subject of the war they are thoroughly convinced of one thing. England is fighting America's battle, and our providing guns, planes, and supplies is the least we can do. We owe them that. They feel superior to us in that, up to now, they have been giving their lives while we have only been giving our gold. And gold, they point out, will be worth nothing if Hitler wins.

The surprising thing to me is that unlike opinion in America, they feel Hitler's persecution of the Jews is not much of an issue at stake in the war. Two of them don't like Jews, one of them is anti-Semitic, and the fourth is more than anti-Semitic. He'd like to see something done about clearing the Jews out of England after the war. Russia, they feel, is dangerous. Questioning the advisability of changing England from a capitalist to a socialist state would be, to them, questioning the setting of the sun or the movement of the tides.

Here are my four British officer friends. Stephen is a second lieutenant in an infantry battalion. In civilian life he would work for the Ministry of Health. He says he really didn't have sufficient income to take a commission, but he felt having a commission would have considerable bearing in his career after the war. He is engaged to a London schoolteacher. Her picture on his dressing table makes her look just about as you'd expect a London schoolteacher to look. He wears horn-rimmed glasses and is very retiring. One senses in him an acceptance of the idea that my other officer friends, Duncan and David, are above him because of their public school background.

Duncan comes from an old Scotch family with an estate near Edinburgh. He was educated at Wellington, which he describes to me as "the fourth best public school in England." He is married to the daughter of a wealthy Standard Oil executive and has never worked for a living. He has wandered around Europe—Paris, Switzerland—most of his life. He is fair haired and blue-eyed, and has Scotch shrewdness and boyish charm. He says he once considered coming to "the States" and marrying an American heiress. Instead, I gather, he got an English one. Judging from her picture she is very pretty, too.

Jack is a first lieutenant in the Sappers, or Royal Engineers, and is not entirely English. He has a French grandmother. He mentions that she was the Countess of Lyons when others get to boasting about their families and background. He was studying engineering when the war broke out. He acts like a kid and seems to be taking a boyish delight in the war. The men in his unit haven't much respect for him because they tell me, "He tries to be one of the boys."

Jack is engaged to a London society girl, but likes to relate his amorous adventures in Paris. He wouldn't, of course, touch the girl he's going to marry until afterwards. Our discussions about the differences between England and America and the morale of the Tommies aboard ship he considers "a lot of balls." The only time I ever see him show any enthusiasm over any subject except sex or cards is when he describes using TNT to blow up things. He describes in detail the excitement he feels when he sends trees hurtling into the air and collapses buildings. "Great sport!" he says. In 1939, he went to France at Dunkerque. David, one of Jack's roommates, thinks he is "really not officer class."

One afternoon, after an especially long game of pontoon, Jack and the other players leave the room. Duncan stands up and is re-adding the score.

"There is nothing," he says sneeringly, "I hate worse than a card cheat." Duncan has suspected Jack of cheating at cards for quite a while. This afternoon, he says, has convinced him of it.

"The man is a cad and a bounder," Duncan says. I am surprised because I hadn't noticed any cheating going on. However, Jack appears to have little or no money and seems eager to win. But the whole thing strikes me as a bit funny because it's so much like a cheap English novel out of the nineties.

The fourth member of the cabin I am genuinely devoted to. He is David Hunt, a First Lieutenant (he is careful to pronounce it "left-tenant") and Commanding Officer of the CMS, Corps of Military Police, aboard

the ship. In civilian life he is a London solicitor who "did a bit of barris-
tering now and then." Most of the officers of the Military Police are
members of the legal profession. He is, by far, the most attractive and
amusing of all the British officers aboard. His family is well-heeled and
he was educated at Harrow and Oxford. He is not only always correctly
dressed but is always perfectly groomed. The best London tailors fit his
clothes and his uniforms. His shirts, he tells me proudly, were made to
order by the shirt maker to the Prince of Wales.

This statement moves me to remark that I didn't see any reason why
Wally Simpson shouldn't have been allowed to become Queen of
England.

"My dear lad," he says, "nothing would have delighted us more than
to have an American woman as our queen. A top drawer American girl,
yes. But a woman who'd had two divorces, who'd been had officially by
two men? Oh no. Even if she'd done a bit of playing around and never
had any divorces, she might have done. But to have a queen whom all
the world knew—no, no, no my boy."

David is an English gentleman. Today, he defines exactly what a gentleman is: "One who is never unintentionally rude."

Virtually everything about David I disapprove of. This includes
almost everything he thinks. Yet he is my best friend aboard the boat. He
could not be more charming. I think it is because he actually believes
thoroughly in what he stands for. One night we are talking about the
skiing and gay life at St. Moritz in Switzerland, as both of us had at one
time spent winter holidays there.

Out loud, I wonder if those days will ever come back again. "My
God, man," David says, "of course they'll come back. That's the sort of
thing we're fighting for."

My main objection to David, and I continually tell him so, is that
he has no social conscience. His ideas simply do not go beyond "the right
sort of people." To David, a coal miner is perfectly happy being a coal

miner. He was born a coal miner so he should stay a coal miner. Conditions are hard for him but you can't do anything about it and besides he's jolly well used to them. The dole keeps him from starving.

When David gives instructions in the evening in his cabin to a non-commissioned officer he assumes a manner. First, he offers the man a cigarette as a signal that there is to be a bit of unbending. But with a certain kind of impersonal charm and eagerness, the manner also says, "There is a wide gulf between us."

"Smarten the men up a bit," David says, "We'll put a bit of side on when the officers come aboard. You know."

David seems to really enjoy acting out these little playlets and does it extremely well. But I keep thinking how surprised he'd be if one of these men were not to say, "Yes sir, no sir, right'o sir," but were just to look at him and say very slowly, "Very well sir, who the hell do you think you are, you smooth talkin' dude?" David simply does not understand that these are guys, people; that they are human beings just like him. Nobody has ever told him. He accepts the English caste system as a scientist accepts the molecular theory. His men loathe him.

It is a wonderful sight to watch him get dressed for dinner. He drenches himself in toilet water after his bath. He takes several minutes tying his tie just right. His lovely Kent military brushes turn his hair into patent leather.

Finally, he adjusts his very smart officer's cap at just the right angle, tucks his Malacca swagger stick under his arm and is off for a before-dinner stroll around the promenade deck. He salutes with a complete dead pan and perfect mechanical precision. A Hollywood actor could never approach David's performance as a British officer.

David has a theory. It is that with the force of your mind you can achieve a mental state where you enjoy suffering. There is no liquor aboard the ship because it's a Navy ship and, of course, there are no women. David says he enjoys this abstinence. Once, in England, a beautiful girl fell in love with David, and he with her although he was married. He could have slept with her; at a house-party, she came to his room and crawled into bed with him. But he resisted taking her and, he says, enjoyed this self-torture much more than if he had taken her.

"America's main contributions to the world are jazz music, women's clothes, and cosmetics," he says. He loves to dress his wife in American clothes. He'd love to have a smartly turned out American girl someday. He likes French and Italian restaurants. His hobby is playing jazz on the piano and singing his own versions of popular songs.

Nothing has ever shaken David. His life has been as smooth as the garden pools of the English estates where he spends his weekends. He is married to a pretty girl of a wealthy family whose picture, in a silver monogrammed frame, rests on his dressing table. She knew he was going overseas two weeks before he sailed. She cried quietly a great deal of the time. He kept up a gay bantering mood. And finally he said good-bye quite casually at the railway station. She was, he says, actually smiling— the light touch to the end.

Being English is one way of explaining David's philosophy of life. He has never doubted that the Englishman is the most superior being in the world. The funny part is you don't seem to resent this in him.

He is so sure of everything. He believes so thoroughly in himself because he is English. Thinking is unnecessary. It's all perfectly clear in the history books, carried on in traditions, and demonstrated every day in the manner of life of the people in high places who rule England.

"Tell me about this American Revolution," he says in all seriousness at tea. "It interests me. I've always wanted to know something about it. You're the only colony we ever lost, you know."

FIFTEEN HUNDRED MILES FROM CAPE TOWN

Today an American sailor jumps overboard. The sailor left a note saying he could not reconcile the way he had seen the British soldiers being treated with what he thought we ought to be fighting for. He said he saw no hope for true democracy in the world. Both British and American officers are careful to pass the word along that the sailor was known to be a crank.

We are being cautioned again about not throwing cigarettes overboard. All garbage on the entire convoy is tossed overboard on all the twenty or so ships at exactly the same hour every night at dusk. By morning it will be scattered sufficiently to confuse submarines about our course. If garbage, cigarettes, and whatnot were tossed overboard indiscriminately it would leave a trail from our sterns all across the North and South Atlantic.

At night we watch the ships in our convoy signaling to each other with helicopter lights. Some of the messages are not in code and the Tommies of the Royal Signals tell us what they are saying. During the day, sailors signal to each other with semaphore flags.

Over the last week or so we have noticed that many of the destroyers are exploding depth charges off their bows. The story around the ship is that German submarines are in this area because they are based in South America and in West Africa.

Tonight, Dennis East gives a violin concert for the U.S. Navy officers aboard the *West Point*. He is a talented virtuoso and, in civilian life, was first violinist for the London Symphony. Standing on the platform, before he begins playing, in dirty shorts and shirt, he looks just like every other one of the five thousand Tommies aboard. The officers are very moved by Dennis's performance and crowd around the platform afterwards to thank him.

He is a private and only permitted to carry his army kit, but regulations have been winked at to allow him to bring along his instrument. He carries it in a specially constructed black metal case that looks like a baby's casket. He has given many concerts aboard the ship for officers and troops without charge. Officially, the British Army has yet to recognize his musical talent.

His commanding officer has already been irked by the attention and adulation that Dennis is receiving. "Having a famous fiddler as a private under one's command," he told one of the AFS boys, "is rather a problem, you know. I really don't know what to do with him."

OFF THE CAPE OF GOOD HOPE

Perhaps it is the atmosphere of Saturday night in town reaching far out to sea, but this Saturday night seems especially gay. Actually, it is, I suppose, just like any other night. It is full of salty dampness; the decks are crowded with Tommies looking longingly out to sea. They are talking about pubs they used to frequent, about their girls or wives or kids, about how long before the war will be over.

From the afterdeck come the slow strains of music and singing. One of the best of the accordion players, a member of the Cambridgeshire Regiment, has brought his accordion out. He is leaning against the muzzle of an antiaircraft gun. Some of the Tommies have gathered around him and when they know the words to his tune, they sing. I put my bedding roll alongside the high metal fence that protects the six-inch gun and look up into the sky wheeling back and forth across the deck.

"'Tis a fine thing to sleep on the deck of a great luxury boat like this with only the stars for a roof over your head," a voice from beside me in the darkness says.

"You speak like an Irishman," I say. "Not many on this ship."

"No, not many," the voice says, "but they say that a hundred and fifty thousand Irishmen have joined up with the English. I have two brothers in the British Army. 'Tis an easy thing to be an officer if you can show papers that you have an education and have been to one of the great universities like Trinity College in Dublin."

We are silent for a time because the accordion player has begun the strains of the "Londonderry Air." It is a tune often heard aboard our ship and there is apt to be little talk while it is being played. The voices of the men singing the "Danny Boy" words to the music seem to blend so easily and beautifully with the sad plaintive melody.

"Has it been long since you were home?" I ask, wondering if by any chance he lives near some relatives of mine in County Cork, whom I once visited.

"After Dunkerque," he says, "I was given a long leave. They call it a survivor's leave. It was a long journey because County Kerry is a long way from London town. And then you have to go to the north of Ireland because no British soldiers are allowed to cross the line. They give you a civvy suit to do this thing. 'Tis a strange thing about the Irish. There's many a soldier in the Irish army gets browned off, as we say, and deserts to join the English. Then, when they get fed up, as you say, with the English they go back to the Irish army."

A tenor voice stands out above a group of Tommies who are singing and the words of the song can be heard very distinctly.

"I suppose," he continues with an almost musical quality in his voice, "that the Irish have always loved to go where there's fightin'. And, if there's no fightin' to be had, they fight among themselves. The trouble, though, has been over a long time in Ireland."

The lights-out bugle call of the British Army sounds. The ship changes her course again. The wind is blowing from another direction. A different star appears above the silhouette of the big naval gun on the port side. In another six minutes the ship changes her course, for we are zigzagging in the night.

My Irish friend is still talking. His name is Michael O'Flaherty and he was a member of the Inniskilling Fusiliers. Their record before Dunkerque was good, but then came the order to evacuate and they fled to Dunkerque with the rest. Michael somehow got a ship at Boulogne but it didn't go to England and dropped him at Le Havre. Then he had to fight his way to Dunkerque. "'Tis an awful sight," he says of Dunkerque, "to see the Gerry dive bombers coming at you and nothin' over your head to protect you."

Michael boarded the *Lancastria* and half way to England she capsized. He slid down her side and was picked up by a fishing boat that took him to Plymouth.

"The people of Plymouth," he says, "gave us a great reception. They cheered us and fed us. Then we went to our regiment's base depot, for you see we had nothing. All our rifles and kit were left behind in France.

The wind sings mournfully in the ship's rigging. We say goodnight and both go to sleep on the open deck.

ARRIVAL AT CAPE TOWN

The convoy sails past Cape Town, out of sight of land. She hugs the eastern shore of the Cape of Good Hope, arriving at the port of Cape Town from the east rather than the west. It is to confuse spies and submarines and to await word from patrol boats that the waters are safe.

Airplane beacons flashing in the sky at four in the morning are the first sign that we have reached the continent of Africa. An MP on night duty wakes me. I get up from blankets on the deck and look over the railing. Officers and soldiers soon come up in pajamas and undershirts to see with their own eyes some evidence that there is land.

After breakfast, the colored boys working in the ship's galleys line up on deck wearing their spotless white U.S. Navy uniforms. Over the shoulders of their inspecting officer they can see the shores of Africa where their ancestors came from. I watch their eyes for some glimmer and listen to their talk. But it's just another port to them.

At two in the afternoon tugs push us sideways alongside the dock. Ambulances immediately remove our dangerously sick. Debarkation officers come aboard wearing uniforms that would put Hollywood to shame. One has maroon trousers, a khaki tunic with a shiny Sam Browne belt, and a bright green armband. Another is complete with kilt and tam

o'shanter, even to a jeweled dagger strapped next to his shin. He is a
Colonel in the South African branch of the Black Watch Officers. These
old English regiments do a version of falling on the necks of fellow officers from the home office. It mostly consists of clearing their throats
and twirling their mustaches.

At four, leave slips are distributed, and at five, troops start filing
down the gangways. It is the first time in almost a month and a half that
our feet have touched land. Everybody heads for the nearest bar.

David takes me to a big ball at the Kelvin Grove Country Club given
for the officers of the convoy by the leading citizens of Cape Town.
Hundreds of girls are waiting in the spacious lounges. Most of them
wear long white flowing evening gowns of light material and dance beautifully. They look and talk and flirt like southern belles.

Elaine Bright, who is descended from an Irish grandmother and a
Dutch grandfather, is, I decide, the loveliest of the Cape Town girls. I
don't let her get away from me. The orchestra plays many waltzes and
Elaine and I dance together. During the intermissions, we sit on a flag-
stone terrace and drink scotch and soda. She is terribly proud of being
South African. Although her loyalties are divided between her English
and Boer origins, she seems to feel America comes next in her affections
after her own country. Because she is the editor of a South African
woman's magazine, she is terribly interested in all I can tell her about
American magazines. She is also very much pleased when she learns I am
a great admirer of Olive Schreiner and Isak Dinesen.

The most popular American officer, in fact the most popular young
man at the ball, is Franklin Delano Roosevelt Jr. He is an officer aboard
one of the submarine destroyers that has been guarding our convoy. All
the Cape Town girls at the dance whisper to each other about him and
try and arrange to meet him.

Suddenly, toward midnight, there is a loud rolling of drums. Field
Marshall Jan Smuts, the George Washington of South Africa, ascends

the platform. To me it is as if he had stepped out of a history book. Actually, he happens to be in town for the opening of the South African Parliament. He is slight in his South African uniform with red shoulder tabs, has a neat little white beard, and, although over sixty, has a spring to his step.

The couples crowd around the platform. The little soldier looks slowly around the ballroom and says he is reminded of the great ball given for the English officers by the Duchess of Richmond on the eve of the Battle of Waterloo.* The officers cheer. Englishmen like to remember that ball because victory came the next day. It was said that many of his Majesty's officers were found dead on the battlefield, the morning after the battle, still wearing their dancing pumps.

With great seriousness Smuts says: "Japan has made no contributions to civilization in our entire history. But at last she has made a great one—she has brought the United States into the war." At this the cheering seems to shake the rafters of the big ballroom. After the ball, the fair and lovely Elaine drives me to a restaurant high on the side of Table Mountain. I had seen the mountain, a sheer, flat-topped rock rising behind the red tile roofs of the town, that morning as the convoy approached Cape Town. The old Dutch settlers told their children that the white clouds that spilled over its edge were a tablecloth made by a giant who smoked his pipe while dining at this mountain table. We sit on the terrace and have coffee and scrambled eggs. Below us are the blinking lights of the un-blacked-out city. Beyond are the waters of the South Atlantic and the Indian Ocean mirroring the moonlight.

"There is little war here," Elaine says. "There is not even conscription. Our boys volunteered to go north to fight in the desert as if they

---

* Smuts may have been drawing on legend recounted in "The Eve of Waterloo," a section of Lord Byron's poem "Childe Harold's Pilgrimage," which relates the events of the night before the battle of Quatre Bras, fought near Brussels, Belgium, on June 16, 1815. Quatre Bras was the preliminary of the battle of Waterloo, fought two days later.

were going on a hunting expedition. We are only conscious that there is anything wrong in the world when the big convoys come through."

"At first," she continued, "I couldn't bear looking at the boyish faces of the Tommies and Aussies and New Zealanders, so many thousands of them pouring in here among us—then disappearing by night. Our life here is so peaceful and beautiful; it is almost too easy to make a living. Why must there be war and hate and fighting?"

"But then," she says, taking my hand, "if it were not for this war I would never have met you." My heart thumps and I want to stay in South Africa, marry Elaine, and have lots of beautiful children. She drives me to the docks. The Tommies are all aboard and asleep in their bunks. They were ordered to return to their ships at midnight. Officers may return at two o'clock.

The next day, Elaine drives me into the hills above Cape Town to the home of a South African intellectual that I shall call Jacques.* We fall into conversation.

Jacques sees my observations and little generalities about the class divisions in the British Army as clues to a bigger and more sweeping picture. The grumblings of the Tommies are part of a great unrest in the world, part of the surge of the revolutionary spirit, of the common man, of the little guy. The "old school tie," England's public school system, is the organized training of a ruling class. The class distinctions are fostered because they are necessary to maintain the capitalist rule of the British Empire. The things I am seeing and learning are byproducts of what Jacques calls "capitalist wars."

The great struggle, he says, is between capitalism and communism. Russia has made great strides as a bulwark against fascism and in pointing the way toward new socialistic concepts of government. America has

---

* Bowen is disguising his host's name to protect him. In the 1940s, the South African Communist Party was in alliance with the African National Congress and in 1950 would be declared illegal in South Africa.

shown the world what can be done toward giving people the full bene-
fits of the new developments in science and industry. But the rest of the
world must catch up, too. There can no longer be a coolie in China getting a penny's worth of rice for a day's labor.

The light in the living room grows dim and I look from Jacques through
the big window to the bookshelves in back of him, to the expanse of ocean
below us. The force of our geographic isolation and Jacques's dizzying
talk bring on an almost godlike feeling of awareness and knowledge.

He speaks of the awakening of the black and yellow races to a consciousness of their exploitation by the white man. Even in Cape Town,
the race problem is fraught with danger. There are one hundred fifty thousand Europeans and one hundred seventy five thousand Negroes. He sees
India and China as great latent forces soon to be unleashed in the world.

All these things, he feels, are part of the death agonies of the capitalist system throughout the world. A new era of socialism is dawning
and the peoples of all nations will live together in peace and in plenty.

Again, Elaine and I dine in the mountains—this time in a big tavern
made of logs. We have big plates of mixed grilled meat, bacon and kidneys,
South African wine, cheese, fruit, coffee, and brandy. Elaine is pleased
because I am so curious about sampling all the country's foods. I don't tell
her that, after the rations on the troop ship, it's not entirely curiosity.

Going down the mountain in the darkness, riding in Elaine's
American-made roadster, we try to sober ourselves from Jacques's brilliant talk. How wonderful it is, I say, to be able to see clearly all the
nations and peoples of the world moving in a definite pattern—to have
such a thoroughly global concept of these confusing times.

"Jacques is like that," Elaine says, "only interested in nations or
masses or ideas in the abstract. I am like you, intensely interested only
in people, in their individual problems and in their little joys and sor-
rows. As for a greater concept, I have a God, my religion in which I
believe firmly, a faith in a God whose will transcends everything."

People seemed to come and go in Jacques's living room, people from all over the world. They seemed to love to tell him things and he is interested in everything and fits it all together. "It's amazing what he has learned about the progress of the war," I say to Elaine.

"Actually, he's absorbed also with a deep love of South Africa. All of his family are Boers and he speaks Afrikaans as I do. He has done much in fostering poetry and literature and is himself a talented writer."

I find myself unable to tell Elaine what I am thinking. This friendship with her, the gentle friendliness of the people of South Africa, the almost painful beauty of its mountains and forests and coastline that she has shown me, make the war the last thing in the world I want to see.

Suddenly, I look at my wristwatch. It is a quarter of twelve. The convoy is scheduled to sail at twelve. We race down the mountain and arrive at the gates of the pier at three past midnight. There is scarcely time to say good-bye, which is perhaps just as well.

Once aboard the ship, I learn that the convoy will not sail until its orders from Admiralty in London have been changed. At ten the next morning the ships move quietly away from the pier and out into the harbor. The city looks lazy and peaceful in the bright morning sun. Table Mountain is hidden by low-hanging clouds.

Standing on the afterdeck, I look at the tall office buildings and wonder if Elaine is looking out of her office window and watching the convoy maneuvering into place for the departure. Just as the *West Point* gains its full speed, a white gull flies out and hovers over our deck for an instant or two, then turns around and glides back to the land. It gives me the shivers.

CONVOY OFF DURBAN

Again we are in the timelessness of green water, blue sky, and the darkness of the sea. The long mess lines wind their way through the ship. We wait with buckets in the morning and evening at our fresh water stations.

Portholes are closed during the hot nights. Only abandon ship and fire drills break the monotony of the routine.

Today word is given out that the convoy is headed for Bombay, India. So the words of the Tommies' song "Bless 'Em All" will have special meaning for us: "A troop ship just leaving Bombay." But why has this convoy, loaded with troops scheduled for the Middle East, been rerouted to India?

There has been much discussion of good times in Cape Town. A surprising number of Tommies were entertained by Boer families. The troops had been warned to expect much anti-British feeling. One Tommy tells me that he became fast friends with an old veteran of the Boer War who had fought against the British. The old fellow was much incensed because of an order recently issued in South Africa ordering the confiscation of all firearms. It resulted in the old sir having to give up two ancient rifles: one a relic of his campaign days, the other a relic of the early settling of the country.

Most of the Tommies tell me they got acquainted with Capetowners who were in the same trade or profession that they had practiced in civilian life. A South African carpenter, for example, fell to talking with a former English carpenter and took him home to dinner. It is a pity politicians from different countries don't get on as well.

Twenty-six soldiers from the convoy deserted at Cape Town compared to fourteen who deserted at Halifax. One Tommy was shot and killed. A U.S. Navy sailor had his ears cut off as a result of going into Section Fifteen, the Malay Quarter. The area had been declared out of bounds and troops specifically ordered to stay out.

Many of the Tommies to whom I talk have decided to settle in South Africa after the war. There is lots of sunshine, they say, and opportunity for a poor man, "and there isn't the class distinctions you have in England." Even David says he'd like to bring his wife there and start a new life. He was told there were great opportunities for English barristers.

It seems like everyone, both officers and men, either fell in love, or had a romantic or intense affair with, a Cape Town girl. Many have photographs of their new ladyloves.

But even the pleasant memories of lazy happy South Africa and her friendly, kindly people fade gradually. There is no passing of time. Our world is only the sea, the sky, and the decks of our ship.

IN THE INDIAN OCEAN OFF MADAGASCAR

The commanding officer (the OC, or what Americans would call the commanding officer, or CO) is presiding at hearings for British soldiers who have been placed "on charges" by their superior officers. The offenses range from stealing to smoking in the blackout, from insubordination to "being improperly dressed."

A short scrappy Sergeant Major (SM) has nine men up in the main hall of the second-class section of the ship. All nine have been standing rigidly at attention for quite a while. He keeps singling out one or the other of them for abuse. He makes them mark time: "Halt! Chin up! Attention there!"

He inspects every man's uniform carefully and discovers something wrong with each one. The Adjutant to the OC calls for the men to come in one by one. The Sergeant Major marches the culprit into a little room. The OC is sitting at a desk. Just as the man enters the door, the SM says, "Caps off!" and before he has time to think or do anything about his cap the SM has knocked it clean off his head.

The Adjutant reads the charge and the OC lectures the soldier and passes sentence. The OC's desk is entirely bare and the offending soldier must stand well away from the desk, out of reach of the OC. The reason for the bare desk is the same as the removing of the hat—so the soldier will have nothing to throw at the officer.

David tells me the whole procedure, which is almost as old as the British Empire, is designed to humiliate the soldier as much as possible. The knocking off of the cap is the final indignity and throws the soldier completely off poise the split second before he faces his judge.

David says the British Army in peacetime is apt to be largely made up of men little better than criminals. He feels that methods designed for hardened toughened men should not really be used on civilians conscripted during wartime. But it works. British officers speak continually with the greatest pride of the discipline of the men in the British Army.

The Tommy does not see things quite this way. He speaks of everything about his life in the Army as "the old British Army bullshit." He especially resents the continual polishing of his brass buttons and his boots and the washing of his webbing (the web belting that holds on his kit) and the general kit inspections. He knows these duties are largely to keep the men busy and get across the idea of discipline.

Every Tommy tells you that commissions in the British Army are obtained because "a bloke has got pull or got his own income or went to one of the right schools." One of the loudest complaints of the Tommy concerns a charge on which he can be placed, known as "dumb insubordination." It means that if you look at an officer and there is something in your eyes he does not like, he can have you court-martialed for having been insolent to a superior officer.

CROSSING THE EQUATOR GOING NORTH

It is Christmas Eve and groups of Tommies move about the ship singing Christmas carols. They are dressed in white underwear tops and blue gym shorts. "Good King Wenceslas" is sung most frequently. Everybody seems rather depressed.

Because of fear of Jap air raids, all the troops' Bren guns are mounted and manned on the decks. Regular antiaircraft gun crews, as well, are on twenty-four-hour alerts.

Christmas morning finds the corridors of the ship decked with Christmas trees, one for each regiment. There are toys on the trees, gifts from the men to the officers: dolls with blond hair, tin soldiers, toy guns, trucks, and tanks. At lunch there is a piece of turkey with dressing and cranberry sauce for everybody. It is good Christmas fare but somehow seems rather forlorn on our mess tins.

In the evening there is a pantomime, which both officers and men have been rehearsing ever since we left Cape Town. A pantomime, it seems, is an old English Christmas custom. It is a kind of musical comedy based on a familiar plot but full of allusions to local situations and characters. Ours is based on "Dick Whittington and His Cat." Hot dogs, the shortage of ice cream, the blackout rules, the officers, the Captain of the ship—all come in for a ribbing. The thing is rather well done because it was written and directed by officers who, in civilian life, were active in little theater groups in their towns in England. Some of the actors are professional, as is the musical talent.

At lunch the next day a very dejected Tommy stares at the hot dogs and beans on his mess tin and says:

"You'd of thought they'd do better'n this on Boxing Day."

"What's that?" I say.

"Oh," he says, "don't you know? It's the day after Christmas." The weather is getting hotter and hotter. The dawn comes up just as Kipling said, "like thunder out of China across the sea."

A TROOPSHIP JUST ENTERING BOMBAY

Black kite hawks wheel overhead as the convoy enters the harbor at Bombay. The rickety airplanes of the Indian Army, old Curtiss-Wright crates, sputter overhead. Two very light cruisers of the Indian Navy, lying at anchor in the harbor, send up signal flags. Dhows with slanted masts and gracefully cut sails glide by. At the tillers are men in red fezzes or turbans, the first Indians we see. The wind blows from the land and you smell the East.

Before anyone is allowed to disembark, the officers take their revolvers to the customs house to have them registered. The stringent check on any kind of firearms in India is because of the constant fear of a mad native uprising.

At noon, troops go ashore and are quickly absorbed by the big sprawling city. They crowd the troop canteens run by the wives of British colonial officers and by Parsi ladies in saris. Wearing their shorts and sun helmets, the soldiers wander the bazaars buying trinkets like any cruise passengers.

Go to war and see the world. It might make a good picture story. I pick out a typical British Tommy, Arthur Bignell, who, back in England, draws ale in a pub at Birkenhead. He has been in the British Army for eight months and is a machine-gunner. On his arm is tattooed a naked woman, a British flag, and a coiled snake which he had done while training at Aldershot. His ambition was always to see the world, then settle down.

I photograph him talking to Indian natives, visiting mosques and Hindu temples, and visiting the bazaars. Afterward, we eat piles of bacon and eggs at a troop canteen. My pushing him around and yelling at him when he's posing with the natives makes him think I'm absolutely nuts. But the whole thing amused him and he had a very good time, he says.

At midnight, I go aboard the ship and stop in David's cabin. He is sitting on the side of his bed, resting his chin on his fists, very dejected. I have never seen him like this and ask him what is the matter.

"I never thought," he says, "there were people who had no home or bed to sleep in. We had a lovely dinner at the Taj Mahal and then on my way back to the ship I saw thousands of them. They were sleeping in the gutters and on the sidewalks. They are so starved and dirty looking. I never knew such want and squalor existed in the world. Is this the magnificent India of which our King is Emperor? Is this stinking, poverty-stricken, country the glittering jewel in the crown of Britain's Empire? God deliver us."

Perhaps, I think while listening to him, David has at last acquired a social conscience.

We have a last cigarette together. He is gay again like he always is. You can't be with David two minutes, no matter where you are or at what hour, without it being like a party. He confides to me what's going to happen to us all. A few special branches of the Army, like military police and medical corps, orderlies known as "draft troops," and the American Field Service, definitely earmarked for the Middle East, are to disembark in the morning. The Eighteenth Division, all the rest of the troops on the entire convoy, has been ordered by the Prime Minister to proceed to Singapore. The city is in grave danger.

David appears to be completely undisturbed by the news.

Duncan, who has just come in the cabin, says; "I hate fighting the Japs. Anything but those frightfully dirty squatty little yellow men. I'd much rather fight Gerries. They're much better sports."

Jack says, "Let's have a go at 'em, I say. They're pushovers for us, as you Americans say."

Stephen doesn't say anything. He just shrugs his shoulders. None of the Tommies will know where they're going until they get there.

We say good-bye, all of us.

"I'll see you in the States after the war," David says, "I've always wanted to take my wife for a visit to 'Amedica.' Cheerio and all the best, Croswell, old man." He is smiling gaily, but in his eyes and handshake there is a reciprocation of the deep affection I feel for him.

Two weeks later a communiqué from the War Office in London announced that the Eighteenth Division of English Territorials, about seventeen thousand men, disembarked at Singapore four days before the fall of the fortress. All the friends we made on the long voyage to the East were either killed or became prisoners of war.

FROM A BAR ROOM ON THE BANKS OF THE SACRED GODAVARI RIVER

On December 30, seven weeks after we left New York for Halifax by train, our unit disembarked from the *West Point* for good. We traveled north and east through hills to Deolali, a British army camp, for a month of training. The place had long served as a holding pen for British Foreign Service men who had done their tour of duty in India and were waiting to go back by ship to Britain. In British slang, "doolally" means "mad" or "eccentric." Life there was so boring it was said to drive some men insane.

From a bar room on the banks of the sacred Godavari River, a tributary of the Ganges, my friend, Shinde Bahadur, ran the eastern equivalent of the corner tobacco store in Deolali's bazaar. His cigarettes are called "biry," and are nothing more than a rolled dried leaf. Most of his products are various fresh leaves, spices, and herbs. He does his best business in betel nuts. You can easily tell if someone has been chewing betel because it makes the inside of the mouth and the lips a bright red. Sidewalks and trees in crowded areas always look spattered with blood, but it's only where Indians have spat after chewing it. It's probably no worse than our chewing tobacco. The stuff tastes like licorice to me.

Shinde insists that I taste all his various spices. One of them makes me kind of dizzy. Shinde is very much irritated because the British Army has issued an order forbidding troops to chew betel nut. He says chewing is a pleasant sensation, good for the digestion, and it's a shame to deprive the poor British Tommies and Sepoys of it. Besides, he says, the order is very bad for business.

Shinde's hobby is photography. My Rolleiflex and Contax cameras, strung around my neck, make me a very distinguished figure indeed, in Shinde's eyes. Late this afternoon, I stop by for a chat with him after taking a few shots of the town and the bazaar. Shinde says he has a picture story for me. In about an hour there's to be a Hindu funeral. Swami Row, owner of a military tailor shop, died this morning, and his body is to be burned according to Hindu custom at a burning ghat beside the river. Shinde is to be a kind of master of ceremonies. He assures me he will see to it that I get very good pictures of this ancient Indian custom. We agree to meet in an hour at Swami's house.

As I approach the Row house, which is not far from the bazaar, I see a crowd gathered outside. From inside the house come sounds of wailing and sobbing. Shinde is waiting outside, and tells me everything is fixed, but the family would like prints of my photographs.

While I'm waiting, two Tommies stroll up and decide to attend the funeral party. They are both wearing bright bouquets of flowers on their battledress.

"We've just been to a native weddin'," one of them says. "Now we're going to see a native funeral. We're seein' everything."

Two sputtering gasoline torches are lit, and the light casts an eerie glow over the crowd. The body of Swami Row is brought out the front door. It is then washed, wrapped in the white funeral cloth, and a blanket of flowers is spread over it. The head remains exposed. The Brahmins keep praying and the family, which numbers about fourteen, continues wailing and sobbing.

The body is placed on a stretcher and four men lift it onto their shoulders. The funeral procession, lighted by gasoline torches, moves out of the town. Two attendants in the procession keep clashing cymbals, another keeps striking a gong, and another swings an incense burner. Other participants toss rice, three kinds of grain, and coins all along the way. Shinde says it shows the futility of earthly possessions. A gang of village kids follows us and scramble over each other trying to find the coins in the darkness. Above the noise of the wailing and the cymbals rise the voices of the priests.

On a promontory overlooking the Godavari River, the funeral pyre has already been built of a wood called amli. There are a few sticks of sandalwood, but if the family were wealthy the pyre would be all sandalwood. Swami's eldest son places a gold coin in his father's mouth to pay his way to the other world. His hair and beard are shaved off, and some of the strands placed in the right hand of his dead father, a final act of supplication. Meanwhile, Shinde is trying to start a little fire with sticks and straw and the coals from the incense burner. He pours some kerosene on the coals but is unable to make a flame. I reach over with a flame from my cigarette lighter. Shinde waves me away, saying that the fire for the pyre was carried in the burner from the family hearth and only this fire must be used. Finally, he puts the embers out entirely with the kerosene. He motions for me to light the straw after all, but cautions me to do it quickly without anyone seeing me. Several tins of kerosene are poured over the pyre, and two pounds of ghee, or butter fat. In the old days, says Shinde, they used to use only ghee to burn the pyre.

The eldest son walks three times around the pyre and then picks up a handful of straw and touches off the kerosene. The flames leap into the air. They are reflected on the quiet waters of the river below us. I get my first smell of burning flesh. It is sharp and unpleasant. Swami's youngest daughter seems the most grief-stricken. She keeps calling to her father. Shinde tells me she is saying, "Where have you gone, oh my father? Why have you left me?"

The fire has caused the body to swell. The Brahmin strikes it with a stick to prevent an evil spirit from taking possession. The movement of the body, as a result of the heat, makes you think for a moment that it has actually come alive. The procession leaves while the flames are still high. Shinde tells me the son will return in the morning and cast the charred bones into the sacred river. It reminds me that I've been swimming in that river every day for the past week.

I would like to visit the inside of a Hindu temple. It will be late and no one will notice us. Shinde tells me about some of the Hindu Gods. There is Vishnu, god of creation; the elephant-headed Ganesh, god of wisdom and learning; Hanuman, the monkey god in the Ramayana who helped Rama escape from the underworld; and Krishna, author of the *Bhagavad Gita*. Shinde says it would be interesting for me to photograph the festival of Nag Panchami in honor of snakes, especially the cobra.

He clears up several things I've been curious about. The Hindus consider sex a fine and holy rite. The blue and green stripes you see on all the saris the women wear are symbols of the two sacred rivers that flow into the Ganges at Allahabad: the Ganga and the Jumna.* The more one hears about the Hindu religion the more colorful and exciting it becomes.

The temple is still as we enter. Shinde and I walk among the moon shadows in the quadrangle. He shows me the various statues of the gods. Then, abruptly, we come on an especially strange-looking statue. I had seen this statue in the houses of Hindus. Shinde tells me this is Kali, goddess of death and destruction. She is also the goddess of creation. I feel that at long last I have reached something that I have always been looking for. For thousands of years the Hindus have worshiped Kali. She is older than Christianity, older than Western civilization. Looking at her as she stands in a niche in the temple gives me a distinct feeling of consolation and relief.

Around her neck are human heads; around her waist is a girdle of human arms. She herself has four arms. The lower left hand holds a severed human head, and the upper hand grips a bloodstained saber. It is said that "one right hand offers boons to all her children; the other allays their fear." Her posture combines the terror of destruction with the reassurance of motherly tenderness.

Never was there a time, I think, when man looked more agonizingly at the skies above his war-ravaged lands, beyond the wings of bombers. What God is it, he cries, that rules the world today? In Kali he may find the answer. The Hindus have known about her for a long time.

A SOLDIER'S LOVE LIFE ABROAD

From India, we traveled north through the Arabian Sea and the Gulf of Suez on the ship HMS *Talma* and then to the AFS Mobilization Center

---

* The Ganga became the Ganges and the Jumna is now called the Yamuna.

for the Middle East (MOB Center) at El Tahag, in the Egyptian desert, for a week of British Army organization and desert warfare instruction. Then we formed a convoy and made our way northeast through the Sinai Desert and through Palestine to Aley in the mountains east of Beirut, where we were to wait until we received orders.

When I rode down the mountain to Beirut on my motorbike on clear early mornings, the sight of the mountains of the Lebanon was so absorbing that twice I almost went off a cliff. The sentries at the Free French encampment halfway down have come to know me and I wave gaily as I whiz past.* Sometimes I race down the steep inclines against a Free French despatch rider or a Red Cap of the British Corps of Military Police (CMP). It's dangerous but it's fun.

I take pictures of an AFS mission sponsored by the American University of Beirut to distribute free flour to needy villages in the hills north of Latakia, but there is not much else to do. Some of us take leave to discover what, if any, truth is in the tales of a soldier's love life abroad. This would make a good essay or a story for *Collier's*. It seems to me that whenever American, English, Australian, New Zealand, South African or any other of the numerous Allied soldiers stationed in the Middle East get letters from their girlfriends back home containing cautions about not falling in love with some mysterious siren of the East, a great "ha ha" goes up. For here in Beirut, the girl situation is complicated. There is plenty of variety but a great scarcity. Male charm and courtliness have risen to dizzying heights as a result of the competition.

In any decent European civilization you can divide girls quite simply into nice girls and regular girls: those who'll listen to reason and those who won't. In the Middle East things are different; it's not so simple. In the first place, you can't even get a look at a Muslim girl. They are

---

* By the spring of 1942, the Allies had successfully rid Syria and Lebanon of Axis-allied Vichy control. From this point on, Free France controlled both Syria and Lebanon until they became independent.

kept locked up in their homes or if they venture on the street, they wear a black cloth over their faces and black dresses down to their ankles. Even if a girl is unmarried, she is never allowed to talk to a man or to let him see her face. If she did let him see her face, she would no longer be a nice girl. No self-respecting follower of Allah would consider making her one of the four wives Muslim law allows him.

A Muslim husband would as soon introduce you to his wife as a European husband would be to show you his wife taking a shower. Not that Muslim and Arab men are not hospitable. They invite you into their houses at the drop of a hat, but these affairs are strictly stag. One Muslim husband apologized to me for not bringing his wife into the parlor to meet me. I had remarked that the food being sent out from the kitchen was mighty good. He said as far as he was concerned he'd just as soon have me meet his wife because he understood such things went on in America. But if he did, the neighbors would gossip something terrible. He showed me a photograph of her on the QT. I took a good look at her. I didn't blame him for not introducing her around. She looked very luscious indeed. As for Alouite girls, gypsy girls, or Bedouin girls, you're as likely as not to get a sickle in your back or find your ears hanging by their lobes if you even turn your eyes in their direction.

Then, of course, there are the brothels.

Most of the soldiers stationed in North Africa and the Middle East solve the girl problem, if and when they feel it needs solving, by going to the brothels. It is the simplest way and the easiest. A British MP, a friend of mine, suggests one day that I go with him on the inspection party that clears all uniformed men out of the brothels every night at 10:30. He makes arrangements for me to meet him at a certain apartment at a certain address and recommends I go a little early to see what it's like before closing.

The famous brothels of Beirut constitute one of the biggest and best-organized red light districts in the world. They occupy several city blocks and one row of the apartment houses faces the city's main square, the Place des Canons. The ground floors of these apartment houses are cafes and restaurants.

Entrances to the houses are on the side streets. The district is rigidly controlled by the military in cooperation with the civil authorities. The British, Australian, and Free French Armies maintain prophylactic clinics known as Blue Light or VD Stations in and among the apartment houses. An orderly is on duty twenty-four hours a day and greets the men cordially. They are not required to register but are merely shown how to wash with germinal soap and then how to apply mercurial ointment.

The orderly at the station I visit is an eager young Australian who was a medical student when called into the Army. He shows me some of the posters of attractively nude girls with the slogan, "Very nice but hell if you don't use a Blue Light package." Australian soldiers are issued little packages of prophylactic materials in a blue box as part of their standard kit. The orderly is very pleased with his job and the work done in this field station by the Australian Army Medical Corps. He says that the rate of VD among soldiers in the Middle East declined from eight hundred a month to twenty a month as a result of Army supervision of the brothels. The soldiers cooperate very well except when they are drunk and forget. He considers that continual education of the men is just as much a part of his job as administration of the station. When he returns to civilian life, he says, he hopes to continue in the field of VD control and is writing a paper on the subject now.

Each brothel unit operates in an apartment presided over by a Madame and a staff of Arab servants who do the cooking and cleaning. The apartments are owned by wealthy families. Most of them are full of cheap modernistic French furniture. There is generally a large living room with bedrooms opening off of it.

The district is divided into two sections: European and Arab. The girls in the European section are Lebanese, French, Greek, Polish, or

Turkish. Some were always prostitutes; others have taken to the oldest profession as a result of the war. One very popular Greek girl is reported to be the wife of a British tank commander killed in the Western Desert. Their appearances and personalities vary as in any ordinary community. All are dressed very well in Paris fashions as business is at its best in wartime.

The Arab section possesses a little of the traditional flavor of the East. The light is dim. The apartments are bare except for low benches and have no central heating. Each girl sits in front of a round iron bowl of burning charcoal embers warming her hands. They are dressed in bright colored flowing gowns. Sometimes they moan sentimental Arab songs. A few of the girls in this district are Negroes. Few white soldiers go into the Arab brothels. They are frequented mostly by local citizens and by Senegalese, Sudanese, or South African native troops. The girls in the Arab quarter are cheaper, charging the equivalent of fifty cents instead of the dollar and a half at the better establishments.

The brothel where I wait to meet my MP friend is in the European quarter. I sit down in a large living room with cheap, shoddy benches all around the walls.

It is filled with Tommies, Free French, American, and New Zealand soldiers, some looking very miserable, some gaily drunk, and others very serious. The girls here are mostly Greek refugees. They sit on one pair of knees and then on another. Now and then a couple gets up suddenly, the girl leading the way, walks into a bedroom, and closes the door. The girl reappears first and ducks quickly over to sit on the nearest pair of knees. Then the soldier appears looking very sheepish and fastening a last brass button on his tunic. His waiting comrades generally greet his return with earthy ribaldry and laughter.

There is much merry talk and horseplay in the parlor. Many of the soldiers have come here merely to talk to the girls. They have neither the money nor the specific inclination. They are simply lonely and want to talk to girls. You see a group of girls and soldiers sitting together talk-ing, apparently as innocently as if they were high school kids killing time in a country drug store.

Nobody seems to object to these purely social uses of the brothels. The demand continually exceeds the supply. The girls welcome in-between periods of laughing and joking with the clients. But you sense beneath the seeming gaiety, an underlying atmosphere of sadness. You feel that under the uniforms, behind the bawdy laughter, are men torn by war from the arms of their wives or sweethearts. They are really not being unfaithful, in a way, but merely trying to cool for a time the burn-ing pain of desire and loneliness.

Just before my MP friend comes in, I notice an American soldier who was a Texas cowboy in civilian life. He has suddenly decided on a girl, picks her up on his shoulders, and trots her piggyback into her bedroom.

At 10:15 my MP friend arrives and takes me down to a French bistro at the corner where the inspecting party has gathered. There are two English MPs, an Aussie MP, a Free French MP, an Arab of the local gen-darmerie, a local official, and an interpreter. They put an armband on my arm and delegate me as an American MP.

We go from apartment to apartment, up and down the stone steps of the buildings. The soldiers grumble when they see the MPs as they always do, but kiss the girls good-bye and file out. The MPs look in clos-ets and under beds to be sure no soldiers are spending the night. In two apartments slightly tipsy soldiers voice objections to this invasion of their liberties. One of them says a soldier never has any fun, adding that MPs always spoil everything. Some soldiers get away with spending the night by borrowing, buying, or stealing a "civvy suit." Anyone in civilian dress may stay the night in a brothel if he's willing to pay the extra fee for such a privilege.

In some of the apartments the soldiers have already been sent on their way. The girls are setting the table for the evening repast. They greet the MPs with girlish glee and fling their arms around them or whirl them around like they were at a country-dance. One English MP has a little act he goes into.

He commands one of the girls to *shifti*, Arabic for "show me." The girl smiles demurely and throws up her skirts, revealing her thighs. "Bloody lovely, oi say," says the English MP. The joke is repeated often.

There are no arrests, although the MPs stop an incipient brawl. A Free French soldier is about to engage in fisticuffs with a Tommy with whom he has been carrying on an inane argument since neither understands the other's language. Both have been drinking.

The inspecting party winds up the night's work at a large beer hall where we are served beer on the house. Looking back over this evening's adventure, I feel again the impression of sadness and dreariness. It will be interesting, after the war, to see the romantic movies Hollywood turns out about a soldier's beautiful love affair with a ravishing siren in some foreign land. It will also be interesting to hear exactly what we tell the gals back home after they've urged and urged us to tell about our love life adventures when we were off to the wars.

SYRIA

By early in the spring of 1942 we are in Syria. I decide I've been without the gentle companionship of girls long enough. Christian girls are easier to get acquainted with than Muslim girls, but Syrian girls are carefully guarded, with Mother always around looking very pleasant but missing nothing. A few Australian or English girls, mostly from the Women's Auxiliary Air Force (WAAF) or the Nursing Sisters, or with the Army Transport Service (ATS), come through Syria on leave. They are interested only in British officers who are so lonely they'll even resort to matrimony. This leaves Arab dancing girls, Christian girls on the loose, and Turkish, Polish, Greek, Armenian, and French refugees.

I take a charming Lebanese girl named Lillian, who works in the Free French Propaganda Section, out to dinner. She is a Christian and was educated in a French school in Syria. We speak only French.

She suggests dining at the Saint George Hotel. The Normandy and the Saint George are the two swankiest hotels in Syria. It's fine, but dinner is somewhere around four dollars apiece. We are served in style with fairly good French food and Syrian wine. At the other tables in the big dining room looking out on the moon-washed Mediterranean are resplendently dressed British and Free French officers stationed in Syria and the Lebanon. Each, of course, is engrossed with a "lovely," the British officer's expression for an attractive babe.

Lillian seems to know most of them. She also seems to know a lot about them. This woman there, she says, is the mistress, as everyone knows, of that Free French officer. It is a great scandal. A man over there, Hashemat by name, has a wife and children in France. The wife is a young girl of good family. Truly, says Lillian, men are fantastic and terrible.

Most of these women are for a sureness in communication with Vichy. Indeed, everybody knows that the British officer who wears the monocle and is sitting at the table by the window is telling the gravest of military secrets to that disquieting woman he is with. Men are also of such grand foolishness.

As I look again at these women, whom Lillian is absolutely truly sure are Vichy spies, it troubles me. Somehow they seem a bit tawdry, not exactly in the best Hollywood tradition. Isn't a spy supposed to be an out and out femme fatale? Why, you swoon if you even look at one.

After the entree, Lillian tells me she is going to get married. She does not know whom she will marry but it will be for a certainty, a French officer. Naturally, because it is war, she has had many proposals. She would prefer a French officer to a British officer because the French officers have much more sympathy and understanding for a woman. American men, of course, are charming. But Americans are like children, is it not true? She would perhaps consider marrying an American if he would take her back to America with him. Then she would live in great riches because, of course, all Americans are of much money.

Nothing worthwhile comes of the affair between Lillian and me largely because I was not of much money. But I would see her around the bars in Beirut now and then and talk to her for a little while. Generally, she was with some British officer on a leave for a week or two from fighting in the Western Desert. Each one would take her out to lunch, cocktails, and dinner every night, looking very calf-eyed and in love. She must have run through about half a dozen during the three months I was in Syria. A couple of times, I tease Lillian about this fickleness.

"It is amusing," she says. "They have many francs in their pockets which they wish to give away. Also, they are sad and lonely. I am a good comrade for them. It is the war."

The most fabulous girl in Syria is Belinda Lyons, who is secretary to Gen. Edward Spears, head of Britain's mission to Syria and the Lebanon. Belinda was in Greece when it was invaded by the Germans and escaped to Syria on a Greek fishing boat. I met her at a dinner given by Alex Waugh, the novelist and a political officer of the Spears Mission. Her conversation is brilliant; she can quote poetry like a streak and seems like a hundred percent dream girl. But I don't have much chance; the competition is too keen. Nothing under a brigadier will do.

I speak wistfully of her to Geoffrey Household, a Field Security Officer in Syria who wrote the novel the movie *Manhunt* was based on.

"Ah ha," he says, "Belinda is like a case of the measles. You have to go through with it. Everybody who comes to the Middle East gets infected. Her fatal fascination lies in the fact that she has an English complexion and voice plus the alertness of an American girl plus the body of an Italian peasant."

The girl who turns out to be the most fun is a seventeen-year-old Arab girl. She has dark hair, a slightly bronzed skin and flashing eyes.

My curiosity about Arab food results in our meeting. I am in an Arab delicatessen shop buying a few francs worth of this and that of their forty odd delicacies when I see her eyeing me with much amusement. We walk out of the store together and grin our happiness at finding each other. She climbs on the back of my motorcycle and we drive, food and all, to a tall cliff outside Beirut that looks far across the blue Mediterranean. Below us we can see a partly camouflaged British coastal defense gun, manned by a crew of Tommies. As neither of us speaks the same language; our conversation is not exactly garrulous. It consists largely of grins, nods, gestures, and hearty laughs. She is the happiest person I've met in a long time. She looks at me then goes into gales of laughter, throwing her head back and showing her sharp white teeth. I am puzzled and look inquiringly at her. "American," she says, "verrigood."

It is the kind of expression of goodwill for my country that I continually hear from Arabs. Somehow, they seem to have found out that Americans particularly are a friendly, easy-going people who don't want anything from them. We sit silently now on the edge of the cliff and munch our food. She uses one word very frequently that I understand. It is *maleesh*, Arab for "it doesn't matter." But the word has shades of meaning. It sums up the entire Arab philosophy. Nothing matters. It is of "little importance." It bears some semblance to "So what?" My Arab girlfriend's family was killed during the bombing in the Syrian campaign and she lives mostly on the bounty of friends or relatives. The war has made food prices soar in the Near East and she says she loves to eat but if she does not eat, it doesn't matter. She points to the setting sun, the sky, the trees and grass around us, and the blue Mediterranean and says, "Verrigood."

My gaze wanders to the Mediterranean. I can see a tiny coil of black smoke rising from a ship far out at sea—another oil tanker has been torpedoed.

The food has made me drowsy and she puts my head in her lap and runs her fingers along the edge of my jaw and around my nose and forehead. She is singing some kind of mournful Arab song but, like most Arab music, it seems slightly off key and shrill. Then it gets dark and a chill sweeps in from the sea.

I take her home and again she rides on the back of my motorbike. She directs me to an Arab mud hut outside the town. It is one of the characteristic clusters of mud huts that suggest bee's honeycomb. An old Arab couple greets us and instantly brings a cup of black Turkish coffee. From their clothes and the furnishings in the floorless room I know they are very poor people. My Arab girlfriend is talking rapidly to them and they are nodding their heads in approval and smiling over at me. They look me over carefully, walking around me, but smiling all the while. It makes me feel as if I'd just walked in from Mars. Finally the lady sits down and looks into my eyes and chuckles, then says very carefully "American, verrigood."*

---

* With Christian girls easier to go out with, Muslim girls not so, and Syrian girls carefully guarded, this "Arab girl" is presumably either from a Muslim sect less restrictive in its practices regarding unmarried women or is a non-Muslim Arab.

2 CONVOY TO THE FRONT

AFS MOBILIZATION CENTER AT EL TAHAG

We are to see action at last. It is May 2, 1942. AFS General Headquarters in Cairo has ordered us to proceed to Libya in the Western Desert, where we are to be attached to the Eighth Army. We travel by truck convoy, skirt Cairo, and arrive at the AFS camp at MOB Center.

Late yesterday afternoon the rest of our unit was brought over in trucks from the station at Ismailia on the Egyptian West Bank of the Suez Canal, six hours after our arrival in the baggage truck. We are to be issued new ambulances, desert motorbikes, various kinds of desert equipment, and attend lectures. There is considerable delay until all the red tape is unraveled. The next morning I get a ride on a Royal Army Service Corps (RASC) truck going into Cairo. Complaints have reached the AFS from the British that the pictures I have been taking for *Collier's* in the Lebanon and Syria violate my photographic pass. I've been given leave to go into the city to straighten out the situation and develop my negatives.

I take all my supplies and most of my personal kit. A smartly turned out British lieutenant is also making the trip. He takes the front seat and makes no move to have me sit up there with him. We get on a very bumpy road paralleling the Sweetwater Canal, to avoid the convoy traffic on the main road to Cairo. The more I am jounced around in back, the more burned up I get. The truck is an American-made Dodge which we have sent to the British on Lend-Lease.

CAIRO

Cairo looks out of place in the Middle East and the British Army looks out of place in Cairo. This big, sprawling city with its personality split between the East and West fills my mind with the descriptions I've read of it under war conditions—its vivacity, its mystery, and its exotic allure. The streets are crowded with Allied officers and soldiers and filled with dull, sand-grey military trucks, staff cars, reconnaissance cars, and water trucks. Military vehicles outnumber civilian vehicles about two to one.

But I keep being more and more conscious of the Egyptians. I keep sensing the utter contempt they obviously feel for the men from the West who have come here to fight and die. In tents, in the big park, at the center of the business district, artillery pieces and sandbags are spread out among the trees and shrubs. The green grass is sliced with slit trenches. How would I feel if Central Park were thus occupied by soldiers from a country thousands of miles away who didn't speak my language?

But, most of all, I am struck by the lonely Tommy wandering around with no place to go. He looks in store windows, sits in cheap cafes eating eggs, bacon, and fried potatoes. He pays fifty cents for a can of American beer, which he doesn't much like but which is all there is. The only girls for him are in the brothels. Egyptian girls are strictly in seclusion. Girls in the women's branches of the armed forces only go out with officers. Every first class hotel, restaurant, or nightclub bears a sign which says: IN BOUNDS TO OFFICERS ONLY.

There is nothing the Tommy can do about all this and he takes it with good grace on the surface. But the prevalence of the OUT OF BOUNDS rule has produced burning resentment of the Middle East. One indication of this resentment is a piece of verse printed after hours on a press used for getting out army instruction booklets. The men themselves distributed it surreptitiously among the troops:

I've fought beneath a scorching sun
On sandy battlegrounds.
Though many a time a town is won,
It's always OUT OF BOUNDS.

Though NCOs and privates too,
Lay dead 'neath sandy mounds
The only place, and this is true,
That's never OUT OF BOUNDS.

Every rank in battle dress
To sergeant major's crowns
Never use each other's mess
Because it's OUT OF BOUNDS

And when in town on well-earned leave
To spend your hard-won pounds,
Unless you've pips upon your sleeves
The best show's OUT OF BOUNDS

I've fought for Britain and her cause
On democratic grounds
But sad to say, and here I pause...
For England's OUT OF BOUNDS

Each and all a mother's son
That fights 'til victory sounds,
Grant the same to all and one
And banish OUT OF BOUNDS.

Even the Tommy's right to whisk the virile Egyptian flies off his face and arms has been interfered with. Egyptians use a horsehair flywhisk, which looks like a small horse's tail attached to a handle. These have been made up for the military with brown leather handles and replace the usual officer's swagger stick. A Middle East order has just been issued, the Tommies say, stating that only officers may carry these flywhisks.

SHEPHEARD'S HOTEL

The front porch of Shepheard's Hotel appears to cover an acre. It is filled with officers and pretty girls sitting at tables and drinking Scotch and soda. I check in at the reception desk with my imposing array of bags and boxes.

It is good to have a clean room with curtains, sheets, and a mattress. This is my first bed in seven months. I take the longest hot bath I've ever taken in my life. Then I get out my best uniform, the one I had made in India, and groom myself until I feel I don't have to say "how-do-you-do" to any British officer. I'm going to the British Army Public Relations Office at the General Headquarters (GHQ) of the Middle East Forces (MEF), to set things right about my pass.

The GHQ of the MEF is separate from the British Forces Egypt (BFE). Both operate and supply armies that are, as a result of the closing of the Mediterranean, thousands of miles away from England. The officers who permanently staff these GHQs spend their off hours the way any army officer serving abroad is apt to spend his spare time—with women. Every war correspondent that comes through Cairo does a piece on the subject of Cairo's high life.

The GHQ of the MEF is the biggest. It includes a large residential section of several blocks of the best Egyptian homes, commonly called palaces. Barbed wire and sentries enclose the area. As a result of the non-bombing agreement between Cairo and Rome, the Holy Cities of the Muslims have not been bombed. There would be hell to pay for the brass if it were.

In the drawing room of one of these mansions I find Col. Philip Astley, head of public relations—also known as Sir Philip, I've heard. He is sitting in a canvas camp chair behind a table covered with a blanket and greets me with restrained cordiality.

"How is Frank?" he says, referring to a letter to him from Frank Gervasi of *Collier's*, which I had forwarded. He offers me a Lucky Strike cigarette, which I accept, and then takes one himself. Then he leans back in his chair and waits for me to begin the conversation.

All I've heard about him races through my mind. He is the son of a wealthy and powerful family in England and was married and divorced from Madeleine Carroll, with whom he lived for a time in Hollywood. One widely quoted story concerned the reason he got the job as public relations chief of the Middle East. It seems the brass hats at Whitehall reasoned that since he had been married to a Hollywood cinema actress and had lived in Hollywood, he would be able to deal most successfully with American newspapermen.

From the beginning of the war, one of the jobs of the War Office in London has been to get the United States to fully understand the importance of getting stuff to the Middle East. Also, to get the American people and the people of the British colonies to fully appreciate the magnificent job Britain has been doing in this theater of war. Furthermore, the Middle East was Britain's only front, the only place where British forces were engaged in actual conflict with the enemy.

Whether Colonel Astley's hands were too closely tied by the War Office, or whether it was his aloof and affected manner, I don't know, but he had succeeded in antagonizing an awful lot of American and colonial war correspondents. The Fleet Street boys tell me they've been able to circumvent him by using their previous connections at the War Office in London.

I look at this man carefully. He is smoking his cigarette in a long ivory holder. In a sweeping arc he carries it slowly to his sensitive mouth, his palm and little finger pointing toward his chin, like Dr. Fu Manchu in the movies. His telephone rings and he nods his excuse to me as he lifts the receiver from its cradle.

"Were they rude to you, Eric?" he says very softly. "How frightful! Well, let it go." He replaces the receiver and sighs with great weariness as if he had just been terribly put upon. He repeats what is apparently a characteristic gesture. With the back of his hand he smoothes his graying and receding temples, like an actor. That's what he reminds me of— an old-time London Shakespearean actor who's down to playing tank towns in the United States.

As quickly as I can, I explain to the colonel that I am not satisfied with my photographic pass, especially the part of it that limits my pictures to the "activities of the American Field Service." *Collier's*, I point out, arranged that I be permitted to take war pictures with the British Ministry of Information in New York and the War Office in London. I don't like going up to the front with my pass reading as it does. I ask if he will help me.

"Quite impossible," he says without moving a muscle of his face. Maj. Henry Oakshott, his aide, is sitting at a trestle table at the side of the room with several other officers. They are taking in everything, I notice. Major Oakshott keeps nodding his head in assent.

"All right, Sir," I say. "I'll do it your way. But exactly how am I to interpret to what extent the activities of the AFS my pictures are confined? Who is to make the decision when I'm on the spot and about to make what I think is an interesting picture?"

"I am afraid," he says, "that is entirely your affair. The Field Security people have been getting after us terribly lately, so you'd better watch your step."

"My dear fellow," the colonel continues. "We have rules here and both you and ourselves must abide by them. You are a member of the American Field Service and only as such can you be permitted to take pictures at the front. Don't go trying to get any action pictures up there. Actually, the British Army does not permit still photographers, except our own official ones, to take pictures in the field. *Collier's* can get all the pictures they want from us through the Ministry of Information in New York. Frankly, I think *Collier's* is trying to use you and the American Field Service as a subterfuge to get exclusive pictures at the front."

"Quite the contrary," I say. "It was I who wanted to put my cameras to work for the British. I have come all the way over here with the greatest good will and been given the assurance by the British Ministry of Information in New York that I would be very welcome. Editors in New York have been disappointed with still pictures out of the Middle East. They are anxious to print interesting pictures, which show that Britain has troops in the Middle East and that they are good troops and doing a good job of fighting the war. After all, I believe in what they are doing. I want to tell their story in photographs. I only want to help."

"But, my dear fellow," he says, suppressing a yawn, "everybody wants to help."

That ends the interview for me. I excuse myself and say, "I guess I better be going." He says for me to come in again and he'll help me about sending my pictures back from the front and getting them censored. That round, I reflect as I'm leaving, was all Sir Philip's.

As fast as I can, I hotfoot it back to the nearby British Embassy where I know Douglas Williams has an office. He has just been made head of the Ministry of Information in the Middle East. Mr. Colebaugh of *Collier's* had cabled me to look him up in case I have any trouble.

"Take it easy and have a drink," says Williams. Before I can tell him my complaint he starts telling me how much he hates the Middle East, how he worked in New York for ten years, how he is an old Fleet Street man, and how he wishes to God he were back in the newspaper business where he belongs. Finally, he gets around to telephoning Colonel Astley. He listens to him a while, then says, "Thank you, Philip," and hangs up.

"Astley," he says, "can't do anything further for you. But I'll give you a tip based on years of dealing with government bureaus. First of all don't make an issue of anything. Don't be too literal about a regulation. Circumvent it. You've got your uniform, you've got your photographic pass, and you're going up to the front. Let well enough alone. Take what pictures you like and I doubt very much if you'll have any trouble."

The Gezira Sports Club is virtually in the center of Cairo on an island in the Nile. It spreads over several acres of cricket fields, tennis courts, and a racetrack. Its life centers around a large swimming pool with a big, canvas-covered terrace beside it. The terrace is full of tables where you can have tea and whiskey sodas in between plunges, and there are chairs around the pool. Sitting on the edge of the pool watching the boys and girls splashing around in the water, I think that it could easily be the pool at the Toledo Country Club on a Sunday afternoon in summertime. The boys and girls look the same and behave the same.

When you want a waiter you clap your hands together as if you were a sultan and yell "Pasha." A seven-foot tall Sudanese in a beautiful gold-embroidered robe that sweeps to the floor comes hurrying to your table and bows before taking your order. It's the "life of Riley."

Actually, although it gives the appearance of being decadent and frivolous, the Club serves a useful purpose. The men splashing around are officers who have had their bodies drained of water over long periods of months while fighting in the desert. The women are nursing sisters who spend twelve hours a day looking after wounded men in the hospitals at Alex, Cairo, and Tobruk. Others are women transport drivers (ATS),

WAAFs who work on ciphers and do clerical work. Most of them are on leave, except those working in Cairo.

You only have to be an officer to get into Gezira. The old school-tie boys among the officers go to the Turf and Field Club, where the entrance requirements are as rigid as for admittance to the Court of Saint James.

At Gezira, on the terrace, I meet Ann Matthews, an Irish girl with the WAAFs who lives somewhere near Dublin. I lose no time in telling her about my Irish relatives in the County Cork.

Ann is with two English girls, also WAAFs. She takes delight in needling them with such remarks as "Britain got her Empire just the way Germany is trying to get hers."

Sylvia, her friend, the wife of an English doctor, says, "Ann, that is a frightful thing to say. I can understand you're thinking it, but saying it when you're a member of the RAF . . . "

"Quite the contrary," says Ann. "I say it because I think it. I came into the WAAFs because I wanted to see the war and was tired of living at home and of everybody else being in the war. I can still think and say what I please."

Ann works all day every other day and all night every other night. We spend every other afternoon at the Club and every other night having dinner and going to a movie or dance until I leave Cairo. I like Ann because I do not have to explain the things I think, say, and feel. On Sunday we go to the Catholic Church together. She looks very attractive in her tropical-weight khaki WAAFs uniform, always freshly laundered. Soon, Cairo is romantic and gay and magic, and like something out of the Arabian nights.

CAIRO AFTER FOUR DAYS' LEAVE

Americans seem to be pouring into Cairo. Most of them are US Army officers, sergeants and technical sergeants, Pan-American flyers, technicians, and the civilian employees of an American contracting firm. Also with them are a few members of the Office of War Information who go about acting very mysterious. It is not uncommon to fall into conversation at one of the bars with a man who flew out of New York just a week ago. It took us three months to get to the Middle East. Meeting a man who is still smoking cigarettes from a carton he bought back home upsets your sense of time and space. The tang of his speech, his little remarks and comments, still bear the fresh flavor of an America that seems, until this moment, a million miles away.

Most of the officers are members of the U.S. Military North African Mission, which has been here since almost the beginning of the war. It is their job to show the British how to use the tanks, guns, planes, and other equipment we've sent over to them on Lend-Lease.

One of the officers of the mission, Maj. Harold Bibo, whom I'd met in Jerusalem, invites me to his mess for lunch. About twenty officers from the mission have rented a large stone mansion out at Mena belonging to a wealthy Egyptian exporter. From the front porch you can look out over the Pyramids. The original servants of the house are keeping it clean and comfortable. High ceilings make it cool. In the main hall, stuffed heads of African game scowl at each other above us. The furniture is carved, massive, and red plush. Everybody is introduced and our hosts set a note of friendliness and informality. It might easily be a fraternity house at a midwestern university.

Capt. Joe Allen of Des Moines, Iowa, who is in charge of the mess for the week, says, "Sit down any place, boys. We've got these Egyptian cooks makin' the food as American as we know how. Pitch right in."

We know what he means. The cut glass, hand-painted china, and array of silverware terrify those of us who've been eating out of cans and off pie tins. We are served fresh fruit compote, roast chicken cut into pieces with a spicy sauce, beans and potatoes, French rolls and butter, cake, cheese, and black coffee.

Maj. Stan Kulak, a liaison officer attached to the American Embassy, has just returned from a trip to Persia where he's been visiting Polish refugees who've been released to the British by the Russians. The poverty and suffering of the women and children have upset him very much. Before we are through lunch he has taken up a collection to be used for certain comforts for the Polish women. All of us are intensely interested in what he has to say:

"So this Polish officer who was in charge takes me to a restaurant to meet some Polish officers who'd just come in through the frontier that day. They were having their first square meal in many months. We wait until they get through toasting each other with vodka and then go up to the table. They stand up very formal and salute and bow and click their heels while I salute them. My friend explains I am an American Army officer. So I speak to them in Polish because my Mother was born in Poland and I used to speak Polish when I was a kid out in Detroit. Well, what do you think; two of those officers start to cry. I sit down with them and we make some night of it."

A bucktoothed Captain from Tulsa, Oklahoma, comes into lunch late. He is an expert on repair and maintenance of General Grant tanks.

"How's the tank school goin', Jim?" Captain Joe asks.

"Pretty good. We've started classes already. Those Tommies are OK. They're willin' to learn."

"Where you eatin'? Officers' mess?"

"Yep and it's the genuine old thing. Those guys sure give me a pain, stuck up as hell. None of 'em speak to me. I ain't got time to get all dolled up and washed like those British officers. I don't have a batman runnin' around looking after me like a French maid."

"Oh ho," says Maj. Syd Berg of Brooklyn, a supply expert, "we're off again."

"You see," says Captain Joe, "talking about the British got so bad around here we had to do something. So we got a box and anybody that started talkin' against the British had to put a *piastre* fine in it. The money went to the Red Cross. We gave it up after a while—I mean puttin' money in the box."

Driving back to Cairo in a staff car driven by a British sergeant, we slow down because an Egyptian shepherd and his flock are crossing the road. The sergeant did not stop entirely but began edging the car through the middle of the flock.

"Damn you, Botts," says an Air Corps lieutenant sitting in front, "there you go tearing ahead without using your brains. Don't you know some of those sheep may be lambing? Don't you ever consider anybody but yourself? That's the trouble with you British, always pushing people around."

"Sorry, Sir," replied the British sergeant, "but I thought you were in a hurry."

"Forget it," says the lieutenant. Then turning back toward us, he says, "I'm sorry, but my family were farmers in Wisconsin and I guess I lost my temper."

The anti-British talk among the American officers I meet disturbs me. Here in Cairo, a logical place for informal liaisons, I see virtually no social intermingling among the British and American officers. Almost every American officer one meets in the Middle East sooner or later gets around to his grievances about the British. The Australians feel the same way, but why?

Sitting at a table at Gezira, I bring up the subject before three British officers and an English girl, the daughter of a British diplomat, and Ann.

"It is to be expected," says one of the lieutenants. "My colonel was talking about it the other day. He said there was only one relationship more difficult than being Allies and that was marriage."

"I'll tell you another difficulty," says another lieutenant named Arthur. "It may sound silly. But in the British Army the officers' mess has rules and these rules are expected to be observed."

"Where are the rules posted?" I ask as innocently as I know how.

"Why . . . er . . . on the bulletin board at the entrance, that is, generally."

"Go on," I say, "I just wondered."

"Well," he continues, "the American officers simply will not wear their dress tunics in the mess. Dressing properly is one of the rules of the mess, you know. This sounds silly but there is the old saying, 'When in Rome do as the Romans do.' Besides, it's terribly important for morale and all that."

"Really, Arthur; I didn't know you were so terribly English," says Ann, her eyes dancing. "Why not let's do as the Egyptians?"

"Well," replies Arthur, "I was born in South Africa, I know, but I went to school in England and lived there so long, I might as well be English."

That night, during dinner at the home of Madame Edward, a wealthy and charming Egyptian woman whose family is mostly in the Egyptian government, she mentions that she is unable to have British and American officers at the same social affairs at her home.

"They actually stand on different sides of the room and sometimes gather in different rooms," she explained. "It makes a hopeless situation for a hostess."

"Why is it?" I ask.

"Oh," she says, "the British are difficult to get along with. You must understand them. They are shy and self-conscious and, I must admit, a bit proud of being English. I'll tell you one incident that helped get the whole business off to a bad start here in Cairo. General Maxwell, the head of the mission, he's so charming you know, gave a tea dance for American and British officers. Well, the American boys introduced, how do you say, 'cutting in.' The English and Egyptian girls loved it. There were too many men and it meant that each girl would dance with so many different men.

"Ambassador and Lady Miles Lampson were there and Lady Lampson was having a beautiful time. She is young and loves to dance. Well, a very shy American officer decided to cut in on her. She was dancing with an English lieutenant at the moment and he refused to let the American officer cut in. The American boy blushed and walked away, but it made the other American officers perfectly furious and the incident was talked about for weeks."

Later, in the Shepheard's Hotel bar, Joseph Levy, a *New York Times* correspondent, tells me he's just as disturbed as I am about Anglo-American relations among the officers in the Middle East.

"Our Ambassador Kirk," he says, "had a meeting the other day of British and American correspondents, morale officers, and officials in order to do something about it. We're afraid there may be fist fights in the bars. The conclusion the meeting came to was that there ought to be an Anglo-American club for officers where the two can get to know each other. I've sent nothing to the *Times*, naturally, on account of the censors. But I have hinted at the matter between the lines in my cables."

A few nights later at dinner at the home of Ray Hare, a secretary of the Embassy, and his lovely wife, I get as good an explanation for the whole thing as any.

"Both the British and American officers," says Ray, "ought to be spanked. It reached the point where some American officers who've never exchanged more than a few words with the British officers are sore at them. The same is true with the British, only they simply assume the Americans are dull and boors."

"I must say," Ray says with a smile, "that there are times, however, when the British can be very exasperating. There are times when one must take a strong hand with them or they'll ride over you or overawe you."

Except for a few pictures I take at Gezira showing the high life in Cairo, I am not doing any work, or any worrying, just having fun. War is sure hell here. Hollywood ought to do a movie with British-occupied

Cairo as a background. It could be full of beautiful Greek refugees, ravishing Italian spies, seductive Egyptian courtesans, sensitive boyish British officers, Arab dancing girls, dashing war correspondents—everything. It's all here, but it is by no means as glamorous as the movies make things out.

Most of the war correspondents hang out on the terrace of Shepheard's Hotel, generally in a group. I've talked with some of them. Ben Robertson of *PM* is the most pleasant. He insists on wearing civilian clothes; he says a uniform makes him feel uneasy. Later, he returned to New York and went to work for the *Herald Tribune*. He flew to Lisbon, but the clipper crashed on arrival and he was killed.

Levy is the most serious and earnest of the correspondents. He is upset he says because his Palestine despatches are criticized by both Arabs and Jews. He is having trouble with his health.

George Lait of International News Service is the most philosophical and easygoing. He is just recovering from malaria, which had him in the hospital for several weeks.

Harry Zinder of *Time* and *Life* seems to be the hardest working and to have the most contacts.

Ed Kennedy, bureau chief at the Associated Press, is very serious about his work and looks continually worried. He reminds you of a young minister in a small midwestern town. The British show him the most respect of an American correspondent because they think the AP is a kind of unofficial U.S. government news agency. They identify it with their own, Reuters.

Harry Crockett of the AP has just arrived in town to replace Larry Allen, who is now a prisoner of war. Crockett will get the coveted assignment of covering the British Mediterranean Fleet. He comes from a suburb of Boston and appears eager and enthusiastic. He seems like a kid and is having a lot of fun getting decked out in a fancy war correspondent's uniform. Eight months later, the minesweeper on which he was sailing was torpedoed. Crockett slid down the side of the capsized hull and grabbed a life raft. But when a life raft finally reached him, he had gone under and drowned.

Joe Doakes of an Illinois paper is the most cynical of all the correspondents.* He brings with him something of the flavor of the Manhattan reporters who hang out at police headquarters. Nothing is sacred. The brass hats are all stuffed shirts. The British are silly. The whole war is a racket. The censors don't know their left ear from a hole in the ground.

"So I write this piece," says Joe today, sitting at a table on the terrace of Shepheard's, "all about how it feels to take a tank ride. Of course, I made it all up. You couldn't pay me to take a tank ride. I make up in detail how the door of the tank banged shut and latched. Well, the censor gives me a big argument about not describing the door of this kind of tank as closing that way. Imagine, it was all made up."

"The best way to begin a piece from the front," says George Lait, "is to say, 'As I write this despatch on my typewriter, enemy machine guns are beating a devil's tattoo on my tin helmet.'" We all laugh.

Much of the correspondents' talk concerns trouble with the censors. They seem to feel that most of the difficulty lies with the individual censor. When a censor is inept and not sure of the "stops"—matters not to be mentioned—he is apt to cut most everything out. A good censor tries to leave in everything he can and still obey the rules and conform to the "stops." Things have been very difficult for the American correspondents here since Cecil Brown went to town on the British about the fall of Singapore and Burma. The censors are very touchy about criticism and about stories of the high life among the British officers.

In general, the war correspondents seem to prefer each other's company. The British and American newspapermen seem genuinely devoted

---

* The disguised name "Joe Doakes" protects the identity of a reporter who submitted a fictional story to his midwestern newspaper.

to each other. The English correspondents accept the colonial and American correspondents as fellow craftsmen and are even in their talk more critical of their own government and its failures in the war effort in the East than American correspondents. They envy the high salaries paid by American newspapers.

There is something almost identical about newspapermen the world over. Even the Egyptian and other Arab newspapermen look like any newspapermen. The war correspondents wear uniforms identical to those of the British Army except that they have green tabs on their shoulders with WAR CORRESPONDENT in brass letters. Embroidered on the cap is a gold letter C. This is a considerable improvement over the last war, the old-timers say, when the marking was WC.

The war correspondents are much sought after socially, and the British officers are eager to buy them drinks at the bars. They seem to expect the Americans to be like something out of *The Front Page*.* It is not because they would like to get publicity, as there is a rule that no one under the rank of general may be mentioned in the correspondents' despatches.

All war correspondents come under the direct supervision of the British Army public relations office at Middle East Forces General Headquarters (MEFGHQ). They are rated as officers with the title of war correspondent. In the last war they were rated as captains, but it caused trouble when the officer being interviewed was above a captain's rank.

Technically, all war correspondents are under the orders of public relations as if they were part of the army. But they can find quarters and eat where they like in cities. Here in Cairo most of them are living either at the Continental or Shepheard's. They go up to the front in parties on

---

* Playwrights Ben Hecht and Charles MacArthur's *The Front Page*, a 1928 Broadway comedy hit set in the pressroom of a Chicago criminal court, featured snappy, streetwise, wisecracking news-papermens' dialogue and a zany, fast-moving plot.

supervised tours of inspection. Conducting officers go along to arrange
what is permissible for them to see. At the front, they dine in officers'
messes and sleep in officers' tents.

Here in Cairo they spend their mornings arguing with censors, getting their cables off or, if they're new, going to lectures on the British
Army, desert warfare, and the campaigns. Day by day news of the
progress of the battles is issued in the form of communiqués. The British
Army, the Royal Navy, and the RAF each has its own public relations
and special censors.

At one o'clock they attend a press conference at the censor's office.
There is apt to be some government or military celebrity available for a
mass interview. Generally, it's rather dull and spiked with overoptimistic
views of the Allied war effort. Mimeographed handouts are passed out
at the end. It is very much like the big business and New Deal stories in
America supervised by public relations experts.

I attend a press conference for Richard Casey, Australia's former
ambassador to Washington, who has just been appointed something or
other in the Middle East.* Nothing much comes out except "everything
is fine, we're sure to win the war." No wonder so many of the war correspondents are cynical. Afterwards, everyone goes across the street to
the bar for a before-lunch drink. All work ceases in Cairo, both military
and civilian, until four o'clock. You sleep or go to the Gezira Sports Club
to swim or drink. Tea is served at five; you knock off about seven, which
is "drink time." Dinner is at nine or ten; then you go to a night club or a
dance.

On the way back to Shepheard's I hear a riotous noise going on in
a cheap Egyptian cafe-ballroom. Men's voices are singing and yelling.
An MP's whistle sounds. I stop to investigate. A crowd of beer-groggy
soldiers is gathered at the entrance. Others, their arms wrapped around
each other, stagger out in twos and threes. Inside, waiters are frantically

---

* He had just been appointed "Minister Resident in the Middle East."

trying to close the place up for the night. It is filled with Aussies, Tommies, Springboks (South Africans), Indians. At the center of the big, table-filled room is a raised platform for dancing. There are no women, only men. Several couples of soldiers are dancing together drunkenly. An odor of sweaty bodies and stale spilled beer hangs over the room. Here and there a drunken soldier is upsetting a table or chair and swearing at no one in particular. Others are trying to wrestle or box each other but are being separated by their mates. Still other soldiers are sprawled out asleep on tables, or hanging limp over the backs of chairs. The MPs arrive and take the situation well in hand. Things begin to quiet down. This is a soldier's gay leave in Cairo, the reward of months of fighting in the desert.

Tonight Ann and I go to the Lonely Officers Dance. A British regimental band provides the music. There are many waltzes and we dance all of them. That was the last time I ever waltzed. I don't know why but there is something that makes waltzes and war go together. Ann knows what I mean.

We get acquainted with a sensitive young doctor just down from the desert who is a captain in the Royal Army Medical Corps. He looks pale and delicate and reminds me of the doctor in *Of Human Bondage*. When he speaks of his life in the desert it seems to make him nervously excited and his eyes dart.

"The great thing in the desert," he says, "is loot. Money is worth nothing, but you trade things. The German officers have wonderful cameras, Leicas and Contaxes and Zeiss field glasses. The best sport is getting Gerry beer. You take a reconnaissance car out at night and locate a Gerry column moving up to the front. You wait and knock off the last truck in the convoy. It's always loaded with beer, nice Munich beer, and lovely."

Later, the young Captain tells us he's been given leave from his medical duties in the desert, a long leave. Ann and I can guess why.

Back at Shepheard's in the big high-ceilinged main lounge with marble columns, the one with the plush benches all the way around, there is a young British Lieutenant playing Gershwin music on a grand piano softly and lingeringly. He looks a little like Noel Coward. Scattered around the benches and on the big divans are English and South African officers with their girls doing a little mild necking. The room is in darkness and officially closed for the night, but the melody lingers on. It makes a very romantic setting.

Ann and I don't say much for a while. Finally, I tell her something that is on my mind. I am uneasy. In the first place, I have a hunch that something's going to happen to me. Maybe it's silly and the result of my superstitious Irish blood, but I feel something coming. It's happened before. I've had a hunch something was going to happen. Then, something happened that altered my life.

Just before my father died, he stood on the platform at the Union Station in Toledo. It was the very start of the Depression and Toledo's banks had been the first to fail. Father was on his way to New York to arrange the refinancing of his business with the home office. I kept clutching at his sleeves. I almost cried out, "Don't go." A week later he died of heart failure on Williams Street in New York.

What is going to happen to me? Something can easily happen. I'm going to the front where the mathematical odds against life are greatly increased. The attack is scheduled to start. Perhaps I am a coward. But I'm getting what I went after. War is why I am here. In fairness to myself, I tell her, it is not exactly fear of death. It is fear of not living some more, not living until I see the end of the war and the days of peace that will follow, not living until I have a son and a home of my own and a wife who believes in me and loves me.

Ann looks at me all the time I am talking. I keep twisting the teacup in the saucer. Then I look directly into her eyes and see sadness, compassion, and deep understanding. Then very slowly, she says, "You are not going to die. I know you are not going to die because you are not the type that dies. In England I worked in the GHQ in an RAF station. I watched the boys come and go when they went on bombing raids over Germany. I watched those who came back and remembered those who did not come back. I knew them all pretty well. Finally, I realized there was a certain type that dies. I can't tell you exactly what the type is. I can't describe them. But I actually got so I could look at a young fair-haired RAF pilot and say, 'He's going to die.'

"But you'll be comin' back, you with that Irish talk you picked up in America. Very soon you'll come stridin' into Shepheard's Hotel and I'll be sittin' on the terrace having a drink, waitin' for you."

END OF LEAVE IN CAIRO

Ann and I sit in the terrace of the Hotel Continental having a Scotch and soda. At a nearby table Harry Zinder is holding one of his regular "drink time" news conferences. He has made many friends in the Middle East and officers continually drop by to tell him an anecdote, a bit of news, or gossip. One afternoon at his table, in quick succession, were an American flyer with the RAF who'd been stationed in Malta, a British Intelligence Officer who'd been interviewing German prisoners at the front, and a U.S. Army Air Corps flyer who'd been bombing German supply lines.

An elderly British War Correspondent I'd met in Beirut joins Ann and me. He's very excited about the coming "flap" in the desert. Intelligence reports, he says, say the attack will take place on June 20.

"Gerry is going to attack all right," he says, "but we're ready for him. We've got plenty of twenty-five pounders. They're just the job. We're sure to stop him with our twenty-five pounders." A South African general and his *aide-de-camp* (ADC) stop by and speak to one of the men at our table.

Both of them begin turning on the charm, obviously for the benefit of Ann. I stand awkwardly by, not sure whether it's up to me to ask a general to sit down and have a drink. Another man at our table finally waves them to chairs at our table. The ADC goes to work on Ann and I listen to the General. One of the jobs of a General's ADC is to line up pretty girls for him. That why, I had been told, ADCs are apt to be very smooth and very handsome. I listen to the General.

"We've got Gerry taped all right," the general says. "But I do wish we were better on signals."

"It would be a jolly good idea," says the ADC turning to me, "if we could give over all the sending of our messages here in the Middle East to some good commercial American firm like your Western Union or Postal Telegraph."

Some more high-ranking British officers, one from Pretoria, one from Rhodesia, another from Johannesburg, also sit down at our table. Ann gets more and more attention. She looks very pretty and blushes each time the elderly officers pay her a gracious compliment. Strange what a pretty girl can do merely by her presence. All the officers are trying to outdo each other in being gay and entertaining. I think of *Gone with the Wind* when all the Southern boys gathered around Scarlet O'Hara at lunch.

Toward 9:30 the officers begin remembering that they were due at a dinner given by Lord and Lady Miles Lampson for Richard Casey at 8:30. Ann and I drift off and have dinner in a tiny Arab café, then go to the movies. We walk back to her hotel in the blackout hand in hand. The lobby is in almost complete darkness and we sit in the dark over cups of tea. Ann says tea makes her sleep better. Our talk is mostly about a trip I'm going to make to Ireland after the war so I can do a book of pictures. She has agreed to go along with me as a researcher. Collecting Irish songs and folktales has been one of her hobbies.

Just before we say goodnight, I tell Ann that I'm leaving the next evening for MOB Center. Word has come that my unit is moving to the front in a day or two. We repeat our plans to see each other and linger until there is no more to say.

I get my last night in a soft bed with clean sheets. All the next day I spend developing the rest of my negatives and filing them away and arranging for luggage and supplies to be stored in the hotel.

At midnight Mort Belshaw and a few other Field Service men and I wait with our kit at the entrance to Casa el Nil Barracks for a truck to take us to MOB Center. There are a hundred or so Tommies also waiting to go back to camp. For all of us it is the end of our leave, and the end of gay days in Cairo.

MOB CENTER

There is a suffused grey light in the tent when I awaken. For a moment or two I struggle to understand why I am not in a bed with clean sheets and why there is no carpet on the floor. My tentmates bump into each other as they grope for their clothes and mess tins. Their scuffling feet churn up the dust inside the tent. It chokes your nose and throat. It is just under another bunch of stuff. Their voices have a rasping sound in the clammy morning. I had forgotten how spiritually important it is to have a room of one's own.

In the mess tent I have a mug of tea and a piece of fried bread with Jimmy King, my commanding officer. I tell him the results of my Cairo interviews. Douglas Williams is right, he says. Play along within the framework of the existing red tape—perhaps stretching a point here and there.

We discuss photographing the convoy moving up to the front. He agrees it will be best for me to hop from vehicle to vehicle and not serve as a despatch rider again. It is too difficult to operate a motorbike and cameras at the same time. My kit can go in the truck with the Bren gun crew. He suggests I get pictures of the AFS operating at the front as soon as possible, then get a ride on a truck back to Cairo to get them censored and off to America. Headquarters in New York is pleading for publicity pictures. Jimmy is so calm and makes everything seem so easy.

It gives you a feeling of security. Tomorrow morning our ambulance convoy leaves for the front. There is a full and active day ahead.

After breakfast we are marched to the gas chamber, our gas masks slung over our shoulders. The professional kidders are hard at work shouting that two or three guys always pass out and that last week a guy died during the testing of gas masks.

Groups of ten men are taken into a sealed tent wearing their masks. They emerge with their masks off their faces, choking and rubbing their wet, smarting eyes. Finally, it is our group's turn to take the test. Inside the tent the only light is from a smoldering can emitting clouds of smoky gas. The can is sitting in a large pan of water at the center of the tent. Ringed around it in a circle, we are in a witches' den, gathered around her cauldron to learn our futures.

The witch, however, is a tall sergeant major with a monotonous cockney accent. He gives us a short lecture on gas as chemical warfare. Then he tells us to lift up the side of the rubber facemask just to see what the fumes smell like. This is only tear gas, he says, and describes the various types of poison gas likely to be used if chemical warfare breaks out. The instant I lift the side of my mask I get a smarting, choking sensation.

That's enough for me. Now he is having us run around the tent three times. This is to get you accustomed to being active with gas masks on. Now we are standing still and he is telling us to remove the gas masks entirely and, with our eyes open, run around the room and out through the tent flap. It is to harden us and get us accustomed to finding our way during a gas attack without masks.

I think fast, take a deep breath while my mask is still on, and memorize where the tent flap is. At his order, I take off my mask with the others, keep my eyes closed, and do a little blind flying to the tent flap. Those who took the sergeant major's instructions literally emerge choking violently, their eyes streaming with tears. With my Rolleiflex, I get some pretty good shots of the boys just as they are coming out of the gas chamber after the test.

After lunch, we attend a final lecture on desert fighting given by a captain of the Royal Army Service Corps on the care and maintenance of military vehicles. He begins like this: "On this map you see the Western Desert where you men are going to do your work. Some of you may find your final resting place on this map."

From the big grin on his face we gather he means this as a joke, but our laughs are not very hearty. The map is hand-drawn with various colored crayons and shows Egypt, the bulge of Cyrenaica in Libya, the Mediterranean's southern coastline. Curving arrows indicate the advances and retreats. "Desert warfare," he continues, "is a paradise for the tactician but a nightmare for the quartermaster."

As the captain describes the campaigns and the seesaw-like shifting back and forth of the lines for hundreds of miles, the enemy becomes one man. Gerry attacked here and then we attacked there. Gerry is "a wily fellow. He is good; he must not be underrated. Rommel, they say, is a decent sort of bloke. Some of our commandoes almost got him at his GHQ during his birthday party. Gerry brings his planes over, then he strafes. His armored stuff made a flanking attack. He couldn't keep up his supply lines. The best way to stop Gerry is to attack his airdromes."

The Captain, I realize, is telling us much less about the situation than I heard from the officers in the bars at Cairo. He then discusses his life in the desert.

"You are a civilized people," he says. "The thing that places us above others is self-discipline. You must continually keep this point of view because you will be subjected to many indignities: dirty diseases, dysentery, desert sores, lack of water for bathing, and generally frightful living conditions. Despite this, you must keep yourselves clean and shaved. It is not only better from a health point of view but it keeps your morale up. By all means keep up your personal appearance. You will learn tricks. You can make a fire by pouring a bit of petrol on a pile of sand and then lighting the sand. You can shave with a half cup of tea. You will learn to always look around you for a slit trench or some hollow in the ground where you can sleep or get protection when Gerry starts dropping stuff in the daytime. Look out for vipers or scorpions; they're apt to be very poisonous. You jolly well won't like sand fleas. Cheerio and all the best."

The rest of the afternoon, after the lecture, the AFS boys make last-minute preparations on their ambulances. Many are still weaving grey tape into the big fishnet camouflage covers for vehicles. In Syria, the tape was green because of the terrain. For the Western Desert everything is brownish grey: the sand, the vehicles, the helmets, even the men and their dusty uniforms fade into the brownish grey sameness. Vehicles are further camouflaged by having sand thrown on them just after they've been sprayed with a coat of brownish grey paint. The camouflage nets spread out in front of the ambulances make nice pattern photographs. I also get shots of the boys making mechanical repairs, refueling, and changing tires.

At dusk I go to the Catholic Canteen for tea. It is the most comfortable of the canteens and the best run. There is a big dining hall and a fine reading room. Father Wickham-George has his study just off the dining hall. He is a sensitive Oxford man, very hardworking, and very gracious. He has made many friends in our unit and seems to have a special liking for Americans. Protestants and Jews, as well as Catholics, come to him.

Father Wickham-George receives me cordially although he is having tea with his batman, who also serves him at Mass. We talk about inconsequential topics for a few minutes, and then I ask him when he can hear my confession. Right away, he says, as soon as he finishes his tea. He presses me to wait and gives me a glass of sherry. Some inner stillness in him makes me relax. The batman takes away his tray and without saying anything, Father puts his halter around his neck, sits behind a prie-dieu and motions for me to kneel and begin my confession.

"Bless me, father, for I have sinned. I have not been to confession for two years. I have missed Mass. How many times? I don't know, Father; I only went every few months."

"All right, my son."

"I have taken the name of God in vain I don't know how many times. I do it all the time every day. I have made love to girls. No, father, none of them were married. I have not written to Mother frequently. I have hated. I have hated the top sergeant in our unit and the public relations officer in Cairo. For these and all the other sins I cannot remember I ask forgiveness. I believe in God the Father Almighty, creator of Heaven and earth, and in Jesus Christ his only son our Lord who was born of the Virgin Mary, was crucified, died, and was buried. The third day he rose again and ascended into Heaven."

As penance I get nine "Our Fathers" and nine "Hail Marys." I tell Father Wickham-George that I will try to come early in the morning before the convoy leaves and take Holy Communion. He says I can go to Communion tonight, after dinner, after the Benediction at eight o'clock, in the chapel adjoining the canteen.

"But I have not fasted, Father."

"That does not matter. The Pope has decreed that soldiers going to and at the front may take communion at any hour of the day or night, whether they have fasted or not." But he would suggest that I fast at least an hour before Benediction.

There are three Americans and two Tommies at Benediction. I join in the words of "Tantum Ergo" and "O Salutaris." Then I take Holy Communion with the others. I get the strange cleansed feeling I have always gotten ever since I had my first Communion as a little boy.

Afterward, we sit with Father in his study and drink his sherry and talk about America and how soon the war will be over. He feels the war will end suddenly. When he says good-bye he gives each of us the little Victory Cross, made of brown plastic. His Holiness the Pope has ordained it shall be given to all Allied soldiers.

There are tears in his eyes when he clasps our hands and says, "God bless you, my son," making the Sign of the Cross. Padres generally seem to be very good guys.

We go through the darkness to our tents. Father Wickham-George has given me something more than a plastic Victory Cross. I do not know what it is, but I know it rings back into the recesses of my childhood. Tucked in my bedding roll, back in my tent, I think about this again. I am no longer afraid. I fall asleep.

CONVOY LEAVING MOB CENTER

Reveille is two hours early this morning because the convoy must get an early start. It is just getting light when we walk away from the mess tent. Members of the mess crew are piling pots and pans into their truck so they can get a good head start on the convoy and have lunch waiting for us.

There is a last-minute assembly for roll call and final instructions. Every man has his vehicle ready and knows his place in line. I stand around our GHQ tent and see to it that my stuff is put into the truck with the Bren guns. The Tommies assigned to the Bren gun crew are supposed to protect us from strafing. They help me load my stuff and promise to look after it. "Right'o, Flash," one of them says, "but you've got to take our photos. I want something to show the old girlfriend back in England."

The light is too dull to get pictures so I stand by our GHQ tent and watch the convoy beginning to come to life. A motor convoy waiting to take off suggests a giant snake casually spiraled on the ground, its body twitching here and there. The men are warming up their motors and backing their ambulances around so that they point in the direction of the ambulance that they are to follow. The staff car moves out first, its headlights and blunt-nosed hood suggesting the darting eyes and mouth of a snake. It moves very slowly out of the camp and up onto the road. Then the second car follows—whiff. Thirty seconds—whiff—the third car goes by. If you are standing close to the path of the convoy, that's the sound rhythm you get: whiff, silence, whiff, silence. You get a feeling of elation, as if it were a big parade, which of course it is. Then the first vehicles of the convoy disappear off into the desert flatness of the horizon.

You wonder how all these vehicles can move as one big body when a hundred or a thousand men are each operating a separate engine. Of course, behind a convoy are days of careful planning. There is a convoy commander and a system of communications by means of despatch riders. There are subcommanders in charge of groups of vehicles. Each driver knows what vehicle he is to follow. The speed is slow, between twenty-five and thirty miles an hour. The last vehicle in a convoy is the wrecker car to take care of breakdowns.

Being part of a convoy gives you a feeling of imperishable power and motion. You feel you yourself have taken on the magnitude of the entire convoy even though you know, rationally, you are but one small cog in it. A convoy moves ahead together, stops together, starts again together, and disperses together. During an enemy strafing attack, the first car turns straight off the road to the left, the second to the right, and the third to the left, fanwise.

While I'm waiting for our convoy to take off, I walk over to another one in the camp adjacent to ours. It also is getting ready to leave for the front. These soldiers are members of the Royal Horse Artillery, now mechanized. One of the despatch riders is lighting up a cigarette. He offers me one. We talk above the noises of his idling motor. His tin hat is cocked on the side of his head and his shirt is frayed. He has been in the desert off and on for two years. His unit has just been undergoing reforming at MOB Center. I ask him how he likes being a despatch rider.

"Bloody Gerry bait, that's what a despatch rider is," he says. "Plenty of 'em left up in the Western Desert. Gerry loves to pick 'em off with whatever he can. But you're on your own more."

"How do you feel about going up to the front?" I ask. The driver of a Bren gun carrier slides out of his vehicle and joins us for a smoke.

"It's all right," the despatch rider says, "but it's a bloody awful strip of land to be fighting over. You can't grow anything on it. It's all sand and dust. Nobody wants it. Yet, we keep fighting for every inch of it. Now if I was fightin' for a bit of the green English countryside, that would be something else again."

"But it's Suez," says the Bren gun carrier. "We can't let Gerry have Suez. England must always have Suez."

A shout goes up. The despatch rider whirs up his motor, the driver of the Bren gun carrier jumps into his seat. They jerk their hands up in a good-bye as the convoy moves off. The slump in the back and shoulders of the despatch rider moving away from me suggests the weariness and resignation in him.

"Soldier, I wish you well," I say to myself.

Walking back to our convoy, I hear a lonely bugle calling in the distance. Behind me I hear the crunching of pebbles made by hobnailed boots crushing pebbles to the earth. It is four guards leading a band of Italian prisoners to their daily chores of digging slit trenches. The sun is just beginning to get warm.

At our GHQ tent, Jimmy King is shaking hands with the RASC brigadier and his staff officers. They are all very grave and formal. I get the picture, but it doesn't say much except that officers are shaking hands. Jimmy gets into his staff car and drives off. Our convoy has now begun its journey to the front.

I jump aboard the water truck and climb up on top of the canvas cover. I can see much of the convoy and this means I'll get some good juxtaposition shots of it against various backgrounds. The trouble from the point of view of pictures is that the vehicles are ordered to keep an interval of eighty yards behind each other. Bunching of vehicles is wonderful for photographers, but a pain in the neck if there's an enemy air attack.

The MPs at the Peace Bridge, which crosses the Sweetwater Canal, converge to check our papers. The vehicles get bunched up here because we're going through Cairo and the idea is not to have the streets cluttered up too long. Cairo is an open city and free from enemy air attack.

The close order of the vehicles gives me a chance to get some good pictures, especially while we are waiting for the MPs to clear us. We drive by King Farouk's Summer Palace and see his lavish houseboat tied up at a canal pier.

Going through Cairo we pass the street where Ann and I used to walk back from the movies to her hotel. In the distance I see Shepheard's Hotel. I wish I were joining the war correspondents for a nice breakfast. The Egyptians scarcely turn around to watch our convoy go by. It's an everyday affair to them. We move out on the road towards Mena, past the Sphinx, and then through a barbed wire enclosure in the vicinity of the Pyramids. It is a big camp filled with Indian troops and motor transport supplies. We refuel and have lunch: a mug of tea, a hunk of bully beef, and a piece of bread.

I get some good shots of the refueling, the mess line in the foreground, and the Pyramids in the background. The back of one of the foreground Pyramids has been repaired, the result of Napoleon's artillery having practiced aiming by shooting at it. Now, in this war, the British are using the Pyramids as an artillery range finder. Soldiers come and go in the Middle East, but the Pyramids and the Sphinx remain, the latter probably laughing.

After lunch we start up again. Soon we are on the road to El Alamein. Here and there we drive close to the Mediterranean. It shimmers in the morning sun, very inviting. The dust is blowing harder and harder as we move into the flat areas unprotected by stone hills. Along the road are other convoys that have stopped for food or repairs. All sorts of stuff is moving up, big Matilda and General Grant tanks on trailers pulled by trucks, supply trucks, fuel tanks, water trucks, Bren gun carriers, trucks loaded with infantry, and artillery pieces, mostly twenty-five pounders. Everything looks alike. It is all the same dull brownish grey of the desert.

We drive through El Alamein. Toward the left is the great Qattara Depression. At about six o'clock we stop at El Daba two hundred miles from Cairo. There is a good water point here. The men fill their water bottles and some of them start taking sponge baths. A Sapper sergeant comes up and tells us to take it easy on the water. I am too exhausted to eat. I spread my bedding roll in the Bren gun truck and go to sleep between a box containing a complete Bren gun with extra parts and a metal case of ammunition.

The next morning we get another early start. Toward noon we stop at a petrol supply dump. It is so arranged that the entire convoy can refuel at the same moment. Petrol tins are spread out over an entire acre as if they were checkers about twenty feet apart. The convoy drives down one lane and everybody pours petrol into their tanks. Then they put the empty tin back where it was and the convoy moves out of the lane and back on to the road. By getting up on top of one of the ambulances, I am able to get some nice pattern shots showing the line of ambulances in the foreground and the tins making a nice pattern that bleeds off to the top of the negative. I shoot it several ways with several duplicates at different exposures to make sure because the picture is a natural.

As our convoy makes its way along the road to Tobruk, we pass towns that tell the story of the campaigns in the Western Desert, Mersa Matruh, and Halfaya Pass. Just a few miles inland from Mersa Matruh is Siwa, where Alexander the Great marched with his troops carrying crockery water jugs. In this war Siwa has seen some of the fiercest fighting in the

Western Desert. You begin to understand the despatch rider's point of view in seeing the war as only a piece of strategic ground that men are fighting and dying to hold. You see the war here as a kind of futile test of strength and endurance in the desert.

Somewhere along this road fifty thousand Persians marched bent on conquest, never to be heard from again. Even before the Suez Canal was built, this forlorn land was fought over. Today, English and South African soldiers bathe in the pool outside the site of the Oracle of Siwa's Temple, where Alexander the Great learned he was descended from deity. It's so much easier to get the overall picture when you're sitting at a desk with maps spread out before you.

Our convoy winds through the streets of Mersa Matruh. All the buildings are demolished and only the jagged, saw-toothed walls remain. Mersa Matruh is the end of the railroad, which reaches from Cairo and Alexandria westward into the desert. The town has a nice harbor and was once fairly well populated. Like in all the North African towns from Alexandria to Benghazi, the civilian populace has been cleared out so that the desert war games may be carried out without civilian interference. At various street corners, red capped MPs serving as traffic police motion us on.

Riding through the streets I reflect that this is the first thoroughly bombed and destroyed town I've ever actually seen. Yet, I seem to remember having been here. Everything is as it should be. It seems to echo some dim far away memory. Is this something from one of my dreams? I find myself saying, "This is familiar. I have come this way before."

Fascinated, I look at the scenes of desolation and destruction in the town. There is a certain incomprehensible satisfaction in the sights. I find a wild beauty in the curves, lines, and planes made by the jumble of the wrecked buildings. Is this perhaps the fulfillment of something depraved in me, an answer to a long-felt desire for destruction?

But we are soon all out of the town and back on the monotonous ribbon of road stretching along the flat, brownish-grey desert with Mort Belshaw, who used to be a newspaper photographer in San Francisco. We open a tin of Australian cheese, which one of the crew slipped to me. As we make our way along the road to Sidi Barrani, we munch on cheese and crackers and talk about girls and dinners we've had. Driving the ambulance is not easy. Since this morning, all windshields have been ordered covered with oil and sand sprinkled on them. This is to stop the glare of the sun on the windshield, which can be seen for miles and easily reveal the movement of vehicles to the enemy. Only a tiny slot is left through which the driver can see to do his steering.

There is not much to photograph except a few signs. It is surprising to see that there are signs on the road to an active front. You had felt that all these locations and distances would only appear on very secret maps, but everything is well marked: Transit Camp No. 8; a sign giving all the distances and directions to Tobruk, Bardia, Siwa, and Sollum; Petrol Supply Depot No. 60; Dispersal Area No. 7. Barbed-wire fences mark off sections on both sides of the road as if there were grazing pastures here. Actually, the barbed wire is not so much to stop infantry advance but to protect our own troops and their vehicles from the land mines. All along the road there are signs saying DANGER LAND MINES.

Passing through Sidi Barrani, I get a jolt from the very name of this godforsaken town. Here thousands of Tommies, Aussies, and New Zealanders gave their lives in some of the fiercest desert fighting.

We see the town of Sollum situated at the bottom of a rising escarpment. We pull into a dispersal area to the left and camp for the night. Some of the boys ride over to the Mediterranean for a swim. I take a walk and get some interesting shots of wrecked buildings. Most of us are thoroughly exhausted and sleep immediately after our dinner of bully beef stew, bread, and tea.

In the morning the convoy begins moving out before sun up. It winds up the escarpment. Looking back at the town and the road below, you see the curve made by the sweep of the beach and the rest of the convoy creeping along the road for miles back like a parade of ants. I shoot it with the Contax, but the dust particles in the air blur the view. Later, this particular vantage point was intensively used by British photographers when they wanted to show the Eighth Army advancing from El Alamein. The road at that turn was solid with vehicles.

From Sollum the land is high, part of the Libyan Plateau. We leave Egypt somewhere along the road to Bardia, and enter the Cyrenacian part of Libya. The drive is even more monotonous and the dust storms appear to be getting more intense. Some of us tie handkerchiefs over our nose and mouth. Now and then we pass cemeteries. Some of them are German, some Italian, and some British. Some are very fancy with stone walls and swastika signs or crosses at the head. Sometimes, along the road, there are single graves with only a gun stuck at the head with a German or British tin hat hung on it.

All graves in the Western Desert look newly made. They will always look newly made because there is no green grass to cover them. The dust-filled wind seems to whip continually at the cross or rifle and the mound as if it wanted to level it off like everything else. Anything that rises above the ground is offensive to the elements in the desert. I remember the lines in the Tommy's poem, "Lay dead 'neath sandy mounds, the only place, and this is true, that's never out of bounds."

We skirt Bardia to the south. There is a good harbor here too. Also a large tented casualty clearing station. The wounded pour from field hospitals stretched along the front from Tobruk to the southeast.

As the afternoon sun lowers, it picks up the gentle ripples of the Mediterranean and makes the blue water sparkle with tiny lights. We round a bend in the road and see, across a tiny bay, the city of Tobruk. But our convoy does not enter the city. It turns on the El Adem road southeast into a dispersal area next to a British ambulance car company. We are protected on the west by a high ridge. A company of South African troops operating reconnaissance cars is scattered about the area on twenty-four hour alerts against paratroops. We are within the perimeter of Tobruk, so far the most impregnable fortress in the Western Desert.

All of us are dog-tired from our three-day convoy ride. But we feel as much like going to sleep as if we'd suddenly been transported by rocket and landed on the planet of Mars. We have a reached a destination of a journey that began many months ago.

At last we are at the front.

The truck finally comes and we pile in along with a half-dozen Tommies. I realize that although I am depressed, I am glad to be getting out of Cairo. It seems wrong now, somehow, to have been there, wrong and perhaps unmoral. It has been an escape as through codeine.

My sleeping bag is still in the tent at MOB where I left it. I unroll it without waking up the others and again sleep close to the earth.

3 TOBRUK

BEFORE THE ATTACK: FIRST NIGHT

It is now May 20. We are five miles south of Tobruk. There are no dugouts for us to sleep in because the British Ambulance Car Company, which our unit is replacing, has not yet moved out. In a day or two they start back to MOB center to be reformed. They've been "up in the blue" (the expression the British use for being in the desert) almost a year. For three weeks the grapevine "desert telegraph," the common soldier's chief source of reliable information at the front, had carried reports that an American ambulance unit was coming to relieve them. Now we're here and they're glad to see us.

Some of the British drivers ask us into their canteen for beer. They make us welcome with quiet charm. Instantly, you respect these soldiers and feel a great affection for them. You look at these kindly, desert-worn, sad faces and you say, "These are men." We Americans are eager, excited, and full of questions. With no trace of condescension, they reply as best they can. By their speech and by their manner, you know that any trace of unkindness or cruelty has entirely been filtered out of their natures. Is this what a year of facing death, a year of seeing little but destruction and suffering, does to men?

Mort Belshaw, who is sitting with us, asks if Gerry has been respecting the Red Cross.

"Both sides," says Blanco White, a Birmingham factory worker, "have been trying to avoid hitting the Red Cross but there has been some bombing and some strafing. Trouble is, ambulance convoys get mixed up with tank columns or supply convoys and there's nothing much you can do about that."

"But," he says as if sensing what we really want to know, "we've not lost many ambulance drivers. A month ago one of our lad's ambulances got mixed up with a supply column and was strafed. The engine set on fire and our lad went around back to take out his wounded. A bullet got him in the back of the neck and killed him."

We are silent for a moment or two and drink our beer. It is New Yorker beer in American Can Company cans. The talk turns to the coming "flap." Here at the front the coming attack is known as the "flap"— something to be regarded as lightly as the wind throwing back the entrance flap of a bad desert tent. It is the same kind of British understatement that causes a soldier who has had his arm blown off to say he got "a bit of a packet." Men have been hearing about the "flap" for about a month. Little bits of information keep coming through.

RAF ground crews hear the pilots talk when they return from flights over the Gerry lines. Gerry's tank columns are forming here and there. The RAF mechanic passes it on to an RAF staff car driver who has told one of the ambulance drivers. Ambulance drivers pick up a lot. They talk to the crews of our armored cars who've been on reconnaissance patrols. They listen to sentries. There have been twenty-four-hour alerts lately. Officers have been excited and called a lot of extra meetings. It all adds up to the same thing—a "flap."

"Bloody silly," says Alf, a tinsmith from the workshop, "this always waiting for an attack. I say why don't we do the attacking for a bit of a change?"

We hear a clanking noise and the roar of a motor. Three of us step outside to see what's up. It is a Honey tank. The driver jumps out and walks toward us with the swagger that marks all tank corps men. He joins us for beer. I ask him if he thinks a Honey will stop Gerry.

"They're a good tank," he says, "and they go fast and you can maneuver them. But they don't have the guns to match Gerry's Mark IV. You've got to get within five hundred yards of a Mark IV to knock him out. He can knock a Honey out with a direct hit at three thousand yards. But I'll tell you, Yank, your General Grants will stop 'em."

The tank driver seems to take great pride in his profession in the tank corps, feels it a great honor to be a member of it, and tells us the corps motto.

A Sapper has joined us from a neighboring camp. The ambulance drivers' canteen is a well-built tile structure sunk into the ground about halfway down. Inside are tables and benches on a cement floor. Because it is so comfortable, it is a popular hangout for men from neighboring units. I am anxious to know if the Tobruk perimeter is well protected by land mines.

"They're all right," he says with a slight Scotch burr to his words, "but the trouble with a lot of our mines is that they were made in Egypt. You can't be sure of them. Some go off before they are planted and we know a lot of them won't go off even after we've laid them."

It is difficult to follow all the Sapper says. To help in the lesson of explaining land mines to the green Americans, one of the drivers goes outside the dugout and gets a discarded Italian land mine. Until this moment it has been used to hold down a piece of blanket that blacked out a window of the canteen. The Sapper takes it and demonstrates. It is nerve-wracking to watch him move the loaded mine back and forth in his hands as he talks. It looks like the top of an electric waffle iron.

"In the bottom of the mine a pin is inserted," he says. "You put the pin in the hole drilled for that purpose very carefully. Then you lay the mine in a shallow hole you have dug with the pin against the ground. Then you cover the mine lightly with dirt or sand."

"The trouble is that these pins don't always fit exactly," he says. "'If you use the wrong size, you're done."

"Gerry's got good mines," he continues sadly, "and good mine detectors. Ever see a mine detector? They're lovely things, very convenient. Look something like a carpet sweeper at the end of a handle. There is a dial you can look at, or you can listen in earphones. When you find out where there's a mine you can dig it up carefully. But sometimes Gerry fools you. When you take up the mine meant to blow up tanks, there's an antipersonnel mine that blows you up."

Everyone has used up his quota of beer, which is about two cans per week per man, and it is time to go to bed. We walk through the camp to our ambulances. Everything is still. The sky is clear and quiet. The stars stand out as if the heavens were set for an astronomy lesson. The desert is grey and the horizons are close. Even the wind is not stirring. Two sentries walk slowly in the distance, their tin hats cocked on their heads, their Lee-Enfields slung over their shoulders.

Most of the unit is sleeping in their ambulances. The instructions are that if Gerry comes over and starts dropping stuff, you jump out of the ambulance and into the nearest slit trench. Not for me. I take my sleeping bag into an abandoned dugout which one of the Tommies has tipped me off to. It is constructed in the shape of a cross. One point is the entrance and the other three places for cots. Tomorrow I'll have to shovel sand out of the entrance. The wind seems to look for holes in which to store sand.

Inside is complete darkness. I look around with my flashlight. It is a well-constructed dugout with heavy beams supporting the top. The floor is littered with a curious array of junk: an empty bottle of Munich beer, an Italian metal water flask, a sheet of mimeographed paper in Polish, some tins of sardines, a tin of Libby's corned beef, several undischarged British cartridges, one tennis shoe, a torn Aussie hat (the kind that looks like a cowboy hat), and two candles, one partly burned. The candles come in handy when I set up my typewriter on an empty petrol tin and work on my journal. It is a quiet night, except for a few bombs dropped over in the direction of Tobruk Harbor.

After I crawl into my bedding roll, I toss and turn, unable to sleep. Finally just before dawn, I light one of the candles and discover that fleas are crawling over my body. The small of my back and the backs of my knees are raw with bites. These are the famous sand fleas of the Western Desert. There's nothing I can do about it now and I fall asleep in sheer exhaustion.

SECOND DAY

I awaken with a start. A shaft of sunlight, like a long moving finger, has suddenly found my eyes. It is like a baby spotlight on me in the darkness of the dugout and is shooting through an air hole formed by a piece of pipe set in the roof. It is nine o'clock and too late for breakfast at the field kitchen.

The rest of my kit, I learn, has gone off with Mort Belshaw's ambulance to carry wounded from Tobruk Hospital. All but one of my cameras are on the ambulance and it worries me.

Fifty feet away from my dugout is an armored car staffed by "Desert Sam" of the South African Division stationed in Tobruk. In civilian life he was a miner in Johannesburg. His Vickers machine gun is mounted and ready in the open turret. He is making tea over a Primus stove as I stroll up, and offers me some. Like so many South Africans, he reminds me of American boys from the south. There is a gentleness about him, an easy friendliness. He speaks with the accent of the South Africans, which is high-pitched and might be a blend of Scotch, Dutch, and English accents. There is about him the burned-out, washed-out appearance of men who have fought long in the desert. From his talk, I learn that he's been through the Abyssinian campaign and several of the British advances and retreats in Libya. I ask him if an armored car will stop Gerry.

"They're not much good except for patrol work or against infantry," he says. "All we've got is machine guns on here, a Vickers and a few Thompsons. These guns were all right in the World War for village fighting, but they're not much good in the desert. They're good against paratroops if they come in the daytime. That General Grant of yours will stop him, though, Yank."

As we talk, two American-made bombers of the RAF sail overhead, back from a raid over enemy lines. We look at them, and then go on talking. Suddenly we hear the buzz of the Gerry planes and look up again. A group of Messerschmidts in V formation is following the bombers. We want to call out to them. The V breaks and they fly about like disturbed bees. Almost at the same instant both bombers start to fall. One lands safely and the other lands in flames. An ambulance hurries in to the burning plane but it's too far gone. No attempt is made to even recover the bodies. Eight RAF men have burned to death. The crew of the other bomber is badly jolted but safe. Later we learn that the bombers had mistaken the Messerschmidts for their escort. In the canteen that night we are discussing the incident when an announcement from the BBC comes that "eight of our planes bombed Derna today, brought down three enemy fighters and all returned safely."

Desert Sam sees his sergeant major walking toward us in the distance, so I say "So long" and take a walk. The thing that strikes me most as I wander around inside the perimeter of Tobruk is the incredible amount of junk that is scattered about. There are all types of wrecked vehicles, tanks, troop carriers, German staff cars, ammunition, and clothing. Here and there much of it is collected into a big junk pile. In most of the junk piles soldiers putter about looking for souvenirs. The idea is to try and find something that has Italian or German words or insignia marked on it.

I stop and talk with the crew of a twenty-five pounder who are camouflaged under grey netting. They are lolling about smoking and talking.
One of the crewmen shrugs his shoulders when I ask him what he thinks
of the twenty-five pounder, which is a modern version of the French
seventy-five used in the First World War.

"They're all right," he says, "but they're bloody difficult to move
about and set up and aim. You've got to transport a twenty-five pounder
with a truck. Then you've got to load it, dig a hole big enough to give you
some protection. Even after you've set up your camouflage netting, your
first bursts give your position away. It doesn't have a very wide travers-
ing arc, which is important if you want to shoot at tanks. If you want to
widen the arc you've got to lift up the stanchion, swing it around, and dig
it again. You need a full crew to operate it and if shrapnel or machine gun
fire knocks out any of your crew, you're done."

"Now it's my opinion that it takes a tank to beat a tank. And you
ought to have a tank with a longer range gun than Gerry's. Tanks can
move around fast in the desert and the armor plates give the crew
operating the guns good protection. We use what they give us," he says,
smiling.

I see ack-ack gun emplacements, armored cars scattered about, and
big inhuman tanks moving along the horizon like giant desert beetles.

All in all, the men I talk with do not seem very excited about the
"flap" but have an air of casual expectancy. In some of the camps men
dressed in blue gym shorts are playing rugby, while others are puttering
over their vehicles or cleaning their rifles and machine guns. They look
like school kids all dressed up in khaki, getting ready for a Boy Scout
expedition.

In the late afternoon Mort returns to our camp and shows me where
he hid our kit in a slit trench. As soon as we lift the rubber groundsheet
that covers the stuff, we know it's been broken into. I have several anxious moments. My cameras and gadgets, worth about $900, are intact,

but my water bottle with a quart of fresh tasteless water from El Tahag has been stolen. This reminds me of my college anthropology class in which Professor Keller told us about the effect of geography on what people value.

Later, in the canteen, one of the British ambulance drivers offers to sell me a beautiful six-shooter for one and a half Egyptian pounds. I take it he picked it off an Aussie officer. Now there's inspection in two days and he does not want to bother hiding it. If the inspection officer finds the gun, he'll pinch it for himself, according to the Tommies. I am very much tempted to buy it as a souvenir but on second thought I cannot bear the thought of having a lethal weapon. The more I see of war, the less I think of the whole business.

A number of boys in my unit have also discovered the junk piles. Already a large number of them are adding Eyetie rifles and machine guns to their kits. They take several damaged machine guns and make one good one. They also find hundreds of rounds of ammunition. They are delighted. They clean and grease all the ammunition they can get and then hide the stuff in one of the convoy trucks. When they go swimming they take along empty petrol tins. They set the tins adrift in the Mediterranean and fire away with the machine guns.

It's great fun. Under the rules of the Geneva Convention, ambulance drivers wearing the Allied Cross brassard are not permitted to engage in combat. But the sport of shooting is in the air. If they can't shoot at men, they'll shoot at petrol tins.

During the Eighth Army advance from El Alamein the following fall, some of the same boys stopped beside the Mediterranean for a swim. Again they shot at petrol tins. Suddenly, much to their surprise, a band of nine Eyetie soldiers stepped from behind some stones and walked toward them, their hands raised above their heads. They wanted to surrender to these playful college-boy ambulance drivers.

FIFTH DAY

Water is something you have always taken for granted. Here in the desert, water is a kind of obsession with us. We talk about it, dream about it, and are always figuring out new angles for getting it. The water truck comes around in the evening at dinnertime and we're allowed to fill our canteens. It's all right for washing, but it tastes like you'd expect from a pharmacist's drainpipe. This is because it has been desalted and purified. Sometimes a friend will give you a drink of decent water from his canteen, proudly announcing that it's Bardia Hospital water he "scrounged" on the last ambulance convoy there.

This lack of water directs your imagination into such visions as swallowing a bottle of Coca-Cola out of one of those ice-filled metal boxes in front of candy stores. Your hand gets cold as you take the bottle, and the stuff in the bottle is so cold you can hardly drink it. Then you remember a cool lake in Connecticut. You swim out to a raft and sit on the edge of it and kick your feet in the nice cool water. You remember fancy tile bathrooms in the homes of people who were giving house parties. You remember cold showers that you took after a track meet, when you stayed under the shower for an hour, letting the water run in your hair, on your face, and down your throat.

This noon I come in on one of the Tommies in our Bren gun crew. He's a batman to an officer of the Royal Army Service Corps assigned to our unit. The Tommy is sitting on a petrol tin outside his dugout staring at a pile of laundry in front of him. I ask him, "What's the matter?"

"My officer bloke has given me 'is clothes to wash," he says. "I don't see how I can wash these clothes without water. I don't have enough water for meself to even shave and wash with."

"Why didn't you make him give you some water or tell you where you could get some?" I ask.

"I did," he says sadly, "but 'e said that was my problem." I then suggest to the dejected Tommy that he scrounge some petrol.

Petrol, I happen to have found out, is being used for many things in the desert besides operating vehicles—cooling beer tins, cooking, washing clothes, and keeping warm on cool nights in winter. Wandering around Tobruk Hospital two days ago, I noticed that some of the men had severe burns. They were being treated by having the burns painted with gentian violet, the new cure for burns. It made them look like creatures out of surrealist paintings. I asked one of the patients how he got burned.

"I was spraying me dugout with petrol," he said, "and some bloke comes and lights a cigarette."

Several other burned patients gave me the same answer. I discussed the matter with a British medical officer.

"It's more than burns they're suffering from," he says. "It's a sickness in their souls. It comes when they can't take life in the desert and won't. I know. They've been coming in here in droves lately—always with the same story. They sprayed their dugouts with petrol to kill the sand fleas and somebody lit a cigarette. It's been happening all along the front. There's just been a Middle East order issued which forbids troops from spraying their dugouts with petrol in the future. The order also states that anyone reporting sick with a burn received in this manner will be placed on a charge of having a self-inflicted wound. Frankly, I have never seen morale in the Western Desert as low as it is now."

Tonight, before going to sleep in my dugout, I try and piece together all that I have seen and heard here at the front. I ask myself if I look for complaints. Soldiers always grumble, they say. Most of the men go about their tasks and get them done each day, then smoke and chat about something inconsequential until time to sleep. But under the surface of each man, if you probe him, you'll find bewilderment, resentment, or a complete feeling of futility. There is no one answer that sums up their

THE AMERICAN
FIELD SERVICE
IN THE
MIDDLE EAST

Now, as in the first World War, the American Field Service is transporting the wounded and sick. There is an immediate, urgent need for volunteers and funds to carry on this humane work with the United Nations in the Middle East. More than ever, we must aid our gallant allies, and our stake in the Middle East is a vital one. Volunteer as a driver or contribute toward the purchase and maintenance of ambulances.

★

Apply for information,
or send your contribution to:
AMERICAN FIELD SERVICE
60 Beaver Street
New York

Unidentified men around table at Shepheard's Hotel, Cairo, a meeting place for the rich, famous, and powerful. War correspondents gathered there routinely.
AMERICAN FIELD SERVICE ARCHIVES

AFS men in Cairo HQ lounge. AMERICAN FIELD SERVICE ARCHIVES

Four women from the Women's Auxiliary Air Force (WAAF) attend the Cairo Amateur Dramatic Music Society straight from duty. LIBRARY OF CONGRESS

Lt. Col. Sir Philip Astley, Director of Army Press Relations for the British in his Cairo office. Astley refused to accommodate Bowen's *Collier's* assignment and confined him to photographing AFS operations. FAMILY COLLECTION

Arab legion camel corps firing exercises. The camel corps had fought with Lawrence and the Arabs and continued in the North Africa campaign, increasingly mechanized. LIBRARY OF CONGRESS

Women of the South African infantry fit gas masks. LIBRARY OF CONGRESS

ABOVE: Soldier surveys Tobruk Harbor, filled with ships, both sunken and afloat. LIBRARY OF CONGRESS

RIGHT: "Tobruk Torch," a newssheet for the "Desert Rats," was printed using a typewriter and a rotary printer. The office moved often due to enemy action. LIBRARY OF CONGRESS

South African mortar gunners in Tobruk—"Desert Rats"—were revered for their toughness.

British map reading and compass bearing instruction. Britain's Long Range Desert Group had been actively mapping North Africa prior to the campaign but the Germans had not. Captured British maps were prized.

Acetylene welder in desert repair shop. Metal smiths were skilled at making repairs, recycling materials scrounged from the dumps that littered the Libyan desert.

Tommies from Ben Ghazi get medical attention on their blistered, callused, swollen feet after 250-mile walk. The last 160 miles were guided by a Sanusi, member of a Libyan Islamic religious order.

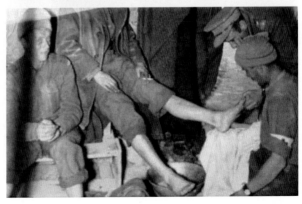

ABOVE: Eighth Army soldiers gather around the crew of a gun emplacement.
LIBRARY OF CONGRESS

RIGHT: Sapper carrying mines. LIBRARY OF CONGRESS

Sappers clearing safety lane by finding mines with bayonets and removing them. LIBRARY OF CONGRESS

AFS men share a smoke, using an old tin can from some "iron rations" as an ashtray. Offering a soldier a cigarette was a routine gesture of comradeship. AMERICAN FIELD SERVICE ARCHIVES

The desert bakery furnished troops with fresh bread and greatly lifted British morale. Tinned biscuits usually arrived after transport as crumbs. LIBRARY OF CONGRESS

Army cooks took a nine-day course to learn how to improvise field rations using ovens made from petrol tins and oil drums. Most rations came in tin cans. LIBRARY OF CONGRESS

The "cave dwellers of Tobruk," defenders of the garrison, point out the only direct hit on the six- to ten-foot-thick rock roof of their dugout. LIBRARY OF CONGRESS

New Zealanders eating in Libyan Desert. LIBRARY OF CONGRESS

Free French soldier drinks from canteen. Most water was tasteless, having been desalinated and purified. LIBRARY OF CONGRESS

ABOVE, LEFT: Bath near coastal defense guns of Tobruk.
LIBRARY OF CONGRESS

ABOVE, RIGHT: Desert shower. Showers were extremely rare and Mediterranean swims highly prized.
LIBRARY OF CONGRESS

Water delivered to desert troops in tins.
LIBRARY OF CONGRESS

LEFT: Holy Communion in the desert. LIBRARY OF CONGRESS

BELOW: The "Dark Angel" of Tobruk still standing in bombed-out Catholic Church. The "Desert Rats" believed that as long as she stood, Tobruk would not fall. LIBRARY OF CONGRESS

Night flares over Tobruk. Photo by Croswell Bowen. WHITNEY MUSEUM OF AMERICAN ART

British ack-ack guns illuminate desert near Tobruk during night raid.
LIBRARY OF CONGRESS

Enemy attack on ambulance convoy. The wounded AFS driver gets away and is treated by drivers from other ambulances. AFS drivers persisted in believing Rommel respected the Geneva Convention and such attacks were either German mistakes or acts of insubordination. LIBRARY OF CONGRESS

A small British patrol in Libya made a successful raid on an infantry unit and received the eager surrender of this driver of an Italian vehicle. War prisoners on both sides of the Western Desert campaign expected humane treatment. LIBRARY OF CONGRESS

Rescued troops after recapture of Bardia dance to gramophone. LIBRARY OF CONGRESS

South African field dressing station inside a Brie (well) underground in Libyan Desert. The patient on the operating table is having dressings put on due to burns.
LIBRARY OF CONGRESS

Wounded soldiers from Tobruk Hospital await transport out of the harbor. Photo by Croswell Bowen.
WHITNEY MUSEUM OF AMERICAN ART

AFS ambulances line up to deliver the wounded to the hospital ship, where they are raised from the dock to the ship's deck on pallets rigged with pulleys.
AMERICAN FIELD SERVICE ARCHIVES

Soldier with amputated leg about to go down steps at Shepheard's Hotel, Cairo. Shepheard's, a "neutral island of Swiss hotel keeping," was a nexus of information and power. Photo by Robert Landry. Reproduced in *Life* magazine, December 14, 1942, but also in public domain. LIBRARY OF CONGRESS

German officer lies dead after raid in Western Desert. LIBRARY OF CONGRESS

Wounded men lie in AFS stretcher lines awaiting transport through "war's reverse supply lines." AMERICAN FIELD SERVICE ARCHIVES

Wounded men await evacuation. Photo by Croswell Bowen. LOOK MAGAZINE

Proposed cover for
unpublished war memoir.

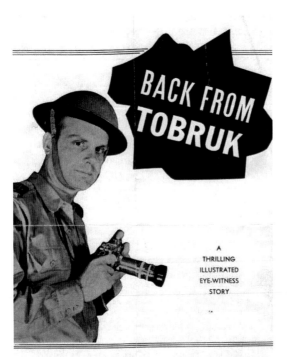

BACK FROM TOBRUK

A
THRILLING
ILLUSTRATED
EYE-WITNESS
STORY

★ **CROSWELL BOWEN**

★ *"WAR IN THE DESERT!"* ★

Out of the scorching hell of the Libyan desert and the fortress of Tobruk, Croswell Bowen, ace photo-reporter, brings back to the American people a magnificent eye-witness account of the savage warfare being waged across the trackless Libyan wastes for the crucial prize of Suez. More than a month before Pearl Harbor, Croswell Bowen as a Collier's representative and as Official Photographer to the American Field Service joined a convoy of 18,000 British troops bound for the East. His unit's war-bound odyssey included service in South Africa, India, Egypt, Syria, the Lebanon, Palestine, and gruelling experience during the savage Axis push into the Libyan desert.

Stationed in Tobruk, he was invalided out just before its fall because of a paralyzed leg. Making his way by ambulance and train to Cairo, and from there by hospital ship to Durban, he recovered sufficiently to embark on a U. S. transport which brought him home.

His story is intended for those who want the real story behind official communiques and censored newspaper dispatches. Bowen realized that the real story of the war, the human side, was not to be found in the fancy, officer-filled bars of Cairo and Beyrouth, but in the dugouts and canteens of the plain soldiers — the men doing the fighting and the dirty work. And it was among these men that he spent his time — Free French colonials, Aussies, New Zealanders, South Africans, British Tommies, Grenadier Guardsmen, Jews, Poles, Czechs, Greeks, Arabs, Indians, and, just before he left, the advance guard of American doughboys now fighting in Egypt.

He lived among the soldiers learning their songs, their jokes, their stories of desert fighting, their hopes and fears and ambitions. And when the Stukas came over Tobruk dropping their "stuff" he crouched with these soldiers in the slit trenches. That is except when he set his camera to get such pictures as the one on the facing page of Tobruk's anti-aircraft barrage by night.

The soft desert night is streaked with tracer bullets and the burst of anti-aircraft shells as the ground defenses of Tobruk open up against enemy bombers trying to lay their "eggs" within the fortress. To take this remarkable photograph, Bowen had to leave his shelter and come out into the open, risking both enemy bombs and bursting shrapnel from the defending ack-ack barrage.

War brings grim contrasts to the Holy Land. A Polish soldier kneels in prayer at the Holy Sepulchre in Jerusalem.

A British "Tommy" inspects a destroyed German anti-tank gun left behind by the Axis forces when they evacuated Tobruk.

★ **Authentic Pictures of the War in Libya and the Holy Land** ★

Book blurb and pictures, publicity material for unpublished memoir.

attitude to the war, or what they're fighting for, or their emotions about being at this godforsaken desert front. The only thing they all have in common, of course, is that they want to go home.

TOBRUK ON SUNDAY

A big troop truck has been assigned to take men from our unit into the town of Tobruk to church. I go along and take my cameras. The Royal Engineers have fixed up two large rooms of the bombed Italian marine buildings for the Roman Catholics and members of the Church of England. Inside the Catholic Church there are not enough chairs and knee benches. Many of the worshippers kneel on the cement floor. There are officers, nurses, and plain soldiers. Churches in the British Army are apparently not marked FOR OFFICERS ONLY, but the officers are expected to sit in certain pews. Two Tommies in the usual shirt and shorts serve the Priest at Holy Mass. Most of the furnishings of the church, the pews, some plaster saints, and some candelabra were brought over from the bombed Italian Catholic Church on the Square.

When Church is out, I take a walk around the town to try to get some good wrecked buildings shots. Wandering through the streets you feel very strongly an unreality and stillness. The Mediterranean sun is bright and gay. May 20 has come and gone and there's been no attack. Everything is so silent except the sharp click of the British Army hobnail boots hitting the sidewalks. You realize that there is a robotic sameness about everyone, for both officers and men wear the faded khaki shirt and shorts of the Middle East. The faces of the men are gaunt and tinted with the pale yellow dust that coats everything.

You walk on sidewalks like those in any town, but virtually all the buildings have been wrecked beyond use. From the debris of furnishings and mechanical things you can tell that here had been a cafe, a store, or an apartment house. Alongside of the regular carved or painted inscriptions on the buildings, the Aussies and Tommies have painted lewd insults and caricatures of Hitler and Mussolini.

The town gives you the feeling of being in another world. You feel that you have entered a stranger's house when he is not there and, from little things you find in his home, you reconstruct the owner's personality, image, and behavior. Here, in the rubble, you see a broken chair he sat in; you see his toothbrush, a few pieces of his clothing, and part of a torn red curtain. Your reactions get twisted. In normal peacetime a wrecked building jolts you, but here the sight of a building more or less undestroyed is a shock.

In the town square I get to talking with an MP who is a former Manchester policeman. He says he hopes I have my pass to take photos. I reach in my pocket and realize I have left it in another shirt. He is an amiable guy and says never mind, but I keep my eyes open for any officer blokes.

We are standing outside the big cement block and plaster Roman Catholic Church. In the main door is a large sign which says, OUT OF BOUNDS—DANGER. The MP asks me if I've seen the Angel of Tobruk. We walk past the sign and into the church. The walls are intact but the windows are blown out. Beams and cross bars, the remains of the roof, cast fretted shadows on the floor. Battered statues of the Holy Family and the Saints, once lifelike even to the flesh on the faces, are strewn about like discarded manikins. A large crucifix, the Christ blown off it, leans jauntily against a wall up on a balcony.

In the center of the chancel, at the gate of a marble altar rail, stands the Angel of Tobruk. She is smiling and serene, untouched except for a piece of shrapnel lodged in her right eye. The MP tells me the Demolition Squad of the Sappers or Royal Engineers moved her into her present location. Rationally, I know it is only a plaster image and that only chance kept her from being turned into talcum powder and lumps of plaster like the other statues. But I get a cold feeling standing there looking at her. The nick in her eye has actually given her personality. I remember her story.

Opposing troops sweep in and out of Tobruk, artillery of both sides hammer the city, airplanes drop demolition bombs, but the Angel remains unharmed. She is lucky for the British side, the men say. She had helped the Aussies hold the siege. As long as she stands in the church, Tobruk will never fall. Some men pray to her.

Her most devout worshippers are the Rats of Tobruk, the gallant men of the Sixth Armored "Divvy," an Australian Tank Division, and the Royal Horse Artillery, a famous English regiment, now mechanized, who, along with others, held off the siege for nine heartbreaking months. The name, Rats of Tobruk, is the result of the besieged soldiers listening over their radios to the taunts of Lord Haw-Haw, who sneered, "Tobruk has held out but there is no doubt but that it will soon fail. The men imprisoned within the perimeter are cowering in their flea-infested dugouts like desert rats. They might as well give up or we'll bomb them out."

But the men never give up and the taunt only serves to strengthen their determination to "stick it." They were relieved, finally, in December 1941.

I keep staring at the Angel, fascinated. I think of some Italian craftsman fashioning her in Rome or Florence and of her being shipped here to be worshipped by colonists in Mussolini's "Paradise."

Then, suddenly, it occurs to me that in the legend of the Angel of Tobruk lies the answers to the questions I have been asking myself. The soldiers are discouraged with their fighting equipment. They are "browned off" with the waiting game being played by the Middle East command. Out of touch with the world, they have come to feel they are merely struggling to hold a stretch of land unfit to live in, to defend a ditch that is far away from home. What to believe in? The Angel. Luck. That's it.

The MP helps me set up my photo equipment so I can take the Angel's picture. I decide, after studying her from various points through the ground glass of my Rolleiflex, to shoot her straight on from the floor. This puts into the picture a graceful curved line made by some lattice in the bombed ceiling from which the plaster has been loose. In the background are two big holes where windows used to be. Even the window frames have been bombed away.

I shoot some interior pictures of the church. Then we go up on top of the YMCA building next door to get a good panorama shot of the entire church showing the bombed roof. In the Y canteen we split a can of peaches. A Sapper sergeant joins us and entertains us with his stories of booby traps. As he warms up to his subject, on which he appears to be quite an authority, we can almost see the incidents he describes.

In one of the early British advances into the Libyan Desert, a British infantry soldier picks up a bright shiny object. "Blimey," he says, "if some Gerry officer hasn't lost 'is fountain pen." He unscrews the top to have a look at the pen point. But he never gets that look. At that instant his face is blown off.

An Aussie soldier sees a chromium-plated thermos bottle glistening in the desert sun. It is lying beside an abandoned enemy officer's dugout. British soldiers are issued cloth-covered metal bottles for water. A thermos bottle is the height of luxury in the desert. He picks it up, unscrews the top to see if there's water or maybe whiskey inside. His hands get blown off.

A sergeant attached to the GHQ of a division that has just taken over an enemy town appropriates a nice little house that will serve as the officer's mess. He looks over the furnishings with an appraising eye. His aesthetic sensibilities are slightly jarred by a picture that is hanging askew on the wall. Fortunately, he is alone in the house for when he straightens the picture, the building blows up.

Another time in another desert coastal town the officers have been living in a house for several days, which also serves as their GHQ. On the mantel is a fine, old Italian clock which appears to have run down. An officer absentmindedly winds the clock. A few turns of the key and the house goes up.

The Sapper pauses in his anecdotes for a moment or two so we can each negotiate a half peach with our fingers, each of us having drunk a third of the juice out of the can. This is the customary procedure in the desert. I take a good look at the Sapper and figure he is the British equivalent of "the life of the party." He seems to really enjoy telling us about these matters.

"How do these things work?" I ask.

"Oh," he says, "you see, it's all a lot of tricks. Generally you fix it so that there is a liquid and a powder in, say, a thermos bottle. When the top is unscrewed the liquid and the powder mix and it blows up, the same with a fountain pen. One good trick is to leave a nice, bright red penny bank lying around. Soldiers will pick up anything that's a bright color. They shake the penny bank and that sets off the charge. The Eyeties used to leave a lot of these penny banks around the desert until the troops got wise."

As our amusing friend the Sapper sergeant talks, I realize suddenly what he really is—a practical joker. He has found a useful niche for his special talents—practical jokes for death. I ask him if by any chance he knows the whereabouts of my friend Major Daly, who is in the Royal Engineers and who is somewhere around Tobruk.

"He's my OC," says the Sapper sergeant. "Would you like to see him? I'll be driving out to my camp in a few minutes and I'd be glad to take you along." The three of us split a bar of chocolate and I thank the MP for his help.

The Sapper drives his truck around the wide bend on the El Adem road made by the harbor. It is a lovely day. South African natives are swimming and sunning themselves on the sandy part of the inlet. In the distance is a hospital ship. An oil tanker is unloading at one of the lesser bombed concrete piers.

"Oh ho," says the Sapper, "they'll be over plenty tonight. There's an oil tanker in. I don't know how they find out, but whenever there's an oil tanker in the harbor, Gerry comes over and drops his stuff."

We pass the newly set up bake shop that's been furnishing troops fresh bread every day, and big barbed-wire enclosures that contain petrol tins, tires, big coils of communications wire, cases of tinned food, and ammunition.

"If soldiers knew what we know," the Sapper says, resuming his favorite subject, "they bloody well wouldn't touch anything they see. Now a very nice place to plant a bomb is inside a lot of papers, especially a lot of papers marked 'secret.' Soldiers always like to read secret papers. Then it's nice to rig up a bomb in connection with an artillery piece or a machine gun nest. Soldiers like to look over strange guns. Then, of course, anything that makes a good souvenir or photographs of nude women. The troops are shown movies telling them about booby traps, but they seem to take no notice of what they're supposed to have learned."

Our truck is ascending a ridge behind Tobruk. Occasionally the wind blows the dust in our faces so intensely it is as if it were a sand-blasting machine. Everywhere troops and tents and supplies and vehicles are spread out. You keep wondering what holds it all together. On the surface everything here at the front looks so hit or miss, so indiscriminate, so casual.

"Troops are supposed," the Sapper continues, "to let the Engineers look over the buildings in a captured enemy town before they go inside. Sometimes just a little jolt can bring down a building that looks all right. Then, of course, there are tricks to making the building come down. For example, you take up a board in the floor of a house. Say it is supported by three beams. You make the center beam a little higher so the board seesaws. Then a bloke steps on the middle of one and nothing happens. This is where the delayed action part comes on.

"You have a battery and some contact points and a nice big charge. You attach contact points to the beam and to the short end of the floor-board. Two wires lead off to the battery and the charge. Maybe this board is over in the corner. It's a nice room and the staff of the general headquarters is there. An officer sets foot on the wrong end of the board and bang—up goes the lot of 'em."

He stops the truck because an MP hails us and asks to see our iden-tification papers. I had heard that German officers with Oxford educa-tions dressed in British uniforms had wandered around inside the British lines for days. Presumably this is to guard against that kind of thing.

"As I was saying when we were interrupted," the Sapper says, "this delayed-action stuff is the best. Maybe there is a drainage pool or rain barrel in connection with a very lovely house, suitable for a nice GHQ full of officers. You run a mat wire into the water. Then you put a piece of metal two inches above the water and attach wire to that. Buried down in the basement, maybe, is a nice big charge of TNT and a couple of dry cell batteries. Maybe while the officers are messing a lot of water goes down the drain. The more water that goes down the drain, the quicker the house goes up.

"Rigging up a toilet is child's play. In fact, we don't . . . " but the Sapper does not finish. We have arrived at his camp and stopped in front of Major Daly's tent. He is not in, but his batman says he's expected back any moment. I take my camera stuff out of the truck and wait. My Sapper friend drives off, probably to go to his tent and dream up some new practical jokes.

When Major Daly drives up, he gets out of his car holding a bathing suit. He's been over to the Mediterranean for a swim. His greeting is very cordial but he does not seem to register my crack, "Major Daly, I presume?"

Probably Henry Morton Stanley's famous remark was not as widely pub-licized in England as in America. We go into his tent and pick up where we left off in Beirut. By the way I must, of course, stay for dinner.

Major Daly is intensely interested in what I tell him I've heard about the attack, what was being said in Cairo, and the rumors.

"I've been so bloody busy," he says, "I haven't had time to pick up all the gossip. Of course, we've been hearing there was to be a flap for weeks."

There has been a terrific amount of work for the engineers to do around Tobruk, he tells me; some buildings have been fixed up for offices and workshops. Other buildings have been leveled. There are still large sections of ground that must be cleaned of ammunition and mines. Great quantities of enemy ammunition must be destroyed. The electric light system in Tobruk is working, although at only half its previous out-put. The officers in Major Daly's unit are having a mess built of salvaged building blocks. Will I come over for a big party they're going to have when it's ready, and represent The States?

I tell him about the brigadier in the RASC telling Jimmy King, my OC, that Tobruk is impregnable now. That it is so well stocked and defended that Gerry won't have a chance.

"I'm not so sure," Major Daly says, "You never know what to expect in this bloody desert fighting. You can be almost to Tunis one day and backed up against Alexandria the next. The old front just seesaws back and forth. They stretch their supply lines, can't keep them open, and back they go. We just do what we're told.

"But I like the desert, for some reason. I'm used to it. I like staying here for months and months and then going away for a few weeks on a bust. I was so bloody glad to get back here after my last leave. Cairo made me sick to my stomach, all those bloody bastards sitting round drinking and chasing women. But by God, I wish I had a woman right now."

In the tent for the officer's mess, I am introduced around to the major's junior officers. They are attractive, sensitive, and boyish Englishmen. Everybody's manners are party manners and they give me a drink of gin, Rose's lime juice, and water. I remark that the water is good and without the funny taste.

"Didn't you know," one of the officers says, "that the engineers always get the best water. We're in the business, you see."

The major sits in an overstuffed chair, taken from a house in Tobruk, beside a fireplace for use in winter. The other chairs are camp chairs. A table made with two wooden horses and some planks is spread with a blanket. The regular officer's mess china with the King's coat of arms is spread out. There are bottles of A1 and Worcestershire Sauce. It is the same officer's mess that has been set up on battlefields the whole world over during the march of the British Empire since the nineteenth century.

The conversation is probably about the same, too. It is polite and strained. Part of the time, Major Daly gets back on his favorite subject of books. He likes Mark Twain and Edgar Allan Poe. Walt Whitman seemed to have Irish qualities about him. Thomas Wolfe was magnificent. But we stop this talk when we see the other officers are politely silent. Finally, Major Daly goes to sleep in his arm chair.

I talk to the officers for a while. I remark that I feel guilty that in the scattered bombings I've seen so far I have not waited above ground to take photographs when Gerry was dropping his stuff on us, but instead dive for the nearest slit trench. One of the Sapper officers says I can get all the explosion pictures I want any afternoon when they blow up enemy ammunition. It's quite a show, he says. Then the talk turns to America. There are the same old questions about Hollywood and gangsters. Then it's time to go home, so I wake up Major Daly. We talk a few minutes and the other officers excuse themselves, leaving the major and myself in the mess tent.

"Major," I say, "won't you please tell me about blowing up the escarpment at Derna? I still want to know, and not for any sensational reason."

"Well," he says very quietly, looking straight ahead, "we had to get out of the town in our lorries, spraying machine gun bullets to keep the mobs back.

"Blowing up the escarpment was quite simple. We planted charges, one on each side of the road. We had wires leading from all four charges to a battery case. I had my subaltern with me and when everything was all clear I gave the order for him to push the plunger into the battery mess and let her go up. My God, what a noise it made, and you should have seen all that debris fly up into the air. We certainly did a good job of it, for the whole escarpment went smashing down. After all, it was a job to do and we did it."

But I am not satisfied. The major has left something out. I ask, "What did you think at the exact moment when you gave the order for the plunger to be shoved into the battery case?"

For a moment or two, Major Daly does not say anything. Then he looks at me with many things in his eyes. "You poor dumb fool," they seem to say. But there is anguish and fear, too.

"I'll tell you, Bowen," he says with a ring of contempt in his voice, "exactly what I thought when I blew up that escarpment. You know I'm an engineer by profession. I know what it means to plan a big engineering project like a bridge, or a road, or that escarpment. I know the heartaches and the sweat and the toil in the labor of men. Well, that's what I thought and I said to myself, 'With one push of a plunger into a battery case I am destroying all of that.'"

I am ashamed that I have dragged this out of him. Trying not to be too obvious, I start talking about meeting in Cairo, getting Ann and one of her WAAF friends, and going to Gezira to swim. He tells me that he's thinking of going into the Indian Army. Auchinleck, he says, has called for officers to volunteer to serve under Wavell.

It is time to go home and the Major gets his batman to drive me back to my camp.

"Come over for a meal any time," he says, "but we'll have some good times when this bloody flap is over. And, by the way, have any of your Americans got that book they say is so good called *For Whom the Bell Tolls?* I haven't a thing to read and I'm getting frightfully bored at night. It's about the Spanish War, isn't it? It's so much more bloody exciting reading about war than it is being in it. Good night."

PERHAPS THERE WILL BE NO ATTACK

The days seem to go by and there is no attack. Perhaps there will be no attack and it was all talk. I try to photograph what it's like living in the desert. With flash bulbs, I take the interiors of some of the dugouts.

I get some pictures of South Africans playing with desert dogs. Some of the soldiers seem to have dogs as pets. When the civilian populace was cleared out of Libya the dogs hid in holes, and later came out and were fed by the troops. They wander back and forth over lines. Probably when they get fed up of sausage or meatballs over with the Eyeties or Gerries, they come back for bully beef.

Some of the dugouts are interestingly gotten up. One Tommy has a human skull on a stick in front of his dugout and underneath is a sign that says, "This is what happened to the last bloke that came in here without permission." Another has a sign on the door that says BOMB-HAPPY VILLA. Looking a little closer, I see that underneath the sign is the name Francesco, who is an Italian who once occupied it. Another Tommy has three doorbells rigged up at the entrance of his dugout. Many others have taken the fans and generators out of wrecked ventilating and lighting equipment for vehicles and rigged up systems for their dugouts. The wind turns the ventilator, airs out the dugout, and charges the storage battery for the lights at the same time.

The British Tommy's natural good nature and sense of humor seems to stand him well in the desert. But then it has always helped him muddle through. General Wavell, I remember, discovered that

German military manuals for the present war exhort the soldiers of *Der Fuhrer* to have a sense of humor. It was pointed out that one of the big factors in England's winning the last war was Tommy Atkins's sense of humor. By way of illustration, the manual reproduced a drawing of Bruce Bairnsfathers, which showed a Tommy sitting beside a wall where a big hole had been blown. "Ole Bill" was jerking his thumb at the hole and saying, "Mice done it." The scholarly writer had appended a footnote which said, "Mice did not make the hole. An artillery shell made it."

Our unit of Americans is learning how to live in the desert. We have licked the flea problem more or less by sprinkling flea powder in our blankets. Many of the boys have learned where there is good water on their ambulance runs and bring it back in petrol tins. We have moved into the quarters vacated by the British Ambulance Car Company and are beginning to consider ourselves veteran desert rats.

The thing that seems to impress many of the boys in our unit is the waste of war. They have seen destruction of buildings, vehicles, and the supplies that have been transported out here into the desert—and for what purpose? In a dugout the other night a boy from Chicago said, "After the hundreds of thousands of dollars' worth of stuff I've seen wasted and destroyed, I'll never again pay any attention to a politician who howls about budgets when somebody is trying to promote a housing project for poor people."

Others in our unit seem to enjoy the experience here as a kind of lark. They are actually looking forward to the attack.

Today I take the ambulance run to Bardia and get a few pictures of the handling of sick men being evacuated. At the hospital at Bardia, I hear that a submarine destroyer has just brought some British prisoners of war who escaped from Crete into the harbor. They were carried to the hospital by AFS ambulances, I am told. They are having lunch in a tent when I find them all dressed in hospital pajamas. Three are RAF fliers who were shot down while bombing the island. Two were left there after the British evacuation. Four are merchant seamen whose ship was torpedoed. Through some kind of underground movement on the island, they were brought together and got a fishing boat that took them off the island. It was overturned during a storm and a destroyer picked them up.

Until they made their escape, they didn't know each other. Each was hiding in the hills dressed in civilian clothes. The Greek farmers sold or gave them food. The farmers, one of the RAF fliers says, charged the German soldiers three times as much for food as they charged the British. There was not much of any guerilla fighting. The Greeks, these men say, are waiting to be rescued by the British. One of the men is the object of some kidding because he went to a Greek whorehouse in one of the towns and waited in line with the German soldiers. "I just wanted," he says, "to get a bit of dirty water off me chest." I take their pictures and we exchange names and addresses so I can send them prints of the pictures.

Going back to Tobruk, I pass a minefield in which some Sappers are working. One of the mines goes up, hurling a Sapper into the air. He lands on his feet, but they are not really his feet for his feet and shoes have been blown off at the ankles. For an endless moment or two he dances around on the bloody stubs, then falls gracefully like a ballet dancer.

THE ATTACK: MAY 27, 1942

Today the attack finally comes. It is the long-expected flap.

It begins quietly enough elsewhere on the front. But for our little unit of Americans its opening is violent and dramatic. Our camp is dive bombed. It is our first bombing. And your first bombing, as we've so often been told, is the worst.

The day starts like any other. We get up as the sun peers above the desert horizon and get our mug of tea and piece of bread with margarine at the camp kitchen. Everything is very still. Occasionally you hear the clank of metal being hammered by the men working at the mobile workshop. Somebody calls from one dugout to another. In the camp kitchen, the rations for lunch are being sorted and cans of peaches and milk are being opened. They are soaking some dehydrated potatoes in water, part of Gerry's supplies captured after a British advance.

A few of the ambulances have been sent on the Bardia run. One or two have been sent to field hospitals, but the cases they carry are mostly bad dysentery or uncontrollable "desert sores." I don't feel much like photographing anything, so I sit in the canteen where it is not so hot. Out of sheer boredom, I eat a can of pineapple cubes.

Then I walk over to the mud and stone hut being used as the AFS GHQ and try and find out if there's any news. There isn't. The boys are filling out the endless British paper reports about strength of personnel, number of vehicles, and ration requirements.

After lunch I go to my dugout, rearrange my kit, and take a nap. When I wake up it's suppertime. Walking to the mess tent, I notice that my shadow is about twenty-five feet long. The lighting at this time of day is wonderful because the sun's rays are soft, and if you expose your negative for the shadows you don't overexpose the sun-lighted part of the picture. I stop and take some pattern shots of a pile of Eyetie ammunition not yet hauled away by the Sappers.

The rations are as dreary as ever, bully beef stew made with dehydrated potatoes. The tea tastes salty as a result of something wrong with the Tobruk water distillery. Dessert is two slices of canned peaches but the cook has spoiled it by adding canned milk, and the resulting mess has curdled.

Peter Glenn from Greenville, Mississippi, has come in from a run over to Bir Hakeim and says there was a tank battle near a position called Knightsbridge and that the MPs were telling drivers that the El Adem road is closed. It is probably one of those rumors that fly about at the front, those of us who are listening to him think.

I walk over to talk with Syd Aft, the Liverpool tinsmith of the workshop crew. He has just finished his supper and is lighting his pipe. He is so English you can almost see the little cottage, hedge, and garden around him. There's a sparkle in his eyes when he looks at you.

"When are you going to fix my cot, Syd?" I say. "You promised."

"I guess we can fix it tonight, Flash," he says with a dead pan. "Maybe you got a nice bit to spend the night with. I'll fix your cot if I can 'ave her tomorrow night."

"She only sleeps with Americans," I reply, "and she's tried all nationalities."

"Ah hay," says Syd, "but she's never 'ad an Englishman then."

We resume our favorite argument, whether a country that calls itself a democracy should have a king and queen. Syd's point is that Americans have Hollywood movie queens. They look up to them and they're nice to see. Well, the king and queen are nice, you see their pictures in the magazines, and they review the troops.

"Anyway," says Syd, "the queen is a nice bit. I wouldn't mind 'aving 'er in bed meself." This, he feels, is the finest tribute he can pay to her, the final proof of his loyalty. His point somehow seems reasonable.

We wipe out our mess tins with one of the little white bags that litter the desert. These bags once contained little transparent squares used in connection with Eyetie artillery shells. I get my cot out of the dugout and meet Syd at the mobile workshop, which is a truck with portable metal workbenches and machines spread around it. At the junk heap nearby, I find a piece of metal out of which Syd cuts an inch-wide strip to reinforce the broken leg of my cot. He is a fine workman.

As he is drilling holes in it for the wood screws, we hear a faint buzzing sound. Moving across the ridge are planes droning steadily.

"Going home," says Syd looking up for a moment and continuing the drilling. "The old RAF going back for their tea. Good blokes, the RAF lads. They won the Battle of Britain."

The blacksmith, his foot moving the bellows of the forge, looks up from a red-hot piece of metal he's heating and mutters, "Famous last words in the Western Desert, 'It's all right, they're RAF planes.'"

Syd chuckles. He decides to make two metal braces for the broken cot leg, one for each side. Then, in the distance we hear the interrupted buzz-a-buzz, the danger signal in the Western Desert. It is the identifying sound of Eyetie or Gerry planes.

"Oh ho," says Syd. "Something's up. We'll 'ave a good look. Watch for 'em coming out of the sun. They like to come at you out of the sun."

Sure enough, out of the sun they come like a great flock of birds. You feel danger; you smell danger; you hear danger. It is thick in the air. It is like the sound of a locomotive gaining speed. The time has come; this is it; this is terror. You feel pulled in all directions, but there is no escape. You stand transfixed, earthbound.

"What do we do?" I say to Syd. Some rigid paralysis seems to have taken hold of my body. I am here in the midst of danger yet I am also far away.

"Take cover," he says, pausing to take a quick pull on his pipe.

He takes me by the arm and together we run to a nearby dugout. We have to push our way inside, for two Tommies are gaping at the approaching flock of birds, to get a last split-second gander.

"Get away from that opening," Syd yells to the two curious Tommies. "Don't you blokes know pilots can see faces better'n anything?"

Just as the Tommies back into the dugout, making way for Syd and myself, I can't resist glancing upward. One of the birds drops out of the formation and dives straight for me. The sound drills into my spine. It is a roar like the grinding gears of creation.

Inside the dugout, huddled with five other men, I find myself trembling and grasping my sun helmet in my hands. We hear a loud boom. The dust churns up inside our little six by six cradle in the earth. The sides of the dugout shake. Boom! This is serious. They want to kill us all.

Boom! They're just dropping those things anywhere. They mean to destroy us. Time begins moving backward through my life. I think of my jobs in New York, college, prep school, the big house in Toledo, the little house on Scottwood Avenue, the rented house on Winthrop Street, and the birth of my little brother.

Slowly, a whirling picture passes before the eyes of my mind. I am being carried up the steps of the porch of our newly built house on Scottwood Avenue. The stork brings me a little brother to play with. Father is walking home from the streetcar corner and I run down the street to meet him. He takes my hand and we walk home together. I am sick for long weeks with diphtheria and Mother takes care of me. The Commodore Vanderbilt rolls into the grimy Union Station, but I feel the thrill of my first vacation from prep school. The family has a big new house outside of town because Father has done terribly well in his real estate and insurance business. It is June after my freshman year at college and I do not tell the family what train I'm coming home on. I just stroll into father's office wearing a brand new Rosenberg's suit made to fit in New Haven. Father looks up and smiles. In that smile is all the love and tenderness in the world. I kiss him on the cheek. There is the fresh, clean scent of shaving lotion about him as there always is. He is proud of me.

One of the men is groaning. Automatically, I begin an "Our Father" and speak the words out loud. But it is hard to keep my mind on the words. I stop and flinch as the explosions sound. "Thy Kingdom come, thy will . . ." I am thinking that dust is getting in my hair. Yesterday morning, at the hospital, an orderly let me have a basin of fresh, clean water. I washed my hair and my face and then my hands. I felt clean for the first time since I've come into the desert. Now my sun helmet is off. The churning dust is grinding into my scalp. I'm getting dirty again.

Will there be any pain if one of the bombs drops into our dugout? Perhaps it will all be over without my knowing that it hit, and I will never know when I die. Suddenly it is silent. It is such a long silence.

"Stay in here, Jim!" Syd calls out, "You bloody fool!"

"It's the blacksmith!" a voice at the mouth of the dugout yells out. "'Es been hit. 'Es lying there and I'm . . ." The voice of a Tommy who's gone out to help a comrade trails off.

We file out of the dugout. Outside, we are unable to see more than a few feet ahead. The billowing dust from the explosions is still settling. The blacksmith is being led to the South African Field Hospital. His whole arm is covered with blood. He was in the London Blitz and takes his bombings casually. When the Stukas came, he merely stepped behind a truck. Shrapnel pierces automobile bodies as easily as tissue paper. One piece has put a hole clean through the truck's engine.

Suddenly, I remember that it might be a good idea to take some pictures. But it's a little late, and the light is dead, so I make just a few shots of the bomb craters and the damage done to the vehicles.

Like everyone else, I am infected by an elation. The Tommies and the Americans are talking and comparing notes on what they did and said while the bombs were dropping. Everyone seems anxious to make it clear that he was scared to death. One of our cooks, it seems, who had been through Coventry, went berserk. He shook his fists at the planes and wanted the pilots to come down and fight him. He'd stop in the middle of his ravings and say he was sorry but he couldn't help it. He was taken to Tobruk Hospital.

Two South African doctors tell me they were having a Scotch and soda when the stuff dropped. A piece of shrapnel went through their portable radio but it kept on playing. They dropped on their bellies on the tent floor. The shrapnel shattered the highball glass on the officer's table and the liquid dripped on his neck. He says he kept worrying about the good Scotch going to waste. A captured Gerry petrol tin they were using to store water in was turned inside out by the shrapnel. Their tent is riddled with holes.

We all try to figure out why the Gerry pilot went for our camp. A stick of about thirty bombs was dropped right through the middle of the area we are occupying. But a big red cross on the ground clearly marks our camp. Tops of ambulances and other vehicles are also marked with a red cross. Why waste good bombs on us?

All we can figure out is that the crane of one of the wrecking trucks, which is camouflaged poorly, might have looked like an antiaircraft gun emplacement. However, there were no direct hits on either dugouts or vehicles. The gasoline dump, which is next to the workshop, would have made a fine show if it had been hit. No one is seriously injured. I get someone to photograph Syd, two of the Tommies who were in the dugout during the bombing, and me. We are all grinning.

All during the night, Gerry keeps up his bombing. We learn later he was setting off British mine fields with dive-bombers. All night long we hear their buzzing. Alone in my dugout I try and think clearly. Why did I ever get into this? But, this sort of thing was what I wanted to experience. Still, to be asking for death by being here seems silly. The sounds of the Gerry motors, the thud of the bombs, the continual explosions— they are becoming pains in my body. Certainly I don't want to die. It's not a question of being afraid to die, though.

I want to get out of this mess and live. I want to live and take more pictures, do another book, and have a wife and babies. This is no place to die. I think of being buried in the New England hills or in Toledo next to Father's grave. I want to be buried in my own land, under green sod, and know that the seasons change and snow and spring come and go overhead.

Perhaps I would feel differently if I were here for some other reason than taking pictures for magazines, taking pictures so that people looking at them can get a vicarious thrill out of seeing what war is like from a Morris chair. Taking pictures so that circulation will increase, advertising salesmen can get more ads, and the magazine can charge more for advertising. If I were here with a gun in my hand, fighting for my country, and knew I were fighting for my country, then that might

make some sense. If I were charging at someone I hated with a bayo-
net or behind a machine gun pumping bullets into the enemy, then that
would give me something to do. But would I like this killing? Who are
these men who are fighting and killing? Who are these men who are
trying to kill us? We don't know them. Would I kill them if I faced
them now?

My thoughts, I realize, are getting the better of me. This is not
healthy. I go over to Mort's dugout. He and several other Americans are
sitting up talking but I can't seem to enter in the conversation. Only
occasionally do they make some mention of the incessant bombing.
They are all smoking nervously. I keep visualizing those pilots overhead
with their goggles on, pulling at levers that may at any moment send a
bomb right on top of me. I curse my goddamned imagination.

I go to another dugout, and then another, but nobody is saying what
he thinks or what I think he is thinking. They are all keeping their minds
off the danger of death.

Finally, I duck into a dugout just as a Gerry flare drops on our camp.
It lights up everything, just like the front of a Broadway movie house
sprayed with Klieg lights on an opening night. Inside are two Tommies
who are sitting on their cots, their heads buried in their hands. One of
them looks up at me and says nothing, but in his eyes is a terror that I
remember having seen on the face of a child whose mother was striking
him in a fit of temper. The other Tommy is talking in a kind of grum-
bling fashion half to himself. Here I will stay. Here are two human beings
who are as terrorized and bewildered as I. They cannot help but understand whatever I do or say. I can speak my thoughts if I like. But I don't
speak my thoughts. Instead I listen to the Tommy's thoughts. Listening
to him, I forget my own fears.

"I didn't want to come," he is saying, "They made me. I was called up.
Me old man said, 'Don't go. Don't let them do to you what they did to
me.' Me old man who came back from the last war, crippled and paralyzed

so he could never do another day's work. Me old lady spent her whole life supporting him and me and the two other kids, too. I don't want to fight. I don't want to be here scared to death all the time. Listen to the bloody bombin' outside. It's goin' on all night."

The other Tommy lights a cigarette, but the more articulate one says, "Put that cigarette out. Don't you know they can see a light miles up in the sky from an airplane?"

The bombing is more in the distance now. I feel better. Perhaps if I go back to my dugout I can sleep. Walking back, a sentry calls and tells me I really ought to stay underground, especially if I'm without a tin hat. The bloody ack-ack shrapnel, he says, is popping everywhere and if a piece of it hits your head it sinks right in.

In my dugout, I go quietly to sleep. Only occasionally do I awaken when there is an especially loud explosion. If I'm going to get it, I'm going to get it. The thought seems to comfort me.

THE FOURTH DAY OF THE ATTACK

Gerry is keeping up his attack. At night, his bombers come over and prowl around dropping stuff here and there, and occasionally lighted flares. The boys in our unit are all eager to get a flare because of the big white rayon parachutes that float them. It makes a wonderful souvenir to give a girl. They even run out of their dugouts during the bombings and go up on the ridge where a flare has dropped to retrieve it.

Today I look at one. Spread out, the material of the parachute is about fifteen feet in diameter. Six metal wires hold up a kind of tray on which four magnesium candles are set. When one goes out, another lights up. The Gerry pilots time the dropping of them very well, and the flame seems to last until just before the parachute hits the ground. The machine gunners around our camp pop at them and their tracer bullets appear to reach the flares, but to no avail. Even if a bullet hits the parachute, it only makes a little tear in the material. But we hate these flares. They violate our escape into darkness. It does not seem fair. It's like someone turning on a light in your room when you are lying in bed naked and on top of the covers.

Artillery is popping around our camp all day. Occasionally, in the distance, a great geyser of dust goes up in the air. It's like the water hurled up by Old Faithful at Yellowstone Park. Generally, such an explosion is too far away to photograph, even with a telescopic lens. If it is too close, I duck into a slit trench like everybody else. These explosions are just explosions. They look just the same as they look in peacetime, when a road excavation is being dynamited.

I know that a man with a rifle, crouching in the foreground, and the explosion in the center of the picture, is a natural for publication. But, somehow it seems pointless to expose myself to this added danger for an explosion picture that still does not say much of anything, except that dust and stones are being hurled into the air at a terrific rate of propulsion. And if a man is crouching in the foreground, he shouldn't be. He should be deep in a slit trench or flat on his belly.

I know I can make pictures here that will knock the eyes out of editors. With little or no danger, I can make pictures of the Sappers exploding enemy ammunition, nice so-called "action shots" that editors will want. There are plenty of soldiers here perfectly willing to pose for me with their bayonets drawn, crouching behind mounds or pointing their guns over the edges of slit trenches. I can get them running at imaginary enemies with drawn bayonets as if they were in an infantry charge. But they'd all be faked pictures and they wouldn't be characteristic of this kind of warfare. It doesn't seem right. Here my sense of values seems to be shifting. The most important thing is not to get the picture. Our first struggle is to exist, to keep from being killed, and to survive. Then, too, it seems crass to be here where men are fighting and dying, merely to take photographs.

Modern war, particularly desert warfare, is singularly unsuitable for photography. The whole essence of this kind of war is dispersal. Keep everything spread out. You try and crowd as much as you can into a good picture. It would be ideal to have one tank in the foreground and one twenty-five pounder and a whole lot of the same thing arranged in the background. Then you'd have a nice pattern shot.

The idea at the front is to keep everything concealed, to make everything blend into the desert, and to prevent anything from standing out. Shadows are avoided as much as possible. Shadows reveal guns and tanks to pilots and show up well on aerial photographs. Unfortunately, shadows are also essential to a good magazine picture.

Tanks at the front move into action, their treads clanging like gigantic chains. They seem frighteningly impersonal. But they are spread far apart. Tanks shoot at each other when they are almost out of each other's sight. They are like battleships firing at each other from miles away. This front is spread out over miles and miles. Tanks must be spread out to cover all the line. If they were bunched together, they'd be a nice target for dive-bombers.

The twenty-five pounders are scattered here and there out of sight of each other. You see a crew puttering about fussing with the gun, loading the shell. They hold still. The gun recoils. There is a puff of smoke. Bang! You hear the sound. This little crew of men seems so cut off, seems to be doing something almost pointless, hurling steel off into the distance at something you can't even see. Certainly, they are in communication with the whole battery by telephone, but you can't hear what is being said.

Infantry move over a piece of ground like a bunch of football players on an open field run. Their bayonets are the only indication of battle. Machine gunners stay in their holes, waiting, waiting, and waiting. Ammunition trucks move in the distance with ambulances and a staff car, but they stay far apart.

Everything about this war is so vast, gigantic, and tremendous. There is no feeling of personal combat. How completely man is licked

by the machine age, even in war. The soldiers each have tiny infinites-
imal jobs, when compared with the whole front. One man unloads a
box of ammunition, another stays at one 50 mm gun on a tank, and yet
another performs a certain mechanical operation on a twenty-five
pounder. They are like workers on the assembly line of an automobile
plant. One man there tightens a certain screw on a certain type of automobile engine all day long. He never feels that he has accomplished
something big that's wholly his. It is so difficult to see the connection
between his screw tightening and the finished engine. And so it is with
the soldier who continually says to himself and out loud, "What am I
doing to win the war so we can go home?"

Yet, everything in the conduct of the battle is so terribly interre-
lated. A fouled spark plug on an ammunition supply truck silences a
twenty-five pounder at the front. A flat tire on a fuel tank truck leaves
a dozen tanks behind during an advance of an armored column. An
infantry battalion can be partially demoralized and terribly weakened
by a food ration supply truck that's lost its way to the battalion's
bivouac.

What keeps everything going? Everything about an army seems
inefficient. Everything seems to go wrong. Still, things happen; things
get done. Everybody advances and retreats together.

These are the things on my mind as I drive about this desert front.
I am being very cautious about where I take out my cameras to take
pictures. This is partly because the pictures would not be much anyway
and partly because I am uneasy about my pass. I know that an irate,
nervous officer could make a lot of trouble for me if he didn't happen
to like my face.

In one way, I would like to see the enemy. I would like to compre-
hend what it is we are fighting and to see the men we are fighting. Like
all the soldiers I talk to, I want to face the enemy and know what he is
like. I would like to photograph him.

On my way back to our camp, I try to collect my jumbled thoughts. I try and fit together what I am seeing, try to make it form into some kind of pattern. It all seems so unreal, like an army on maneuvers, like a big game. You do not feel any strong emotion of zeal, hatred, or exhilaration.

Then, as I am walking along near a wrecked troop carrier, I see a glove. Inside the glove is a hand, blown loose from an arm at the wrist.

I feel something now. I throw up.

AFS GHQ, THE TENTH DAY OF THE ATTACK

All week long the attack has continued. From reports and rumors, the BBC news announcements, and official communiqués that come over our battery radio, we get a very confused picture. We can't figure out which side is winning.

Word has come that Rommel may have broken through the Gazala line. Since early this morning, June 5, we have been cut off. The Bardia and El Adem roads are closed and Tobruk is surrounded just as it was during the Siege. How long will we be cut off from the world? My first thought when I hear the report is that I won't be able to get my film developed. However, no official word of this has come through yet. But, then, you'd expect the official news to be late in arriving.

A few days ago Jimmy King talked with some British officers who said Gerry was definitely on the run and that the General Grants are performing admirably. Some of the soldiers hear, on the other hand, that the Grant is being knocked out right and left. It seems that Gerry has turned up with tanks that have 88mm guns on them. The Grant has 75mm guns. Furthermore, the Grant's gun is mounted on the side, fairly low down, and can only swing in a 45° arc. The Gerry tank can swing all the way around. To increase the arc on the Grant, the whole tank must be maneuvered. Then, too, there is talk about the Grants not moving backward fast enough, which is important in maneuvering.

The soldiers seem discouraged and verging on a slight jitteriness. They don't know where and how Gerry will attack next. I have heard at least a dozen British soldiers say, "Why can't we do the attackin' for a change?"

This is all very bad news, but I do not seem to feel anything one way or another. You go about your daily tasks of washing, shaving, eating, arranging your bedding roll, and talking to the boys just as if you were on a camping expedition. Somewhere, perhaps, there is a world of order and civilization and comfort. Somewhere crops are growing, girls are laughing, and people are eating on tablecloths, but that is far, far behind. This is suspended time in an unreal, dreary world, highlighted with terror.

I wander into the AFS GHQ tent and sit over in a corner. Jimmy King is sitting at a trestle table typing out a memo. As usual, he is immaculately dressed and looks as if he just stepped out of a bathtub.

Somehow he appears at his best as the noise and confusion reaches the greatest intensity. Jimmy is a young man, and he has impressed me as one of the most bored young men I have ever met. In New York and in London, his charm and good looks have made both men and women fall over themselves trying to do things for him, trying to see a lot of him. He has a beautiful wife, an adequate income, and an entrée into the smartest and most fashionable social circles. What's more, he's had his pick of beautiful women.

Watching him confer with his officers, give orders about ambulance convoys, and discuss the men's problems and grievances with them, you have the feeling that he has come into his own. As I have learned to know him on the long voyage here, I kept sensing in him an inner propulsion toward self-destruction, a searching for chaos, excitement, suffering, and death. There is in him, I believe, a deep weariness and feeling of futility. He has been an editor of a magazine, a business executive, a playboy, and a pet of the rich and powerful. He sees no sense in the world, no meaning to life. Now in all this hell, he actually glows.

One of the ambulance drivers comes in and wants to speak to Jimmy. He is an amusing guy whom everybody likes, but he gets drunk. Every opportunity he had from Halifax to Cape Town to Bombay to Beirut to Cairo, he gets thoroughly soused. It would not matter, but after he gets a few he begins to insult people. He seems to have a predilection for stuffy British Colonels.

"I want to be sent to the front," he says, "I'm sick of making the Tobruk-Bardia run. I want to see some action."

Jimmy handles the situation very well. He explains that there really is no front in the sense of a front-line trench with the enemy a hundred or so yards away. Wounded come in from scattered tank encounters and from direct hits on artillery positions. With bombers flying back of the lines and long-range artillery and ground strafing, everywhere is the front. But he will see to it that the man gets an opportunity to take some special assignments.

"They all want to get up to the front," Jimmy says wearily. "They seem to expect some kind of movie version of trench warfare. Generally, it's the unreliable ones, the ones that are always getting into trouble that want to be sent into the center of a tank battle or something."

"Actually, you know," he says, "the boys you don't see much of, the inconspicuous ones, are the best. They do exactly what they're told. They get their work done. They go wherever you send them. They are the ones who keep things going properly. And yet they are seldom recognized as the heroes in war. They seldom get the medals."

Tom Wentworth of Fall River, Massachusetts, comes into the tent. He's had an amusing experience today. His ambulance was passing a section of ground not far away from where some Gerry engineers were digging up land mines in the British mine fields. From entrenched positions several hundred yards away machine guns are firing. A Gerry was lying wounded in the minefield. A Gerry Corporal with him waves a white flag at the ambulance. Tom's ambulance mate takes out a handkerchief, sits on the front fender of the car, and the Americans drive through the minefield to the Gerries.

All the firing stops as if it were a football game and the whistle has blown. The Gerry corporal unbuckles his belt, holster and pistol, walks over to Tom, and hands it to him. The three of them help the wounded man into the ambulance, and the corporal gets in too. He wants to surrender. They take the wounded man to a field hospital tent, then go hunting for someone to take over the Gerry prisoner. Nobody wants him, but they finally buttonhole a British officer who's willing to send the Gerry prisoner to Tobruk in a truck that's going there anyhow.

Some of the other drivers come in, back from the Bardia run. The road, then, is open. We are not besieged. They tell us the story. A German staff car, attached to a tank column doing an encircling movement, suddenly finds it is on the Tobruk-Bardia road. The officer and his driver believe it is a road the German column now commands. They take an MP as a prisoner and move on up the road and inform several drivers of vehicles they are now in German territory.

The news passes by word of mouth up and down the road. The Director of the YMCA canteen halfway between Tobruk and Bardia decides to dispose of his stores of good things—cans of pineapple, peaches, chocolate, and cigarettes—before Gerry takes over. All the soldiers that stop by, including a number of AFS ambulance drivers, take away armfuls of stuff.

In a few hours the Germans in the staff car are disillusioned and they in turn are taken prisoner. Traffic resumes its normal course on the Tobruk-Bardia road. A number of AFS men return to our camp bearing gifts.

After the others have gone to dinner, Jimmy tells me a piece of bad news. It seems an order was sent out by field security to pick me up. I should not have talked to the escaped British prisoners from Crete. No one is allowed to talk to anyone who has come in from enemy territory until they have been interviewed by the field security. Well, a field security officer gets to the hospital at Bardia just after I leave. He is hopping mad because he received the impression that a war correspondent was running around loose without a conducting officer. War correspondents at the front are not allowed out of sight of a conducting officer, generally a public relations officer. He also understands that I went posthaste to Cairo and sent off a hot interview to the American press. He wouldn't know, of course, that any war correspondent who cabled to his newspaper an interview with escaped British prisoners would be fired by return cable.

Jimmy tells me he has explained to the field security people that I am taking pictures for the AFS and not interested in getting spot news or sending cables.

"I explained to them, Flash," he says looking at me out of the corner of his eyes and smiling "that you were, however, possessed of a very strong curiosity about everything you came up against.

"You know you've got to be awfully careful here at the front. With the attack, these British officers get very sticky about rules. They get jumpy about everything.

"I'd suggest you get your work cleaned up here as quickly as you can and then go back to Cairo and send your pictures off to America. The AFS office in New York is crying for publicity pictures. We're also counting on you to do some press liaison work for the AFS with the American war correspondents in Cairo. They don't seem to understand what the field service is doing over here. We're in a rather curious position now that America is in the war. People are wondering why we all aren't in the American Army."

As we part, he suggests that I go out tomorrow with the convoy of ambulances that is going to evacuate the wounded from Tobruk Hospital to the hospital ship *Londonhovery Castle*, which came into the harbor tonight. They want to clear all the sick and wounded out of Tobruk as soon as possible. There might be some good shots at the pier.

After dinner, back in my dugout, I think about being with the AFS at Tobruk. Actually I have no business here. Either I am in the war or not in the war. There is no longer any justification for being a photographer, an observer, a taker of notes, an eager listener. My country is in the war. I feel an emotion I thought I would never feel. I want to serve my country's armed forces.

The U.S. Army Military North African Mission needs a photographer to document their work here in the Middle East. Several of the officers in Cairo said it could be arranged and I'd probably get a commission. That's where I belong. I won't have to do any actual killing. I will be doing useful work and still doing my own kind of work. The thing is settled in my mind and it is easy to go to sleep.

The next day I photograph the evacuation of the wounded. They were taken on invasion barges out to the mouth of the harbor. The harbor was so full of sunken hulls that ships could not come to the wharfs. But most of the wharfs were bombed to hell. These pictures later turned out to be the best studies of wounded men I had done. I had a bad fall on one of the invasion barges, but my Rolleiflex was not touched.

Back at camp, I went over to the hospital and got the wound on my leg painted. There was a danger of desert sores, as there is from any cut when you're in the Western Desert. I spent the night with a couple of orderlies at the hospital who took out their stored canned stuff and we had a feed. We went swimming in the Mediterranean, and I photographed the old Turkish wall, where I saw Eyetie signs.

In the morning, I heard a Tommy across from me at breakfast say, "Big load of stuff today." He and his mates were the morgue detail. They told about tying up the hands and feet of the dead soldiers and then turning them over to the graveyard detail.

That night I photographed, with time exposures, the Tobruk anti-aircraft barrage. The tracer bullets made nice streaks of light on the negative; the bombs made semicircle flares.

I kept going to the South African medical officer (MO) at the field dressing station, as I could hardly walk and the pains in my leg got worse and worse. I was also getting terribly sleepy all the time and was very irritable.

4 FLIGHT FROM TERROR

SEVENTEENTH SOUTH AFRICAN FIELD HOSPITAL, NEAR TOBRUK

I can barely walk now. All week the pains come and go. It is worse at night. They keep me awake. That means I have nothing to do but listen to the steady airplane bombing and the intermittent artillery fire echoing among the wadis. Some of the men seem to enjoy it. They say, "By God, this is great stuff. I hope it keeps up." On others, the strain is showing in their faces. To me the whole thing seems pointless. I simply cannot fathom what adult world would produce this.

The morning after the awful night a week ago, I hobbled over to see the South African MO who gave me the pills. He is very nice and looks my leg over casually.

"What you need," he says, "is to go back to Cairo and stay drunk a while and have a woman. I guess it would do us all good." He marks my sick report ticket "bomb neurosis." It is this war's term for "shell shock." Everything, it seems, not marked GSW (gunshot wound) up here at the front is marked "bomb neurosis." The reason for this is that so many men are "battle wise." They have a way of developing strange aches and pains in their backs or in their heads, just before an attack, or when the going is too rough. Sometimes they throw something out of joint or wrench something.

"All wounds," the orderly says, "are not from enemy bullets. You can fill a tin can with sand, then fire the bullet at your leg through the can. This way you don't report to the MO with powder burns."

The MO is very vague about telling me specifically what he means when he says the pains in my leg are from my nerves. I ask him if it is rheumatism. There is a story among the soldiers that sleeping on your rubber ground sheet can put pains in your legs. He says it is not rheumatism, that it's just my upset nerves. But I sense in him an uncertainty as to exactly what the trouble is. I detect in him a feeling of futility. Later, I learn he is a drinking man. He begins at the officers' mess at dinner and keeps it up until bedtime. "Rum is a fine thing," he says. "Not too much mind you, but just enough."

As for myself, I am not satisfied as to whether these pains in my leg are or are not the result of something in my mind. If only Maj. Alexander Kennedy, the British Army psychiatrist I met on the trip over, were here again, I could talk it over with him. As I understand it, the inference in all these "bomb neurosis" cases is that your mind consciously or unconsciously makes something go wrong with your body. You lose your voice. One whole side of you goes numb. You lose the use of a leg or an arm. You imagine any ailment that will take you away from the firing line. But, I reason, if I know this to be the case, how could it be true of me? Of course, it could be entirely unconscious on my part, but I have studied and read and talked about this sort of thing. It couldn't happen to me.

Anyway, I'll be damned if I'll leave here until I find out. Jimmy King, who has been swell about this, says he does not blame me. The time has come for me to go back to Cairo with my negatives. Transport back is available now. But if I go back before I know more about what's causing the pains in my leg, I'll always feel I ran away.

In the meantime, I sit around at the camp. I can walk only with the greatest difficulty and using a stick. Today, Syd brings me a walking stick he "scrounged" somewhere. It belonged to an Eyetie officer once and, after the capture of Tobruk, it was used in the British officers' mess as a poker. It is slightly burned at the end. I try and take a few pictures around the camp, but to get pictures you've got to get around freely. I seem to have lost my zest for taking pictures. The whole show here keeps looking sillier and sillier.

This afternoon I pack my kit and make arrangements to go back in an AFS truck that's taking one of our maintenance boys, who used to work with General Motors in Detroit, back to Cairo. I'm sick of the uncertainty. After a soak in a hot bath at Shepheard's for two or three days, the pains will go away and the seemingly dead nerves will come to life.

I get Jimmy King to write out a note to the South African MO that I'm going back with the AFS truck and to request that I be given my medical papers so that I can report to an MO in Cairo.

The MO reads the notice and says, "I want you to go back to Cairo hospitalized and under our supervision. Whatever this is, the effect is the same. You are sick and need care."

"Thank you, Sir," I say, "but I think I prefer to go back with the AFS truck."

"This," he says, "is an order. And if you don't go back with the medical corps, I'll have you placed under arrest and sent back." I know I'm licked. But with the knowledge I get a feeling of relief.

I hobble back to Jimmy, and he says to go back and get my negatives developed and get them off to America and he's sure they'll be fine pictures. He says he'll see me again in Cairo shortly and to take it easy.

At the field dressing station the MO gives me a card to the Seventeenth South African field hospital. Why I'm not sent directly to Tobruk Hospital puzzles me. On the way, I stop and say good-bye to Major Daly, who is sorry to hear I'm sick. He tells me not to deflower all the women in Cairo. The way I feel now I'll settle for just having the desire to go on living again.

A few days later when Tobruk fell to the Germans and Italians, Major Daly was taken prisoner.

The Seventeenth South African Field Hospital is a concrete dugout about twenty feet in the ground. Inside, it is like a cylinder sliced in half. It used to be an Italian ammunition dump for the defense of Tobruk. My duffel bag, bedding roll, and photographic supplies are checked on through the medical corps baggage detail, but I keep my leather bag of cameras with me and put them under my head as kind of a pillow. According to regulations, when hospitalized you're only allowed to keep a cloth bag of toilet articles with you, but I insist that my cameras stay with me. For having them to hold on to seems to give me a feeling of security.

There are about sixty beds on either side of the dugout with an aisle down the center. It is very quiet, and when the bombing starts the noise is muffled because we are so deep in the earth. A couple of MOs, one of them a colonel, come around and look at my card and say I'll be all right.

In the morning the colonel and two of his officers turn up and ask me if I would like to take pictures of their field operating room. I say I guess I will if they think I can. An orderly helps me get my camera stuff set up. I take photos of the operating room, the orderlies bandaging wounded men, some stretcher bearers carrying a wounded man into the tunnel leading into the hospital, and some views of the hospital camp, camouflaged in the desert. Every so often my leg gives way completely and I kneel over on my hands and knees. Those pictures, oddly enough, later turn out to be rather interesting medical corps shots.

"You know, my boy," the colonel says, "I could have you walking all right in fifteen minutes if I set about it."

I feel like saying, "Then why in hell don't you set about it?" Anyway, it's become clear why I was routed to this field hospital instead of being sent directly to Tobruk Hospital. The MO at the field dressing station messes with these officers, and they thought it would be a good idea to have their pictures taken.

TOBRUK HOSPITAL

A South African ambulance takes me late this afternoon to Tobruk Hospital. A feeling of relaxation has come over me now that I know there is nothing I can do but lie on my back and wait. I am not allowed to get up to even try and walk. On the drive over, a big Gerry artillery shell lands near the road, and a great geyser of dust shoots into the air. I think it's too bad I didn't have my Contax ready to shoot it.

My stretcher is put on the floor of the hospital receiving room with about twenty sick and wounded South African and Imperial (the term used to differentiate English from other British troops) soldiers. The mills of the Royal Army Medical Corps grind exceedingly slowly, but you get down to the line somehow. We wait until the doctors can check us in. A charming, boyish second lieutenant MO looks me over and gives me the "I could have you walking in fifteen minutes" line. He has me try and take a few steps, then says, "See, you're walking better already."

In the ward, an orderly washes my face and hands and brings a ration of beef stew, which I feel too sick to eat. The nursing sister in charge of the ward is the gayest person I've seen in a long time. She is no spring chicken, but character and decency shine through in her face so that she is beautiful. I watch her closely when a badly shot up driver, whose ammunition truck was just machine gunned and strafed, is brought into the ward. The man has a couple of bullets in him, and a few pieces of shrapnel. In his face is a kind of fixed staring terror. She takes his chin between her thumb and forefinger, and points his face directly into hers.

"Come, lad," she says, "Give us a smile. You look as if you 'adn't a friend in the whole world. You'll like this ward."

"Orderly," she calls over her shoulder, "why haven't you brought this man a spot of tea and some jam. That's what's the matter. He's not 'ad is tea." The flicker of a smile works at the man's features. I watch the sister's face as she walks down the aisle to another case. That sort of thing, I realize, is costing her more than physical strength. The grim line of her jaw reveals what she's thinking.

And she's right, because the wounded driver dies during the night.

Two beds away for me is a German prisoner. He is one of the hopeless fanatical Nazi types. Nurses and orderlies are thoroughly irritated with him because whenever he wants anything he says, for example, "Heil Hitler, a glass of water," or, "Heil Hitler, a cup of tea." He's been doing this for two days. This afternoon, the head sister in the ward has laid down an ultimatum and either the Gerry prisoner can ask for things like anyone else, or he won't get them. For the past half hour he has been saying, "Heil Hitler, the bedpan." His request is greeted with silent glances. Finally, he says, "The bedpan, please." And gets it.

The MO for the ward and the sister are making the evening rounds. He is an older man, a colonel, and his bedside manner is a witty seriousness. He looks at my envelope, fastened to my chart, and sees, of course, "bomb neurosis." Then he pulls back the blanket and tests the reflex in my knee and then my ankle. Neither responds. Then he pricks both my legs all the way up and down with a pin. The pricks in both legs feel the same, which is what he wants to know.

"Put down," he tells the sister in a low voice, "that the knee and ankle jerk are missing. No sensory loss. Obviously—but, hold on, I'd better cover myself. Say, 'does not appear to be functional.'"

When he has gone I realized what I had suspected all along. There is something going wrong with my body and it hasn't got anything to do with my brain. If this thing is not in my nerves, what is it? It may be something very serious, and something permanent.

There is a big skylight window that runs along the upper part of the wall opposite my row of beds. The glass has all been blown out and been replaced by a thin transparent gauze. It is dark outside now, and the skylight frames a pattern of clear desert stars. The ward is silent except for the breathing of the men and a few coughs and groans. The heat of the day has gone, and now and then you can smell the salt water. I sleep fitfully.

The droning is far away at first. I am wide-awake now, listening to hear if it is the steady drones of our planes, or the interrupted buzz. It is the latter. Bang! The flashlights sweep across the skies outside in the window frame. The ack-ack barrage clatters and the tracer bullets make graceful arcs between the stars. Everybody in the ward is wide-awake. Several men are groaning. "Why don't they go away and let us sleep?" a voice calls out.

A sister has come into the ward now and holds a tiny flashlight. She goes from bed to bed. When she comes to my bed I can hear what she's saying, apparently to all the men, "Pay no attention to it, lad. It's far, far away. Probably up toward Benghazi." An orderly comes into the ward. "Sister," he says, "you'd better not let the MO find you in here. The order is that sisters must go into the shelters during air raids." The sister continues her rounds. She is lying to us, and most of us know it, but the men have quieted down anyway. The thudding of the exploding bombs does seem a little more distant now. I go to sleep.

AMBULANCE CONVOY, TOBRUK TO BARDIA

They are trying to evacuate the sick and wounded out of Tobruk Hospital as fast as they can. If Tobruk gets cut off again, it will be a nuisance having disabled men around. From points all along the line, at the regimental aid posts and advanced dressing stations, the wounded men converge on Tobruk Hospital. The operating rooms are working here twenty-four hours a day. Some of the surgeons have not been to bed in almost a week. One MO tells me that the surgeon's job is a lot easier in this war because you don't have to worry so much about infection. You just spray sulfanilamide powder all over the wound. If you cut off a leg or an arm in time, and see to it that you cover everything with sulfur powder, there isn't the worry about gangrene there used to be with the old Carol Dakin solution. Of course, the solution had its points, and was certainly an improvement over what they had in the wars before the last war. Now, I reflect, the old Carol Dakin solution is just plain Zonite. Wars do accomplish something.

This morning I am evacuated by ambulance convoy to Bardia. The ambulances are from my AFS unit. Tom Stix, a college boy from Cincinnati, Ohio, is the driver of mine. He is surprised to see me. My three ambulance mates are a Tommy with a head wound; a "wog," or Arab boy, who somehow got left in the desert and wandered over a land-mine that blew both his legs off, and an Australian who got a bullet in his bladder apparatus. The Aussie can't control his urinating. He has to hold a tin can, which he uses every few minutes so he won't wet up his stretcher and blankets. Every so often Tom stops and empties the tin can. The Aussie asks him why he doesn't take a swig out of that can of nice English beer.

The Arab lies under his blanket, and the blanket is flat against the stretcher from just below the waist on down. The Arab can't speak English, but can only grunt and groan when he wants to convey to Tom to please go easy on the bumps.

TENT HOSPITAL AT BARDIA

There are enough representatives of both Allied and Axis forces in the hospital to hold a peace conference right here and now. About thirty of us are lying on stretchers on the hard, packed sand and clay ground floor of the tent. There are seven Afrika Corps soldiers and two officers, eight

Eyetie soldiers and three officers, nine Tommies, two Springboks, a U.S. Air Corps gunner from Detroit, and myself.

Two medical corps orderlies are in charge of the upper racks of the tent. A member of the British Army stands guard as a sentry. His name is William. One of the orderlies is a wisecracking limey. He has just gone through the kit of an Eyetie officer and has discovered a civvy suit. He puts it on and goes into a kind of vaudeville routine of singing and dancing.

"Oh, ho," he sings, "I'm just a bloody civilian. Look at me in me nice lovely civvy suit. Playing the Palladium, I am."

"Better look out," the other orderlies say. "You'll get the glasshouse if some officer bloke comes along here and finds you in a civvy suit." The glasshouse is what the Tommies call a military prison.

It is strange to see anyone in civilian dress. All of us stare at the gay Tommy as if we had never seen a civvy suit before. He has found a swagger stick and waves as he sings a song:

I've got sixpence, jolly jolly sixpence,
I've got sixpence to last me all my life.
I've got two pence to spend and two pence to lend
And two pence to take home to my wife.

No cares have I to grieve me
No pretty little girls to deceive me
I've got two pence to lend and two pence to spend
And no pence to last me all my life.

Another orderly comes in the tent with a sentry and asks if there are any Eyetie officers present. They take away our three Italian officers. One of the officers trips on the stretcher of a Gerry. The German looks at him with contempt, and mutters, "Swine." All the Italians are unshaven or bearded. The Germans are clean-shaven and have taken their shirts off. They seem proud of their sun-browned torsos.

On the stretcher next to me is a British sergeant who is in field security, and whose job has been to question Gerry prisoners as soon as they are brought into the lines. He is being evacuated because of an undiagnosed infection that has turned both his hands into a mass of scabs. He says he is just as glad because he was captured a few months ago by the Germans and they got his field security identification card with his name and picture on it. He escaped, but if he ever got caught again, he says the Germans have the right under international law to shoot him. I ask him what conclusions he has come to about the German and Italian soldiers he has talked to.

"The Eyeties," he says, "don't fancy the war at all, and thoroughly hate their Gerry allies. Most of them seem to be peasant farmers or workmen, like masons or carpenters. They want to be helpful but are hopeless for getting military information because they don't know anything.

"The Gerry prisoners are brighter. We have the most trouble with the arrogant Nazi type. He is sullen, and apt to be insulting. Naturally, we cannot do anything when he tells us we are stupid English swine. But it's bloody irritating. I'd say about thirty to forty percent of the Gerry prisoners are the disagreeable Nazi type.

"About sixty to seventy percent of them are rather decent human beings. They have no illusions about Hitler and all they want is to get back home and see their families in Germany."

He points out different Gerry prisoners in the tent as illustrations of what he means.

While we are talking, we hear planes overhead. One of the Gerry prisoners mutters, "Luftwaffe." The other Gerry prisoners look very annoyed. At first, the field security sergeant and myself smile at the idea of Gerry planes bombing Gerry prisoners until we realize they also might get us.

The sergeant says that just before he was hospitalized, a German officer drove up on a motorbike with a sidecar and wanted to know where he could give himself up. He had been cut off from his tank column.

"I got in his sidecar," the sergeant says, "and directed him to the nearest prisoners' stockade. He offered me a cigarette from his gold cigarette case. I hesitated, but such a hurt look came over his face that I chanced it and smoked one. It was all right. He turned out to be friendly, but very cocksure. He said he didn't mind being a prisoner because next week Rommel was going to take Cairo. 'Shepheard's Hotel,' he said, 'was going to be the Afrika Corps's GHQ.'"

Then he began to tell me the English and the Germans were the only good people in the world, and ought to run the world together rather than against each other. I knew this was some kind of propaganda so I took no notice of it.

The orderly brings us beef stew and tea. It is getting dark. Tonight we sleep with the enemy.

BARDIA TO MERSA MATRUH

The next lap on the road back has begun. The discards of war are loaded into British army ambulances and start the journey to Mersa Matruh.

On the rubber rack, next to me, is a very sick fellow patient. His eyes squint tightly; the muscles of his jaw harden as he clinches his teeth. Turning over on his right side, he utters the low-pitched call of men in pain. His T-shirt is torn and stained the deep brown of congealed blood. The left sleeve is empty, and the arm meant to go in to it is wrapped in bandages under which blood is oozing in several places. As he turns, his face comes into view from my berth. It is sun browned, the left side is bruised and swollen, his hair is black, and his eyes are dark and sad. He tries to smile in friendliness. He seems to be only a kid.

"You'll excuse me please," he says in a German accent. "The bumps are not good for my arm."

"How old are you anyway?" I ask, smiling back but wondering if it is proper to be friendly with a German prisoner of war. Should my manner to him be one of outrage? Should I denounce him? He belongs to the gangsters and outlaws of the world. I should hate and despise him.

"Nineteen years," he replies, offering me one of the cigarettes issued to German and English wounded alike.

"And how long have you been in the German army?"

"Two and a half years. I have been in the desert almost eighteen months. It is a pity I was taken prisoner for I was soon to get leave to Germany. I would have been able to see my fiancée."

With some difficulty, he takes his wallet out of his left breast pocket, and hands me her photograph. Her name is Hildegard. She is well dressed with a smartly tailored wool coat of a light shade, a large brim hat, high-heeled shoes, and silk or rayon stockings. Her hair is blonde, and she is slightly on the buxom side. She could easily be an American college girl.

"It will be perhaps a long time until I see her again," he says, sighing. The sigh seems to echo hundreds of sighs I've heard from American soldiers, British, French, Poles, Australians, New Zealanders, the sighs of all the many fighting men of the Middle East. They show you a picture of a wife, sweetheart, son, or daughter. It is always the same sigh as the picture is returned to the same left breast pocket, over the heart.

Our ambulance is leaving Sollum. We can hear the wind clamoring and beating at the metal walls. Little eddies of the powdery desert sand are blowing into the cracks of the door and window. The patient below me coughs. Outside, a big convoy is passing us as it moves up to the front: staff cars, trucks full of infantry, despatch riders on their motorbikes, petrol trucks, trucks pulling trailers with General Grants and Matildas on, and last of all the workshop truck with its crane arm pointing to the blue sky. It's stuff to stop Gerry's latest attack.

The enemy is staring at the ceiling in our ambulance, talking quietly. Now and then he grips his wounded arm and holds it steady as we pass a rough section of bombed road. His name is Otto, and he is an only child. Before the war began he had lived a year with his parents in Brazil. His father was an agent for the distribution of Bosch electrical products.

The family returned to Germany just before the war, and both father and son were conscripted into the army. Otto was trained for the Afrika Corps and sent to Libya. The father, after serving on the Western front in its advance into France, was transferred to the Russian front, where he was killed this past winter.

"I have only my mother left now," Otto says. "I hope this crazy war will soon end so that I can see her once again. But it is a long way to Germany from Egypt."

Our ambulance stops suddenly. The door is flung open, revealing a group of smiling Tommies of the Royal Army Medical Corps. They have news that Cologne has just been bombed. In their hands are plates of bread and beef stew, and mugs of hot tea.

One of them, glancing at Otto, says, "Hello—a Gerry."

"Hey, Fritz, who is going to win the war?" says another Tommy.

Otto smiles feebly. He does not reply. The mess crew, busy with the plates, move on to feed the wounded in the next ambulance.

Otto's face is wet with tears. "What's the matter, Otto?" I ask.

"My mother, she . . . lives in Cologne," he says.

Then Otto asks me to speak to the first doctor we run into, because his arm is hurting him terribly, and he'd like a narcotic.

"Right-o," the MO says, when I tell him the Gerry prisoner is in pain. He calls an orderly, who brings a tray of bottles and syringes and puts them on the floor of the ambulance. Rubbing a portion of Otto's leg with cotton soaked in alcohol, the orderly fills a syringe and hands it to the MO.

"Are there many Americans in the desert?" the MO asks, plunging the needle into the calf of Otto's leg.

"A couple of hundred of us are at Tobruk," I say, "We're members of an American ambulance unit."

"We hope there'll be a lot more of you soon. Cheerio, and all the best." He moves on to inspect the patients in the next ambulance.

"Then America is truly in the war," Otto says. "We heard but we were not entirely sure. And you are an American, then?"

"Yes, Otto, I am an American. What do you think about America coming into the war?"

"It is not good for Germany," Otto says, as if he were thinking carefully about his words. "But I do not understand why America should fight Germany. I liked America. They build many fine machines there. I had hoped to visit your country after the war. Why do the Americans want to fight Germany?"

"Well, I suppose," I say, wondering what one ought to say in a case like this, and also wondering if I actually know exactly why, "for many reasons. We feel Hitler had no right to invade weaker countries, or bomb civilians, or persecute the Jews. We feel his treatment of the Jews and the burning of books was a terribly uncivilized thing. Tell me, do you think Jews ought to be persecuted?"

Otto shrugs his shoulders. "Such things," he says, "I have nothing to do with. They are political matters. I do not concern myself with politics. I do not like politicians. They cause wars. I only asked to be allowed to do my work. At first I was in the Luftwaffe. That was good. I like working on airplane engines.

"Then I was put into a tank. That is hard work. Every night, even after battle, we must work on our tank until it is in good order. I like machines. I hope the British let me do mechanical work in Egypt. Then the time will go fast. When the war is over I will go to Germany and see my mother and marry my fiancée. Then we will all go to Brazil. I like South America. It is beautiful there.

"What a terrible world this is. Everything is crazy. All the countries are fighting. I am glad I do not have to fight anymore. I am glad I am out of the war."

The low droning of airplane motors overhead penetrates the roof of our ambulance. Both of us instinctively clench our fists and close our eyes.

"RAF," I say.

"I know," Otto says. "I know the sound of their engines."

"And I know the sound of your Stukas and Messerschmidts, too." We both laugh. The droning fades away.

Later, the convoy stops again. We are given mugs of warm tea. A group of Tommies gathers around the door of our ambulance. Our prisoner of war is a social success in the Allied lines. They keep pressing cigarettes on Otto, and bars of chocolate.

He tries to respond to their kindness, but he is really too sick to do much more than smile a thank you.

"'Ows old Rommel?" a Tommy with a very cockney accent asks.

"How is Wavell?" Otto replies.

There is a quick silence. None of the Tommies wants to mention that Wavell is in India. On the other hand, there is a rumor that he is returned for this new push. Maybe Gerry's intelligence has caught up with him.

"I say, Fritz," a serious Tommy says, "how do you like the desert? You get enough water on your side?"

"We get good water," Otto says, "but I do not like the desert." Everyone laughs in agreement.

"I say, the sausage and cheese wrapped in cellophane they issue on your side are bloody good. I 'ad some of your beer, too. Not bad."

"We have had some of your bully beef," Otto says. "I myself do not care for it."

The laughter is almost hearty now. Someone calls out that the convoy is ready to move off. The Tommies collect our tea mugs.

"Here, Fritz," the serious Tommy says, "keep this package of Woodbines. English cigarettes, for a change. Good trip, lads." Otto thanks him shyly, the doors are slammed shut, and we move promptly up onto the road.

"I like the English soldiers," Otto says. "They are gentlemen. They are also brave. But they are badly treated, and they do not have a chance against our tanks and guns."

"What you think about the Italians?"

"They are no good. They are dirty and full of bugs, and do not know how to fight."

Otto seems to have fallen into a fitful sleep. Now and then he talks at random. His school life in Germany was happy. He loved travel and games. He and his fiancée took long hiking trips together. His mother was very good to him always. Then he speaks of his capture.

"We were attacking when a twenty-five pounder struck my tank and set it afire. When I jumped out, I was hit by machine-gun bullets. The Free French captured us, put us into a lorry, and took us away. This place on my face, an Austrian officer with the Free French hit me with his revolver. It was very bad. I did not even know the answers to some of the questions he asked me. I was glad when they finally sent me to an English hospital."

Our ambulance is slowing up.

"It has been nice to talk to you, Otto," I say.

"You are a good comrade," he says. "I hope we will be together in the hospital. Or perhaps we will meet when this terrible war is over."

"Any prisoners of war in here?" a Tommy carrying a Lee-Enfield rifle says, flinging open the door of the ambulance.

Outside, in the late afternoon sun, I see a hospital tent with a sign "POW." We are far enough behind the lines so that they are sorting out wounded prisoners of war from allied wounded.

"Good-bye, comrade," Otto says, as his stretcher is pulled along its tracks. He raises his good arm in a farewell gesture. He is the enemy, and I feel no hate for him. I even wish him well.

After I got home, I gave a short talk at a war bonds rally in the New York offices of a large Hollywood movie company on what the war was like. I told the employees of that company about the Tommies, the Springboks, the Aussies, and about Otto and some of the German and Italian prisoners of war I'd met. I told how curious the Allied soldiers were to find out how the soldiers on the other side of the line were faring and how they kidded around with the prisoners and gave them cigarettes, candy, and food.

The audience seemed interested, but afterwards one of the big executives called me aside. "That stuff about prisoners of war—it's interesting and true," he said. "I know, I was in the last war and we know what it's like. But you mustn't tell anybody. You've got to create mass hate. You've got to tell the people that these German soldiers are monsters and that you despise them and they must despise them and to buy war bonds so as to help kill them. Your job right now is bond selling. That's why you're here. I know about appealing to the masses. I've been in the business a long time."

MERSA MATRUH

They have found room for me in a medical ward tent, and four South African natives are carrying me on a stretcher. I can see a little of the tower of Mersa Matruh. It is less forlorn than elsewhere in the desert. A few palms are bending to and fro with the wind. In the distance, the zigzag-topped wells of the bombed town reflect the light of the morning sun. Hospital tents rise out of the sand dunes. The wind picks up the grains of sand, and they bite into your face and arms like tiny needles. This is part of the Libyan plateau. The wind gets a good start, but it does not behave exactly like winds elsewhere in the world. Only in the Libyan Desert does the dune "form parallel lines with the direction of the prevailing winds." I remember bits from the research on this area, which I did as background for photographs I had hoped to take. "Before the dunes of the Libyan Desert were explored, dunes parallel with the wind were unheard of. Between the dunes the soil is left bare several kilometers wide. The Libyan dune is typically oval shaped.

"Silica is the main constituent of sand; it is evident therefore that the material of the dunes is dried from the withering of arenaceous bits. . . . The combination of wind and sand forms a denuding force of great power. The sand is capable of planing and grooving the exposed surface of the hardest rocks." I remember that much knowledge was accumulated and shared on those matters by English, Italian, and German scientists during peacetime.

It is good to be taken inside the hospital tent and away from the sun and wind-driven sand. The floor of the tent is covered with canvas. Sandbags are built around the entrances to the tent to keep the sand from coming inside. The patients are lying in two rows on stretchers. We are all still in our uniforms.

In the afternoon, the wind increases, flutters the tent flap, and beats against the canvas walls. Orderlies step inside hurriedly, brushing the sand out of their hair and eyebrows. Somebody says it's a bloody *khamsín*, the dry, hot wind that carries sand and dust from the desert and can create an electrical disturbance that renders compasses useless. Even here in the tent, the air is filled with a fine dust. Your nose and throat seem caked with grit. It is no use trying to get the dust off of your face or out of your hair. It becomes part of your skin. You wonder if there will ever be water to wash away the dust and sand from your body. It even gives a ghostlike appearance to all the men, because it coats their faces and uniforms. Everybody is miserable, but nobody complains. In any case, this is much less of a hell than the terror at the front.

Tonight the pains in my leg are more intense than they've ever been. I ask the orderly for a narcotic, and he gives me a tiny glass with a white powder dissolved in it. After a while I can tell what he's given me from the lack of effect it has on me. It must be just plain aspirin, not one of the heroin powders I've been given before. I stick it out a while longer, and then get up and hobble out of the tent into the open.

The moon is shining brightly, and the wind has stilled. Everything looks magic, like some garden of paradise. My mind is crystal clear.

I stumble in the sand. It feels soft on my hands, as I tried to break the fall. Then in the distance I hear the drone of airplane motors.

Perhaps this is not Mersa Matruh. Perhaps it is the lost oasis, the white city of Zerzura. Archaeologists believe it might be very near here. It is a wonderful place, this "oasis of little birds," and there are palm trees and springs. There is peace and beauty. Perhaps if I keep walking I will find this lost oasis, for which so many have searched, and the water from the springs will take the pain out of my legs.

Better still, I will get, somehow, to the Siwa oasis. It is only a hundred or so miles south of here. It was from the oracle there that Alexander the Great learned he was descended from God. No one would hear the oracle for the noise of the bombing. But I could photograph the temple to Ammon, god of prophecy. He solves riddles. His voice is the oracle, and he would explain to me why there are wars. He will solve the riddle of this war and tell me who will win.

In my mind's eye I see things that cannot be there. Troops are marching over by some trucks. Something is very wrong. Time has the years mixed up. They are not our force's troops. They are Alexander the Great's troops, and there they are carrying their own water in big clay jugs. There are some more soldiers going by, and they are in another kind of uniform. Yes, they are the Persian troops of King Cambyses, more than fifty thousand, and they will go into the desert and they will never be heard of again. Perhaps some British desert patrol will come across evidence of where these soldiers perished, or perhaps a bomb crater will turn up bits of their armor.

An Arab woman is sitting beside me now. She throws her head back, opens her mouth wide, and laughs.

"Why are you laughing?"

"At you," she says, "because you are so incredibly naïve."

"Who are you?" I say.

"I am Cleopatra. How silly you are about men in time. Men have not changed at all these centuries. Nothing has changed. And you are looking at me strangely.

"You thought the war was going to be a romantic adventure. Now you find it's a dreary, sordid business. You thought your civilization had advanced. It always remains the same. The Libyans always fought the Berbers, and then when that ended the Libyans fought the Egyptians. Then the Romans fought the Jews over in Palestine. Nothing is new. Hitler says the Norse gods are on his side, and you say the Christian God is on your side. Yet, Rome is on the wrong side."

She is laughing. It is such loud laughter I am sure she will wake up the others, and they will find me here. It has awakened someone. It is the orderly.

"Dat is not goot, my boy, that you should be out here. You are sick. You have been talking to yourself. Come back and I will give you something to make you sleep."

"You talk like a Dutchman. What are you?"

"I am a Boer, and I speak Afrikaans."

"Then what are you doing here? You are on the other side. You're fighting the British."

"Come with me, boy. First, pull yourself together. Everything will be all right."

He is gentle and he is good. He puts his arm around me, and leads me back into the tent. And he gets a glass with something bitter in it and I swallow it. He sits by my stretcher and talks quietly. I do not understand the meaning of his words, but they are soothing words and I know he is my friend. Now I am happy because the pain is gone and I am falling asleep at last.

MERSA MATRUH TO EL TAHAG BY HOSPITAL TRAIN

Early this morning we are loaded onto the hospital train, which has been made up at Mersa Matruh, the end of the line. Toward noon we start up, but I am scarcely aware of being on the train because an amiable MO has given me a pill of morphine. He says I can have all I want on the train ride. It is wonderful to feel no pains in my leg, and to wander back and forth in a dreamy, misty world on soft clouds. I can make things happen so easily in this dreaming world. I am dancing, or making love, or eating a wonderful meal. I can go anywhere I like. I am lying on the grass in Connecticut at my farm. I am swimming in the lake. There is nothing wrong with my leg. The war is over. Everybody is happy.

Somebody says the train has stopped because we're at Alexandria. Then, in the afternoon of the next day, our train stops again for a long time and an ambulance takes me to the receiving tent at Number Six General Hospital at El Tahag. My stretcher is put on a two-wheeled cart, and three laughing Italian boys, prisoners of war, wheel me to the wooden hut in which my ward is located.

NUMBER SIX GENERAL HOSPITAL AT EL TAHAG

One of the first things I ask for is that word be sent to Father Wickham-George that I am here. He comes and sits on the side of my bed. He asks about my AFS unit at Tobruk. We, he says, are his favorites. The strain of seeing so many of his boys coming down from the desert "shot up" is telling on him. His eyes reveal how deeply troubled he is.

"But there is one good thing about all this," he says. "Boys that have not thought anything about their religion since they were children are coming to me and asking me to hear their confessions. So many of them who have never had any religion, or never paid any attention to their religion, want to know how they can begin now. Most of my spare time is taken up with talking to converts."

Just before he leaves, he hears my confession. I have little to tell him, except that I have cursed and used foul language. I also tell them that I am worried about my faith.

"Many times," I say, "since I have come out of the desert, I have doubted that there is a God. I have had many moments when my faith left me. I can't stop my mind from wondering how any just good God could permit all the pain and suffering I have seen."

"Your faith," he says, "will always come back to you. There are moments of darkness for all men. War and all its evils are not the ways of God. It is man's work, and he must pay for it, for he has visited these things upon himself."

We talk quietly for quite a while. A new stillness seems to take hold of me. Finally as he is about to go, Father says, "God bless you, my son. When I say Mass, I will offer our prayers that you will be well and whole again. I will bring you communion in the morning."

A VISIT FROM COLONEL LISTER

The MO in charge of me here is probably the stuffiest person of any nationality I've ever run into. He can't make up his mind what's the matter with me, and he won't admit it.

Of course, "other ranks" in the British would not even think of addressing a medical officer. As a patient explained to me today, "If you asked your MO what was the matter with you in the British army, that would be an effrontery, because you would be assuming that he was interested in what was the matter with you. It simply isn't done."

Some of the patients in my ward are able to stand up and move about. They spend most of the morning before inspections tidying up. When the MO and the nursing sister make the rounds these boys stand at attention.

"Feeling better?" says the MO, and always the answer is "Yes, sir."

The patient is not allowed to tell the MO what pains and aches he has unless the MO asks him. Being an American, I know that I can get away with a little more than they can, and I am doing my level best to find out exactly what is wrong with me.

The MO, who is a major, has put me off so far with, "I'll tell you later. We'll see." From my questions he knows that I know my symptoms can be interpreted as either from "bomb neurosis," or a fall, or a germ. I continue to run a fever, my throat is sore, and I feel sick. I'm not supposed to do it, but I have been reading my chart. I just have to find out what in hell is the matter with me.

The other day my MO jabbed a needle into my back and took a specimen of my spinal fluid. I notice on the report of the examination of the specimen that protein was found in it. I don't know what this means, but from the fact that it was noted down I can tell it's important.

The next day after, my MO sends for me. He is sitting in a tent about one hundred yards away from the hut I am in. I hobble over with the help of a stick. I sit down in front of his desk, and he begins a lecture.

"There is nothing wrong with you, except what is in your mind. You Americans are incredibly naïve. None of your unit was trained for the front. Our men are trained, prepared. No wonder you went to pieces, and this happened to your leg."

He doesn't say anything, and I don't either. Then, out of a clear sky, he says, "Do you hate anyone?"

"Yes," I say. "I hate the top sergeant in my unit. I hated that colonel in Cairo who wouldn't let me have the kind of photographic pass I wanted. Also, I hate this war after what I've seen of it."

"You know," he answers, "even I hate someone. I hate Australians. I think they are the most incredibly awful people in the world. They are coarse and rude, and absolutely hopeless. But you've got to control your hate. It can make you sick, you know.

"Throw that cane away. Go ahead and walk. Get it out of your mind that anything is the matter with you. You're safe now, and you don't have to worry. Colonel Lister wants to have a look at you, however. He'll be around in a day or two."

On my way back to my ward I try and walk without a stick, and to ignore the paralysis of my leg. I fall on my face twice. But, I think, if this thing is in my mind I could lick it. It is inconceivable that this could happen to me, but the MO seems to know what he is doing, and if he says it's so, it must be so. But after I lie down in my bed, I know I am sick, not only sick in my body, but sick in my head.

Two days later, Colonel Lister comes to my bedside. He is short and thin, with a shy, sensitive face. Something is wrong with his right eye. He opens up his little bag, and begins tapping my leg, my knee, and ankle many times with a rubber mallet. He brushes my skin with a metal brush, and asks me if I feel it. He takes a steel instrument that is blunt on one end and sharp on the other. He pushes against sections of my leg, and asks me if I can tell which is the blunt end and which is the sharp end. He tells me close my eyes, reach my arms up, and touch my middle fingers together. He asks me to close my eyes and touch the end of my nose with my index fingers. During the examination, I ask him if he's any relation to Lord Lister, the scientist. He is.

"The family are still operating the old pharmaceutical house," he says. "How do you happen to know who he is?"

Later, I learned that Colonel Lister was a gunner in the last war, and was wheeled into an operating tent in France. The surgeon in charge did not know the name of the patient whose eye it was now his job to remove. But when he looked at the young gunner's face, he saw that it was his son.

Colonel Lister's hands moving over my legs suggest the hands of a pianist moving over a keyboard. When he is all done, he smiles and, tapping his temple with his finger, says, "Nothing wrong with you up here. I've got several ideas as to what is wrong with your leg, but I want to think about it for a while. Also, I want Brigadier McAlpine to have a look at you."

I believe him, partly because I want to believe him, but also because I know from watching him work that he knows his job, and from looking into his eyes that he means only good to his fellow man.

For the next week, I keep being told by MOs who drop by, nurses, orderlies, and some of the patients, that a brigadier is coming to see me. Brigadier McAlpine, they say, is a famous Harley Street specialist, and in civilian life it would cost hundreds of pounds for him to even cock his eye at you.

The great day finally comes. It is late afternoon, and as the brigadier and his staff of about a dozen colonels, majors, and captains enter the ward, there is a hush. They are very resplendent in their uniforms, and some have red tabs on their lapels. The least imposing of the lot is the brigadier. He comes over to my bed and, shaking my hand, says, "An American, eh, veddy glad to see you."

He performs virtually the same hocus-pocus on my leg that Colonel Lister did. During the ceremony, all the brass hats pay strict attention to everything the brigadier does, except Colonel Lister, who smiles encouragement at me from a distance. After the examination, the staff assembles at the other end of the ward and holds a conference. Finally, the brigadier comes over to my bed.

"I understand," he says, "that you'd like to go to the Fifteenth Scottish General Hospital in Cairo because Major Kennedy is there. Your leg is not the result of anything upstairs, you know. Cheerio. I'll look in on you in Cairo."

That night I take a look at my chart. The final verdict is poliomyelitis—infantile paralysis. Crippled for life.

The next morning, I stop my MO as he is making his rounds and say, "Isn't it poliomyelitis?"

"What in the world," he says, "makes you talk such nonsense? Of course, you read your chart."

"Is it my mind, or something else?" I say. "I must know."

"It is not absolutely certain," he says. Anyway, if you want to ask anyone you'd better ask Brigadier McAlpine. You'll see him in Cairo."

5 PANIC IN CAIRO

FIFTEENTH SCOTTISH GENERAL HOSPITAL, CAIRO

This is the best hospital in the Middle East. Beautifully designed, big and modern, it forms a quadrangle open on one side to the Nile. My bed is on a balcony looking out over the river and a road running parallel to it. They're pulling stuff out of Syria and Palestine and shoving it up into Libya to try to stop Gerry. All day we watch the armored columns whizzing past the hospital. Many of the trucks are loaded with Aussie infantry. Bare to the waist and unshaven, they yell like cowboys as they pass by.

Early these mornings, after daybreak, an orderly comes around and fills our mugs with hot tea. Bless them for this. But waking up for these sick men is waking up to despair, and often to pain. Sometimes the chill of the morning wakes you up; sometimes it is a pleasant dream, which has become too real. The tea tides us over until they bring breakfast around.

The orderlies who bring us tea also bring us news of the battle. Security would be horrified if they knew how much news is carried over the grapevine telegraph among the plain soldiers. Most of the news comes from the drivers of the ambulances, who pull in with loads of wounded from the front. They eat at the same mess with the orderlies, and spill all they know. Each man has heard or seen something different, and, over the table, it is all fitted together. Later, when the orderlies come to work in the wards, they share the news with us. It's not good news. Knightsbridge has fallen, and nothing seems to stop Gerry. Everybody agrees that he can't possibly get past Hellfire Pass. But each morning the feeling of insecurity increases.

Major Kennedy, my British psychiatrist friend, comes to see me today. The Brigadier had told him about my leg. I know the problem in my leg is not "shell shock." But still, I think of Jimmy King, my unit's commanding officer, who seemed to come alive during danger, and of the men I'd seen break down from it.

"I guess, Flash," he says, "you've seen a thing or two since I saw you last."

"Sandy," I say, "you deal with people's minds. What is it doing to the minds or spirits or egos of men, especially those who can't take it, or who, like me, are knocked out of it? Isn't it a waste that so many of the men crack up and have to be sent back? Why hasn't modern psychiatry invented some measure of a man's ability to take front line duty?"

"Good officers," he says, "generally do this. They carry on periods of training in which they get their men seasoned. They pick out the ones for combat duty they feel will be able to take it. The rest they transfer out of their units. It all works out.

"I am troubled not so much about what it's doing to the men now, but what will happen after the war has ended. Some men develop a taste for blood and killing. They like the excitement and the noise and the danger. When the war is done they will not give it up, and because they can't find it in civilian life they will provide it for themselves. They will drink heavily, and there will be murders and shootings.

"War changes men's values. They are going to think table manners and etiquette are not so important. They are going to think less of

material possessions, and they will not fuss and worry over making deci-
sions. I'll tell you what I mean. You take an officer who has five minutes to make a getaway before the enemy has surrounded his position.
He's got kit worth about $500 to load into his staff car. He decides
damn quickly between saving his kit or saving his life. In general, you'll
find that men who've been to war will lead more abandoned lives."

Sandy's talk is even more interesting now than it was when I first
had met him. Before he came to Africa, he had dealt with bombed civilians, and now his experience has been much enlarged by dealing with
soldiers who have been subjected to bombing and shelling at the front
in the desert. He has insisted on being given a fancy office here at the
hospital in which to carry on his interviews. There are bookcases, pictures on the wall, a carpet on the floor, a desk and chairs, and a fine electric fan.

"When the boys come into my office," says Sandy, "it is important
they think I'm God. You see, after we get them a bit pulled together, I
have to tell them they're ready and able to go back to the front. I have
to explain about the war, and how they ought to feel about it. Generally,
I explain it a little more realistically by pointing out they've got to go
back, and it's more expedient to make the best of it. Well, I put my subject in a chair with the light from the window pouring into his eyes.
Then I have the fan blowing on him just enough to be disconcerting.
This places him at an immediate disadvantage when he sits down, and
throws him off guard. It generally works.

"In fact, it worked on a certain brigadier from whom I was trying to
get a better job. He said he'd discuss the job when he came around to
the hospital. I got him into my office, into the same chair as my patients,
and before he left the room, I had the job I wanted."

An orderly comes and tells Sandy he's wanted at his office. He tells
me he'll be around again, and that he's glad the trouble with my leg was
not a "bomb neurosis" as he didn't think I'd likely be a subject for one.

One friend, who comes to my bedside every night, has given me something that I doubt can ever be taken away from me. It is an unshakable belief in the dignity of man. In civilian life he was a South African farmer. He'd been operating an armored car in the desert for a year, when he got a week's leave to Cairo. The train he embarked on at Mersa was bombed, and then the ambulance that picked him up was also bombed. Shrapnel hit him in the back and head. He has been in bed so long, and been so sick, that his legs and arms and body are skeleton-like.

During the last two weeks, he's been getting out of bed, and, walking with two canes like a run-down jerky toy, comes and sits beside my bed. According to the MO, according to all the rules of medicine, it was impossible for this man to walk. It is sheer will power. He comes to entertain me and cheer me up, and he does. But I am ashamed when I realize that what's wrong with me is nothing compared to the way he's battered up. His conversation reveals his deep love and nostalgia for England, although he's never been there. His great-grandfather was a Welshman, who settled in Johannesburg. The family has all been farmers. My friend often jokes about the two things that worry him most.

"Imagine getting blown up on a leave train," he says. "Think how I'll feel when my grandchildren say, 'And what did you do in the war, Granddaddy?'"

Then, too, he'll sometimes say, "What a mess I am to turn up before my wife. I wonder if I have any right to go back to her this way."

But someone in our group is always quick to reply, "She'd be happy to see you any way you are, lad, as long as you're alive. She'll be glad to have you back, all right."

The farmer looks from face to face, with a deep, sad smile, and says, "Do you honestly think so?"

This evening, none of the rest of the group is around. My friend shows me a tiny, worn book of selected prayers and Bible readings. His wife gave it to him just before he sailed "up north" to fight in the Western Desert as a volunteer. He carried it in a pocket over his heart through all his campaigns. Just after he was bombed and sent to the field hospital, the orderlies took off his uniform to put pajamas on him. Although he was almost unconscious, he had just enough strength left to ask the orderly to give him the little book out of the upper left pocket of his shredded battledress. During the bumpy ride in the ambulance to the hospital in Cairo, and until he finally reached the operating table, he held the book in his fist.

"I kept thinking of my wife," he said. "It was just as if she were with me, and I was holding on to her hand. I honestly believe it was my holding on to that book that brought me through. I suppose it's silly, but I believe it."

We talk about our lives and our homes until the light dims. The evening chill bothers his legs. Just before he gets up to go back to bed, he looks out over the Nile from our balcony and says, "This is the time I like best on my South African farm. The work for the day is done. I sit on my porch with a whiskey soda. I can look out over the veldt and see my cattle grazing peacefully in the half-light. Perhaps I shall do that again someday when the war is over. Hope you sleep well tonight, lad. Good night."

After he has gone, I think about all the examples of the brotherhood of man I've seen from the mountains of the Lebanon in Syria, on ship convoys, in the desert, and in hospitals. All during the travels in this war I've listened to men pouring their hearts out to each other. Here, perhaps, lies the hope of the world of tomorrow. When the great leaders sit down at the peace table, it might be helpful if a few of them had spent some time as patients in military hospitals and had seen how men from all over the globe can treat each other.

THE MAD DESPATCH RIDER

In a special room, which opens on the balcony near my bed, is a lad who has been unconscious for three months. Until a week ago, he lay on his bed as if he were dead. Lately he has been groaning and howling like an animal.

Two nights ago, he gets out of bed and comes out on the balcony. His hair is long and golden, and his face looks like a skull. In his eyes is a wild, staring look. His body suggests the body of a slum child I once saw, who was hopelessly stricken with rickets. I remember Kasper Hauser, the Bavarian prince, who was confined in a castle dungeon all his life.

"My father," he says, "will give me all the money I want. But that bitch, Joan, she keeps coming around here with that bloody wog. Get out of here, Joan, and let my father come here, because I have a job to do. Let me go. I have a job to do. Those bloody wogs ought to get out of the way so I can see . . . Ah, but that is the finest sight you'll ever see when you drive around the bend in the road, and there's Huddersfield . . . no town in England like Huddersfield, but now it's full of wogs. I've got a job to do and . . ."

The orderly gently leads him back into his room. I have a name for this patient—the mad despatch rider. Three months ago he was serving in the desert, and one night, during a movement, was given a "signal"— a message to deliver to a tank corps commander. Streaking across the desert on his motorbike, he crashed into a reconnaissance car. He was flung from his motorbike and lay in the desert darkness all night. In the morning, he was picked up and carried back of the lines to the base hospital. Apparently, as he regained consciousness, he still had the anxiety of getting the signal through to the tank commander.

There is nothing the doctors can do, no operations or treatment. They say if he stays alive he may get all right. As it is with so many of the difficult cases, you just let nature go to work patching up man's destruction of man.

They've had to do everything for the despatch rider: feed him arti-ficially or by spoon, wash him, and diaper him. The nurses and orderlies have turned over most of the duties of looking after him to a walking patient. Since I've been here, the walking patient on the job is a clumsy, tough cockney, who looks like a saloon bouncer. Often, when he's around talking in our group, he will suddenly say, "Excuse me, I've got to go look after my kid."

Morning and afternoon the despatch rider receives two callers: a blind Sepoy of the Seventh Rajputana Rifles from India, and a Fighting French soldier, who is blind in only one eye. The cockney is pleased to have them call on his kid. Listening to this little social gathering makes me want to pinch myself to be sure I'm not in some strange, never-never world of my cloudy imagination. None of them speaks the others' lan-guages, which are English, French, and Hindustani, and of course, the gibberish of the despatch rider. But they seem to have very pleasant lit-tle gatherings.

This morning, the walking patient brings his charge out on the bal-cony and puts him in a chair. The despatch rider has the manner of reigning prince with his flunkey, and orders the walking patient around with sweeping gestures of his skinny arms. Just then, the MO and the matron in charge of the wing walk up. The despatch rider looks coolly at them, as if they were the swine of the earth.

Flicking his hand in the direction of the MO, he says, "You bloody bounder—you want to let a wog cut my hair! No wog will cut my hair, and neither will you. You are common, you know. I wouldn't let you touch me if you were the last doctor on earth. My father will come and get me, and give me all the money I want, and take care of me. He'll make me well. Then I've got a job to do. Did you know? I've got a job to do, and I'm going to do it."

The MO grins, but it's rather forced. He shuffles his feet, and looks at the floor, and twirls his stethoscope around his arm. The other patients are taking in every word, and watching the MO to see how he takes it. He's not a very popular MO, and the words of the mad despatch rider are, for some, unspoken words in their own minds.

But the despatch rider is not through. He turns to the matron, and pointing at her, begins to howl with laughter, "You bloody battleaxe . . . you fat old bitch . . . why don't you bring my Joan to me so I can take her into my bed? I don't suppose you know anything about that sort of thing. But it's bloody fun."

The MO coughs, and says to the matron, "He's really getting much better. In this stage of the case, one can accept most any sort of thing." They push on with forced casualness.

Our mad despatch rider is now the hero of the ward. He does not stop talking. His mind wanders back and forth between Egypt, England, and the Western Desert. Time is jumbled up. People who should be in England are in Egypt, people who should be in the desert are in England. The war is won and lost, and lost and won. Joan is the most beautiful girl in the world and then the worst bitch. But Huddersfield is the most beautiful place in the world, and father will take care of everything.

At intervals, however, he pauses and looks very serious. "I have a job to do, you know." A look of urgency comes into his eyes. This moment of seeming lucidity seems to be recurring more often. A nurse comes by and says he must go back to bed, and that he must not get too elated by talking to us.

Tonight, a young Lieutenant drops in to see the despatch rider. When he comes out of the room, I speak to him, and he walks over to my bed. He is the OC of the boy's unit.

"Rather odd, you know," he says, "but if he had delivered that signal an entire unit would have been cut off. We didn't know that Gerry . . . but it's rather complicated explaining the details. Bloody curious, really. Nice boy. Hope he gets well soon."

LEAVING CAIRO

For two weeks now, ambulance convoys have been coming up just below my balcony all during the night and all during the day to drop their loads, the blokes who didn't get away in time when a shell set their vehicle or tank on fire. Sometimes you see a driver jump out of his ambulance which is far back in the line waiting at the hospital receiving entrance, and run into the hospital. He returns with an MO. They open up the back door of the ambulance, and the MO has a look. But generally you see them shake their heads. It's too late. A hundred and fifty man miles of ambulance space wasted.

These drivers bring news. But it's all bad news. On June 21 we learn that Tobruk has fallen. Surely, the grapevine telegraph has gone haywire this time. The next day, Rome radio says, according to Cairo newspapers, that Tobruk has fallen. Then, the next day, the War Office admits that Tobruk has fallen. We are sick at heart. Tobruk would never fall. Surely the siege was not in vain. Yes, the men who died to hold that forlorn desert spent their lives for nothing.

Then, as the days go by, the names of the places Gerry is taking get closer and closer: Devil's Cauldron, Knightsbridge, Acroma, Sidi Rezegh, El Duda, Gambut, Bardia, Fort Capuzzo, Salum, Hellfire Pass, Buqbug, and Sidi Barrani. What's the use? The Gazala Line is smashed to hell, but Bir Hakeim, one of the strong points, seems to be sticking it.

Most of the patients brought down from the front and into our ward are dazed and bewildered. Tonight, a supply truck driver walks into the ward. He drops his kit bags beside his bed and starts to take off his shoes, as if he were in a dream. He looks all right otherwise. I ask him what's the matter.

"This is the third campaign I've been through," he says. "I've been in the Army seven years. I always thought I could stick anything. But last week I began to get faintin' spells when the stuff started droppin' around me. I just went blank, nearly run the truck off the road. I don't understand. Neither do the MOs."

"The retreat is coming off all right," he says. "The coast road is jammed with vehicles, but fortunately we have air superiority. The boys are all 'browned off,' however. What in hell is the matter with the blokes runnin' this war? All we ever do is wait and retreat."

"Don't worry, soldier," I think. "Forget all about it. Everything will come out all right. Go to bed and sleep. Let others take care of you now. You are safe here—for a while."

But we're not so safe as the days tick by. The Mersa line does not stop Gerry and he is at El Alamein. Some of his stuff is fifty miles from Alexandria. Some say he can drive a division into Cairo within twenty-five hours. Orderlies who work until after dinner are irritated because an MEF order has just been issued that troops must be off the streets of Cairo by eight o'clock. My night orderly tells me he was standing around a corner near the Continental Hotel the other night and some "wogs" sneered at the soldiers. One of them said, "The British are no good. They can't stop the Germans." There was a free-for-all. A Tommy was stabbed and killed. The accumulations of incidents like this have resulted in the order.

We are told that if the Germans enter Cairo, we are not to worry. Everything will remain the same—there will be the same orderlies and some of the same MOs. The only difference will be that the OC hospital will be German.

The American Embassy is burning documents. The GHQ of the Middle East Forces is also burning documents and already making preparations to move up into Palestine. It is reported in the papers that Egyptian troops will join the British at El Alamein in the defense of the Nile Valley. The next day the Prime Minister, Mahmoud an-Nukrashi Pasha, denies it. All the soldiers say Generals Ritchie and Auchinleck will get a bowler hat for this or, in American, get fired.

Some of the war correspondents are clearing out by plane. A boatload of women and children has already been evacuated. An order has been issued that all sick personnel who will not recover in five weeks are to be evacuated to South Africa. All my news comes from orderlies, the walking patients, and my visitors. Some of it comes officially from newspapers.

Capt. John Ogden of New York City, attached to the AFS GHQ here in Cairo, turns up and gives me news of my unit. They got out of Tobruk just before the coast road was cut off. They stayed a while at Mersa, camping on the beach. At the moment, they are at El Alamein. My friend, Mort Belshaw, was captured by the Gerries. He had a brand new Leica on him. Captain Ogden takes my undeveloped films to get them processed and cleared by the censors.

A U.S. Army intelligence officer attached to the Fourth North African Military Mission, a major who lives in Baltimore, arrives at my bedside and says the British Defense Security Officer wants to look over my photographs. He says he doesn't know what the score is, but he's got to play ball. All I can tell him is to find Captain Ogden. I am very upset because this looks as though my photographs will become hopelessly embroiled in army red tape.

This afternoon, Ann Matthews turns up. I had told an RAF patient I'd like to see her, and he managed to get word to her at the RAF GHQ that I was here. When she arrives, I am wrestling in my bed with a wash-cloth and a piece of soap, trying to take a sponge bath. There is a kind of screen around my bed that is supposed to hide me. I yell to Ann that I won't be a minute. In my haste I spill some of the dirty water out of the basin onto the bed. Then a gust of wind blows the screen over, revealing me sitting up in bed, washing my armpits, and my leg, which has been set in plaster, propped up at the foot of the bed. Finally, I'm ready to receive her.

She sits in a chair beside my bed. She hasn't got on her uniform. It is her day off from the RAF.

"I knew you'd be comin' back," she says. "But I'm sorry you had to come back like this."

There is a long silence. Neither of us thinks of anything to say. There are so many things I want to say to her. I look around nervously. The guys in the beds around me are not missing a thing.

"I brought you some candy," she says, handing me a box of Turkish paste. "I love Turkish paste. And here are some magazines. There are some American magazines, too. I tried to get what I thought you'd like."

She is looking at me with pity. From what she has probably heard about the war in the desert, she must think there is some kind of screaming cauldron out there. To myself, I think, "You can only think of war in terms of fire and noise and smoke, and some vague kind of hell. But it's not that. It is a lot of things all added together, day in and day out. It's boredom, and terror, but terror is only part of it. It's living in the ground like animals. It's being dirty and eating out of a filthy mess tin a dog wouldn't eat out of. I think, Ann, it is mostly that war is the greatest insult in the world to the dignity of man. But I can see you don't understand, I wouldn't even try, because you are far, far away, and we have lost each other."

I can explain none of this to her. She chatters on, "I should love to see America after the war. It must be simply a fantastic country. I suppose it's because I've seen so many Hollywood movies."

Mac, an Edinburgh barber whose arms are crippled with rheumatism from lying in slit trenches while working as a Sapper in the desert, is standing beside us, grinning.

"Going down to the canteen, Flash," he says. "Would you like anything?" I could kill him for this, but after all he just wants to talk to a pretty girl.

"Ann, this is Mac," I say. And to myself, I think, "You wouldn't be seen dead with him in Shepheard's Hotel, Ann, but he's just like all of us—a poor, dumb, bewildered victim of something he didn't have anything to do with. One of these days he and I are going to find out who causes these wars. You'd better watch out then, because he'll probably make mince-meat out of those fancy officers you've been drinking with out at Gezira."

"Cairo is simply filled with Americans," Ann is saying. "The other night I met an Air Corps captain from—how do you say it? Alabahma."

Below my balcony, I see the walking patients who got leave to visit for the afternoon checking in at the entrance. Some are minus a leg, some an arm. A lot have their arms in slings, or have bandages on their heads. And there is the usual blind man being led by a partially blind man. They are happy because they've had a nice afternoon at the Egyptian equivalent of an English pub. Can you look at them, Ann, without an overwhelming feeling of responsibility? We are the intel-ligent and the strong. We'll do all right. We're in. But . . . don't you think . . . ?

"Isn't there something I can bring you?" she is saying. "It's so diffi-cult to know what you men need. I suppose the Red Cross takes care of everything. I'd better be runnin' on. I work from eight until midnight tonight. I do wish I could tell you some of the things that are going on that I've found out from decoding RAF signals. It's terribly exciting. I'll try and get up to see you in a day or two."

After she has gone, Chico, who works in the operating room and who got to be a friend of mine on the convoy out, comes to tip me off to something.

"The day after tomorrow they're going to ship a couple hundred patients out of the hospital down to Suez. A hospital ship is waiting there and it's bound for Durban." My name is on the list of those to be sent.

"You ought to be bloody glad to get out of the Middle East," he says. "They'll treat you fine in Durban. Very democratic it is. The girls are wonderful, I hear. They can't do enough for you. Be sure to have your stuff sent on from Shepheard's. I'll attend to everything."

For me the war is over. I feel a sharp nostalgia at the thought of leaving the Middle East. There is so much I can still learn from this strange, bewilderingly magical part of the world.

But I am glad, really, for I will be going home.

6 WAR'S REVERSE SUPPLY LINES

CAIRO TO SUEZ BY HOSPITAL TRAIN

A British fighter plane swoops down over our hospital, its engines roaring like staccato thunder. It comes so close to us we think it's going to plunge into the Nile. The patients groan.

"That sort of thing," says trim Mrs. Scott, an English nurse's aide, "is known as reassuring the civilian populace, at least that's what my officer friends tell me."

Here in Cairo, with the threat of German occupation at our doorstep, the despair is weary and deep-rooted. It is apprehension at the possible collapse of a world we believed in. The danger is not only across the Nile out in the desert but, as the soldiers say, the "wogs" are ready to turn on us at the slightest opportunity. They say it's in the look in their eyes and their muttered insults as they pass in the streets. We have lost face with them and for a very simple reason: we are not the victors in battle. We are no good because we are losing. Those of us who are chained to our beds by illness can't even cling to the faint hope of fighting, or fleeing to safety. Our despair is resignation.

All day long people come and go in the ward. Many of the orderlies were my friends on the convoy out and on the boat to Suez. They come around to tip me off about official papers and lists on which they've seen my name. I'm definitely leaving tonight or early in the morning. It's supposed to be a great secret, but everybody tells me about it except the officers. They behave as if nobody knew what was up but them.

The U.S. Army Air Corps major brings me my films from the Defense Security Officer. Captain Ogden comes to say good-bye on behalf of the Field Service. A lady from the American Embassy, a friend of Ray Hare's, comes around to see if there is anything she can do.

Many of the "base-wallahs" from MEF GHQ are already packing to leave for Palestine. They are the "gabardine swine," a name that arises from the Biblical allusion and also from their resplendent gabardine uniforms. Things will remain just about the same for them in Jerusalem because they'll move into the King David Hotel.

General Auchinleck has ordered European civilians out of the city and five thousand women and children have been evacuated by boat.

At three in the morning, I am awakened by Jim. He is the best orderly, as far as I am concerned, in the entire British Army Medical Corps. He gives me some heroin powders for pain and takes my arm. "You'll be leaving in a half hour, lad. Have you everything ready?"

He helps me put my toilet articles in my kit bag. Then he brings me a cup of hot tea. It is damp, cold, and dark. Below my balcony the ambulances are already being loaded with patients. Finally the stretcher-bearers come for me. They are gentle in their handling. Down in the lobby of the hotel the stretchers with the men lying on them make a mosaic of rectangles on the floor. Jim comes along.

"All the best, Yank. You ought to be glad to be leaving the bloody war. I'm coming to the States after the war and I'll look you up. Take care."

The driver of the ambulance, which takes me to the station, is a South African ATS girl with red hair and red freckles. She insists on lifting the stretchers herself. She jokes with the patients, asks if everything is all right, and do we want anything. She asks us if, by chance, any of us saw her brother at Tobruk. He's probably a prisoner of war by now, but she wishes she could find someone who ran into him before Tobruk fell. She gives us cigarettes, casually touches each man's face or his hand. We had felt dirty, unattractive, and like pieces of cargo. In five minutes this girl has made us feel like men and heroes. We are in love with her before we reach the station.

As we are carried through the big Cairo railroad station and down the platform to the waiting hospital train, I get, for a moment, the familiar feeling of the surge of any big metropolitan city. But Arabs wearing the tarboosh and their nightgown-like robes remind me it is still the East. As I am carried down the line of the waiting platform, I see an orderly standing outside one of the cars calling out, "Any officers there? This car for officers. Bring officers this way, please."

Trains are beautiful and exciting things. I know there is another younger generation than mine that seeks the skies and wanders the clouds in airplanes. Its dreams take place in the ether waves among the radio beams that guide planes at night. My love is the great express trains that web America, that glide up and down the Hudson and slip across the Mississippi and skim over the Nevada desert. She rides the gleaming rails and cinder beds that cut swathes through America's forests and skirt her mountains.

Trains have always made me aware of time and have cut the events of my life into neat chapters. As I take this ride from Cairo to Suez, I know my life is being cut in half this time. Before this ride and after it, I die and am born again. Suspended in time and space, I pass—on a stretcher—from one world to another. Time stops to give me the lesson of what lies in war's outhouse. It is going backstage with war and finding out that glory and honor, those glamorous leading ladies, are second-rate whores. It is learning that in war the little guy's life and health come very cheap.

Our train does not go direct to Suez. It goes to Alexandria first. There it picks up the excretion of the hospitals and then along the Suez Canal at all the RAF Stations. Through the window I can see them being brought aboard. And then to El Tahag to take what Number Six General has to offer. Above my bunk they've put a man who can't control his bowels or anything else. Orderlies come occasionally and wipe up the mess.

Rat-tat-tat-tat-tat. The train is again crossing a series of tracks running at right angles to our tracks. The steel wheels click sharply like the staccato of a machine gun. The men curse and growl. For many of us these sounds produce pains, real pains. The association of ideas is still too strong in our minds. Will they never stop going back and forth over these crossings? When will we get to the hospital ship?

The orderlies are so rushed they can't answer all the calls for "the bottle." Some of the men can't hold their urine any longer and let go in the blankets. The windows of the train are kept tightly closed because a *khamsin* is blowing up. The stench of festering wounds and the smells of men's bodies fill the car. The MO saunters through and I talk him into a couple of codeine pills. All morning, all afternoon, and into the night, we pick up the useless, the sick, and the wounded from all over Egypt. I think over a lecture by a young captain on the subject of the Royal Army Medical Corps: "Our purpose is not to save a life but to restore men to the fighting front. This must be kept in mind throughout these lectures. War is conducted for one purpose: to win. Humanitarian considerations are secondary."

We are the failures, the discards. We are a military liability. We've been seventeen hours on the hospital train.

It is ten-thirty at night when our train arrives at Suez. Ambulances take us to hospital barracks much like those at El Tahag. We are handed basins of water to wash with, then fed, and given little glasses of liquid narcotics.

There is news here. The orderlies tip us off that the *Queen Elizabeth* has just landed with a couple of fresh divisions from England. American tanks and guns have also just come in. There's a good chance of holding Gerry off.

A little joke is going the rounds of our ward. It seems some Tommies were standing on the dock when a transport loaded with American soldiers waving from the decks pulled up at the Suez pier yesterday.

"Come on, Yanks," one of the Tommies yelled. "We'll teach you how to retreat."

As I fall asleep I hear a U.S. Army bugle call taps. Gladness warms me inside. Nothing can ever happen to my country and I'll be taken care of.

HOSPITAL SHIP LEAVING SUEZ

Orderlies wake us before light. This is the day our ship sails. Ambulances carry us to the docks where we see the harbor. It is filled with ships flying the flags of many nations. The air is damp and salty. We smell the familiar odor of a ship's food supplies, meats, vegetables, bananas, oranges, and eggs. They are being hoisted aboard our ship, which is the *Londonhovery Castle*. It is the same hospital ship I photographed at Tobruk taking away wounded just before the town fell. A big newly painted red cross is on her side.

Our stretchers are carried to a table at which two officers sit. They give each patient a little colored wooden stick with a number on it. You hold it up with your fingers and the orderlies direct your stretcher-bearers to the proper place for you in the ship. All these weeks, all the way from Tobruk, I have been on my back. It's a new angle from which to see the world. Never in my life have I seen so much of the sky. I've certainly never seen the rigging of the ship against the sky, nor the ceilings of the promenade desk, nor the ship's corridors, nor the way our steel bunks are fastened to the joists supporting the deck above my ward.

My ward is just above the water line. The bunk ahead of me is a bad spine case. A shell fragment ripped away the lower vertebrae. To my right is a bomb neurosis case. He keeps getting out of bed and walking like a monkey. He says they're looking for him. They want to shoot him for spilling a glass of water. In civilian life he was a carpenter from Johannesburg. He takes off his army sneakers, puts them back on, then takes them off, over and over again. Then he takes off his pants, folds them neatly, unfolds them and then puts them back on, and then starts the process all over again. I watch him do these things, completely fascinated. When the ship engines begin to throb and she starts to move out of the harbor, he falls asleep like an exhausted child.

OFF PORT SUDAN

We have left the Gulf of Suez and are halfway down the Red Sea. It is steaming hot and getting hotter. Soon we will be at Aden, which is the hottest place in the world.

This morning one of the men in my ward dies. His heart just stopped ticking. They have pulled the sheet up over his head but haven't taken him out yet. He was an old soldier; been in Egypt for fifteen years. His wife and two children are in Syria. Some kind of army red tape ordered him back to England because of his weak heart. There is no conversation in the ward. When two orderlies finally come with a stretcher, they put a Union Jack over the old soldier's body and carry him out. His body is laid on a plank with one end on the railing. It is sewed up in canvas, and discarded fire irons are placed at the foot of the bag. Two soldiers, an officer, and a member of the ship's crew stand at attention.

The Padre reads the burial service for Catholic soldiers. "We humbly beseech Thee . . . that Thou deliver him not into the hands of the enemy, nor forget him forever. . . . Let our hearts be deeply moved at this sight of death; and while we consign the body of the deceased to the deep, let us be mindful of our own frailty and mortality, that we may experience a merciful judgment and everlasting life, through Christ our Lord. Amen."

The Padre looks at the member of the ship's crew. The crewman raises his hand to someone on the bridge. The engines are stilled for one minute. The soldiers tilt the board up over their heads. The canvas sack slides out from under the Union Jack and crashes into the sea.

The patients down in my ward listen to the stilled engines. A friend of the old soldier walks into the ward. He tells me he watched the whole thing from the upper deck even though he wasn't supposed to. "Impressive," he says. "Why, those sons of bitches don't even know how to bury a bloke at sea. The poor old bastard took two somersaults before he hit the water. A bloody outrage I call it. And him in the British Army all these years."

ADEN

It is so hot that the nurses and orderlies fight their way through the heat in the ward. The patients lie in their bunks entirely stripped except for a pajama leg thrown across their loins. This morning the matron makes the rounds with Sister Heyward and tells us we must keep our pajamas on. "It doesn't look well, really," she says.

After the inspection is over, Sister Heyward returns to the ward and tells us we can keep our pajamas off but we must put them on during the matron's inspection.

"Absolute nonsense," Sister Heyward says. "Some people think this hospital ship is being run for the doctors and nurses. I happen to think it's being run for the men."

"You know, Yank," she says as she stands at my bedside, "I don't like this war. I liked the last war. That was a friendly war. I worked in hospitals all over France. Everybody was friendly and we had good times. But in this war they just don't seem to have the spirit they had in the last war. In this war everyone seems to want to look out for himself. I just don't know what the world's coming to."

Sister Heyward was a young nurse in the last war. She might have been good looking. Now, in this war, she is old and horse-faced. The men have an easy friendliness with her in which there is no trace of sex. They look at her as they would look at their mothers or their mothers' friends.

The young nurses in this war are having flirtations with the officers or getting married to officers. Sister Heyward didn't get a husband in the last war. She has never married and from her gruff, spinsterish manner, you know she has accepted the idea she never will.

Unlike many of the other older nurses, she has turned whatever bitterness or frustration she might have felt into a violent championing of the patients. She clashes continually with the doctors and nurses. She is so completely sincere and outspoken and generally so very right that she has her way. Even the matron, a severe disciplinarian, is afraid of her.

Until this morning I loathed the matron. She noses around the ward on her inspections, stands at the foot of the bed, and smiling sweetly says, "And good evening. Feeling very well . . . that's good."

It is an inflexible custom that you smile and say, "Good evening, matron. I feel very well, thank you."

Several nights ago, I was feeling terrible and also irritable. When the matron came around and smiled and said, "Feeling very well?" some devil in me makes me say, "I feel terrible. I never felt worse in my life." The look of amazement on her face might lead you to believe someone had just slapped her derriere. She hurried on to the next bed.

"She hasn't been so shocked," one of the participants nearby says, "since the Prince of Wales ran off with that American girl."

This morning, however, something occurs that clearly indicates the matron knows her business. She is making her rounds rather casually. Elsewhere in the ward an MO and a nurse are dressing a wound. The matron passes a man who is sound asleep. She is about to pass his bed when she pauses, turns around, and touches her fingers to his forehead. Instantly, she calls the orderly, the nurse and the MO to the bed. The nurse and the MO begin rubbing the man's arm. The matron takes his temperature. It is 108°. The orderly brings a wet sheet and a bucket of ice. The patient is as close to death as is possible. The four of them work on him for an hour and before our eyes they bring him back to life. His wounds had weakened him and the last of his life was ebbing away from heat exhaustion.

I ask the matron, as she passes my bed, how she knew he was so close to death. "I don't know," she says. "I just didn't like the look of him." Nobody else in the ward had noticed anything.

The stink of the wounds festering inside all the plaster casts is getting worse and worse. One tank corps gunner comes around and sits on my bed two or three times a day. He is full of fascinating information, but I can hardly breathe for the smell. His shoulder and arm and side are all in a cast. He says the trick of letting wounds fester inside a plaster cast for several weeks is something new in this war. You just clean up a wound, put bandages over it, and then close up the whole thing with a plaster cast. "Then the wound rots inside the cast and all the badness is allowed to come out," the tank gunner says.

A pal of his from the same medical ward is often with him. He's got gnats inside his cast because the bone is infected and the gnats eat all the infection off the bone. I put my ear down near the cast and I can hear them. He says it itches quite a lot but he's gotten used to it and considers the gnats his friends.

OFF THE SEVEN BROTHERS ISLANDS

Today the MO decides it would be good for my leg to get into a tub of hot water every morning. I have watched the orderly carry some of the other patients into the bathroom in his arms. But he shall not carry me. The idea of another man taking me in his arms as if I were a baby is revolting. I tell the orderly to get me some crutches and I will somehow get to the bathroom on my own. I have been on my back all the way from Tobruk to Cairo to Suez to here. I was carried aboard this ship on a stretcher, placed in my bunk, and have not stirred from it for two weeks. I resent it bitterly.

Why did I have to get crippled at this time in my life? Things were just beginning to look good. I was acquiring a nice skill—photography. I was getting to where I could walk into an editor's office and say, "Here are my pictures. It's a good story and you can take it or leave it. It's good." I got my best pictures because I could move around fast on my feet, climb up any hill, and crawl along the ground. I suppose I can maybe still do studio work, take pictures of fashion models flaunting their wax limbs under artificial light, or take portraits of people who are only interested in a flattering likeness. What a way to end.

They can't do this to me. My body has always been a good machine incapable of being touched by anything. It is inconceivable for me to be a cripple, to be pushed around, to be pitied, to be helped.

The orderly tells me the bath is ready and someone else is waiting for me to get through. I throw back the sheet, take off my pajamas, and put my legs over the side of the bed. For a moment I am dizzy. I look carefully at my leg. It has shriveled into a horrible little toothpick. It reminds me of the way the Kaiser's arm dangled from his shoulder. My ankle cannot hold up my foot. My shin and ankle make a straight line. I loathe the sight of my leg.

Charlie Walter, whose arm was shot off at Hellfire Pass, stops by my bed. He has been to the canteen and is carrying three bottles of lemon pop, two chocolate bars, and a tin of cigarettes with his one good arm. A chocolate bar and a bottle of pop are presents for me. I marvel at the way he manages with his left hand. "I beat the game," he tells me. "I was already left handed when I got my right arm shot off."

Charlie gets around on the ship a great deal. By watching the section of the deck where they hold the sea burials, Charlie keeps track of the patients who die of the heat as we make our way through the

Red Sea and the Gulf of Aden. He also knows that the nursing sister with the frizzy red hair in the next ward meets an officer patient every night on the promenade deck and necks with him. The OC of the ship, according to Charlie, makes jam down in the galley and sells it to the officers' mess. It's his hobby and he likes to turn a penny here and there.

Charlie is sure he will not be allowed to leave South Africa and go back to England before the war is over. He claims "the authorities" feel that soldiers minus arms or legs returning to England are bad for civilian morale. This is, I suspect, another piece of British Army folklore and there is no way of checking its truth. If it were true, it would probably be ordered verbally, and "unofficially" carried into practice.

Tonight Father McLean, the Scotch Catholic priest, comes down for one of his talks with me. He is not very sympathetic to my mental struggles with faith and my distress at trying to reconcile the war with the church. The war just is, according to him, and there's nothing you can do but accept it.

"I've done my best to cooperate with Rome," he says. "I took three Italian padres to Turkey on an exchange ship. I kept them in cigarettes. I gave them candles for saying Mass. I bought them drinks. It all came out of me own pocket.

"When we got to Alexandria and took our British prisoners on board, we got no padres. I was so angry I nearly blew up. I knew of at least six British padres who'd been captured in the desert and were in prison camps in Italy.

"You can bet that when I returned to Egypt, I went immediately to see the Papal Nuncio at Alexandria. He represents the Pope, you know. As soon as I mentioned my complaint about receiving no English padres in exchange for the Italian padres, he said, 'Oh, my dear Father, this awful war. This stupid war. Eet is so difficult. The Holy Father is so distressed.' All that sort of thing.

"I looked him square in the eye. I pointed my finger under his nose and said, Look here, monsignor, I want none of that 'dear Father' nonsense. With all due respect to your high office, I am telling you that if I don't get me at least a half-dozen English padres and get them quick, there'll be trouble.

"I'm a good Catholic priest, to be sure, but I also wear the uniform of a captain in the British Army. I know what's fair. Good day, Sir."

Father McLean's face is flushed with anger from just telling me the story. He doesn't see anything funny, ironic, or sad about it. He's just mad. Also, from his conversation, I suspect he just doesn't like Italians.

For the first time in my life, I don't feel the need to take sides. Whether it's the war or my illness, I don't know, but these days I see everything in the world as if I were remote from it, as if I were looking down from a cloud.

THE MOZAMBIQUE CHANNEL

We crossed the Equator going south a few days ago. The occasion passed without remark. We are sailing south between the island of Madagascar and the colony of Mozambique. It is getting cooler but the hazard of heat has been replaced by the threat of German submarines. At night we are under intense blackout with all portholes tightly shut. Hospital ships may move freely and safely according to the Geneva Convention but our captain is taking no chances. Several Allied hospital ships have already been attacked this year. Here in the Mozambique Channel, reports of the sinking of Allied merchant ships come into our radio room every day.

The radio operator pays me a visit every night and relates these interesting bits of information by way of entertaining me. Last night he told me a German raider is in the vicinity. An American merchant ship was torpedoed yesterday afternoon. Knowing about these things upsets me because I have been nursing my hunch that something else is going to happen to me before I get home safely.

Every day now we have lifeboat drills. A bell sounds and the orderlies pass around cork life preservers to the patients. If a patient is too
sick to put on his own life preserver, the orderly wraps it around his
shoulders. We sit up in bed until the all-clear signal is sounded. I can't
help but speculate, during this interval of a half hour, on the prospect of
removing five hundred patients from a sinking hospital ship and loading them into lifeboats. I also keep wondering if I could make my way
to a lifeboat by jumping on one leg.

One of the orderlies in the next ward was on a British hospital ship
that had an oil bomb dropped on it while carrying wounded from
Tobruk to Alexandria. He heard the explosion and then saw his entire
ward enveloped in smoke and flames. He ran through the smoke and
flames up a hatch and onto a deck. He jumped overboard and was picked
up by a lifeboat. Something seems to have happened to his mind because
he keeps quoting some lines from the Bible having to do with the Lord
leading a man through smoke and flames to salvation.

Most of the patients seem to show signs of improvement after we
leave the blazing heat of the Red Sea and the Gulf of Aden. More
patients seem able to get up on deck for an hour or two. The smell of the
wounded does not seem as pronounced as it was. Matthews, the bomb
neurosis case in the bunk next to mine, is beginning to have moments of
looking almost normal. He looks at you as if he were seeing you for the
first time. Today he speaks for the first time during our three weeks' voyage. Without any warning he turns to me, his face lit up by smiles and
in a loud, clear voice, says, "There's no reason why the English and South
Africans have to kill each other. They can live together in peace and love
each other."

He's been taking a photograph of his wife and kid out of his wallet.
He stares at it, puzzled. Then he puts it back into his wallet and puts
the wallet carefully in his pajama pocket. He has shown it to a few of us.
Both patients and orderlies have helped Matthews over this dark period

in his life by being friendly, natural, and gentle. We have said to each other many times that Matthews will be entirely well when he once again sees his wife.

An orderly in the "padded cell" ward has told me of two of his cases I would not be so hopeful about. One is lucid and moans. The other is violent. The lucid one was a truck driver in the desert. One day, when he was driving up to the front in a supply truck convoy, some Messerschmidts came out of the sky and bombed and strafed his convoy. None of the drivers had time to dive to the ground in safety. In the truck ahead of the lucid case was his best friend. He looked up when the planes had gone and his pal's truck was on fire. He ran to the truck and saw his friend being asphyxiated and burned inside the cab of the truck. He started for him but the flames kept him away. The paint started to peel on the truck and he knew that the spare tins of petrol would soon go off. He stood and watched, dazed.

Just then an officer drove up in his staff car. The lucid case ran up to him and began explaining that it was his pal, he had tried to save him, the flames had been too hot, he was his pal and so on and so on. Now in the padded cell, the lucid case moans and keeps explaining to the officer why he couldn't help his pal from being burned to death.

The violent case was an infantryman. He and fifty other of his comrades were ordered to take a certain position in the desert. They knew they couldn't take the position and the officer who had ordered them to take it knew they couldn't take it. But they went ahead anyway, because all along the front it was important that all the orders be carried out. It was the front as a whole and not just one group of fifty men that mattered. Most of the infantrymen were mowed down by machine gun fire.

Just before the last few reached the position, the violent case saw one of his comrades standing rigid and helpless because he had been hit. He uttered a low cry of "help." The cry echoed in the mind of the violent case. He remembered that once in London, at the end of the day's work, a group of people were waiting to cross a street. A bus rolled up and one of the men in the crowd was pushed in front of the oncoming bus. Just as the man was hit he uttered the same low cry of "help." The violent case took off into the desert when his mind coupled the two incidents. Apparently it has set up some uncontrollable frustration in him.

He is kept in a straightjacket most of the time and when he is turned loose in the cell, attacks the orderlies. "It is filthy," the padded cell ward orderly tells me, "looking after him. It isn't human. We can do nothing with him."

When I returned home, I recounted some of these case histories to Army psychiatrists. They pointed out that always there is some oblique, unexpected reason that seems to set a man off who has been under battle pressure. Some hold to the school of thought that no soldier cracks up just because of his being under fire. Always, they said, it is something in his past life, some emotional thing inside him that sends his mind off. These officers continually said, almost violently, "There is no such thing as shell shock." Then I myself came to believe that perhaps nature was merciful in these cases. Perhaps it was releasing soldiers from the bondage of too great a strain on their minds and sensitivities.

ARRIVAL AT DURBAN

The first time since I spent those few days at Cape Town eight months ago, I enjoy the comfort of being in a land I feel is not entirely alien to me.

This morning at dawn we drop anchor just outside the harbor at Durban. Toward noon we moor alongside the docks. A hospital train is waiting to take patients to Johannesburg. The orderly in charge of baggage tells me that all my kit and boxes of photographic supplies are still intact. He says I am down on the list as going to a hospital in Durban.

Early in the afternoon, the stretcher-bearers come for me and I am carried down a steep gangplank to a waiting ambulance. South African Red Cross ladies stand at the foot of the gangplank and pass out bars of chocolate to the patients as they are disembarked.

The ambulance takes four of us to Addington Hospital, which is only a few blocks away. We are checked into the military wing. It is a big state-owned hospital occupying several city blocks.

My first caller, after I am put into one of the wards, is an American sailor. His ship was torpedoed in the Mozambique Channel. His name is Jim Adams and he comes from Sioux City, Iowa. In civilian life he worked as a gasoline filling station operator. "Sure am glad to see an Americano," he says in his Western drawl. "Nothing but Limeys around here. They're nice fellas, these Limey sailors, but I get homesick for a real American.

"I was on duty about four in the morning. I had on the earphones that connected me with the observation lookout on the bridge. We were manning the six-inch guns aft. First I knew something was up when I heard the alert order over the phones. Then the battle-station alarm went off.

"There was a terrible explosion. As far as I can figger I was blown about fifteen feet in the air. I landed on my right knee on the next deck down. One of my buddies helped me to a lifeboat. There was a little wait before they dropped the lifeboat into the water. I kept thinking if my knee wasn't hurt so bad I could take a quick run down to my locker and get the ten five-dollar bills I had in the watch pocket of my best trousers. But that would have been takin' an awful chance with my knee so bad. I sure hate to think of those bills bein' nibbled away by fish."

Jim and I talk on through the afternoon. He tells me what it's like in America now that war has been declared. Both of us recite all the discomforts connected with our sicknesses.

"Why, that sure is terrible," Jim says when I have finished.

"Why, that sure is terrible," I say when Jim has finished.

ADDINGTON HOSPITAL, DURBAN

It is sometime past ten o'clock and our ward has been put to bed. We all wake up suddenly. There is a frightful roaring outside. The men in the ward groan as they awaken.

"God damn those planes," one says, "Why can't they do this some-where else, out of our hearing." Another man mumbles a string of curses.

"There's no end to it," a tank commander near my bed says. "They keep on and on."

A nurse comes into the ward and turns on the light. Wouldn't we like some Ovaltine? She returns with a pitcher of the steaming stuff and pours us each a cup.

"You silly boys," she says, "You know it's only practice. They say they're doing it to get accustomed to diving for the docks at night."

Almost objectively, I note that my distress at the noise of the dive-bombing takes the form of definite pains in my back. It is exactly at the lower third of my spine. It should be impossible, I reason, for noise to produce a pain in one's body. Yet it is there. Probably it is the association of ideas. I had pains at Tobruk when the Stukas came over and it was the real thing. Now I associate the noise with the old terror I knew before I was evacuated.

About my helplessness, however, I am not objective. I use crutches to get to the bath down the hall in the morning, but I still have to ask someone to help me into the tub. The trip down the hall and back exhausts me completely. I am beginning to grasp the full significance of what it means to be a cripple. In my dreams I often run; sometimes it's a track meet. I trip and fall. The fall awakens me. In other dreams I am waltzing around and around with a beautiful girl. We are waltzing so beautifully that the other couples have stopped dancing to watch us. Then I make an especially difficult turn and wake up in my hospital bed.

Three cubicles away from my bed is an Englishman named Evans who is without a leg. Eight months ago he was advancing his tank into battle and a German antitank gun made a direct hit. His tank burst into flames but Evans and his men were able to jump out just in time. Machine gun bullets greeted them. The bone and flesh of Evans's leg were badly tat-tered. It was not until much later, when he had been evacuated here, that the MO told him that unless they amputated, the leg would probably drain for about twenty years and still not be right. Evans signed a paper that it was OK to take it off.

We have often discussed being crippled. I admire his mature and philosophical attitude about facing it. You simply accept it, he says, and make the best of it. One night we are alone in the ward.

"I've been thinking about the glass of beer," he says, "we always used to have after a Saturday afternoon of playing cricket. Talking over the game was always the best part. I shall miss that glass of beer."

Wendy, one of the day nurses, has become a good friend of mine. She is engaged to an RAF flier up in the Western Desert. On her afternoons and evenings off, she likes to go out with some of the soldiers who are passing through Durban by boat or plane. Wendy likes to discuss the vagaries of the male race with me. Why, she says, do all the men you meet these days ask you to marry them? They were not so free and easy with their proposals during peacetime. She notices that the reaction of the men going to war is about the same as those coming out of it—they want to settle down and have children. Wendy has also discovered that certain gentlemen of the Allied armies are not above telling a girl they are single when in reality they have a wife and children at home. Some of her girlfriends were deceived in this manner, says Wendy.

Wendy's father was a rubber planter in Singapore. She and her mother were evacuated just before the city fell. Her father stayed on. She is particularly bitter about the fall of Singapore because of this incident, which happened just before she left.

One afternoon just before the fall, her father was looking over his plantation, which was just in back of the city. He saw a number of British Army staff officers inspecting one of the streams that flow through it. Her father asked them what was up. They replied that they were looking the terrain over to see if the Japs could land tanks from invasion barges onto it.

"And what is your conclusion, gentlemen?" he asked.

"It would be quite impossible," said the brass hat in command.

"You'll give me a tank and a barge and I'll show you how it's done," Wendy's father replied.

But the officers chose to ignore him. This was the way the Japs eventually took Singapore. One of the tragedies of the surrender, Wendy says, was that all the guns were turned over to the Japs intact.

Jim Adams comes around to see me this afternoon. He has found a U.S. Navy ship that's going to take him back to America. His kit is already aboard and he expects to sail tomorrow. Under his arm he has a package of Camels, which he thrusts at me. "I knew you was awful sick of these here English cigarettes so I got these off the PX on my new ship."

Jim has also brought along another present for me. She is a little blond girl about nineteen years old. Too shy to say much, she blushes whenever either of us looks at her.

"She likes Americans," says Jim. "I figure that now I'm going home, I'd leave her to you."

"That OK by you, Honey?" he adds, putting his arm around her and giving her a friendly hug. Her reply is a deep crimson blush.

The day after Jim sails, delegations of American soldiers come up to the ward to call on me. They have just arrived on a troop transport en route to North Africa. It seems Jim met them in various Durban bars and made each one swear they'd call on his sick friend in Addington Hospital. They are very interested in meeting me because, as they put it, I've "seen action." They sure want to see some action themselves.

"How is it?" one asks. "I sure envy you. I wanna get in it as soon as I can."

I feel very old and they seem like babies somehow. I think of myself not so long ago. I, too, wanted to get in it.

7 HOME FROM THE WARS

DEPARTURE FROM DURBAN

There is nothing for me to worry about. I don't have to think. My life is ticking away in a delightful routine of meals on trays, Red Cross ladies who bring us chocolates and books and magazines, pretty nurses, visitors, and gossipy walking patients. I won't ever have to face any kind of reality again because I am helpless, a cripple. I just won't get well. The years ahead will pass smoothly and effortlessly for me. The world can take care of me. I am a victim of the war.

This is a bad state to be in. I am getting to like this escape too much. As I go on thinking about how easy it would be to die in a hospital and yet go on living, a Red Cross lady comes by. There is a twinkle in her eye that lets me know it's all right to ask her what is the best bar in town.

"The Seaside," she says. "I'm driving by there in a little while in my car. Would you like me to drop you off?"

All I have to wear is a trench coat, my forage cap, and my slippers, although now, because of the brace on my leg, I only need one slipper. I put the trench coat on over my pajamas, take my crutches, and start off with the Red Cross lady. The farthest I've gone so far has been to the bathroom. This is my first venture into the outside world. I'm supposed to have a pass to leave the hospital, but we just walk out the main entrance as if it were the most usual thing in the world.

The Red Cross lady has to speak to another Red Cross lady and then go and get her car. I prop myself against a stone wall just outside and look at the world again from an upright position. Two Limey sailors are talking to a little blonde girl with pigtails. She is telling them that her father is nice and understands her but her mother is awful. She won't let her wear long dresses, makes her wear this big straw hat, and the silly school uniform. The sailors seem as young as the girl when I look again at their faces.

My Red Cross lady brings her car to the curb and drives me to the Seaside Hotel. She declines my offer to come in and have a drink. Her children are at home waiting for their supper.

Wendy, my favorite nurse, is in the bar. She has on a red print dress.

"Would you like to meet two of your countrymen?" she asks. They are an army captain from New Orleans and a purser in the Army Transport Service from the Bronx. I drink three bottles of ale and am gloriously happy.

"Did you know we were gonna take you home?" the captain says, grinning at me over his highball. "All you need to get well is to be back in the good old USA. We've got a big empty transport and we're gonna put you in the colonel's suite."

"That's a very nice thought," I say, "but from my experience with the British Army it's going to take about six months of red tape before I move again. They understand what to do with English personnel, or Australian personnel, or South African personnel. But I'm American personnel and they haven't gotten around to that one yet."

"Then we'll Shanghai you," says the purser.

During the next two days I speak to my MO and a couple of officers at the hospital about going home. They all say they'll see about it, but nothing happens. Nobody wants to take the initiative. On the third day, Wendy tells me that it was all fixed for me to come aboard. If I'll just get to the ship, they'll take me home. But I must arrange about it today because the ship is probably sailing in twenty-four hours.

Again, I get up and throw my trench coat on over my pajamas, put on my forage cap and, using my crutches, go down to the main floor and call on the OC of the hospital's military wing. He is a portly South African with a big black mustache. It is immediately apparent that he's had too much lunch and too many highballs. I explain that I have a ship to take me home and may I please be discharged from the hospital to the ship. He is so distressed at the problem I present that I feel sorry for him. After thumbing through a pile of army orders on his desk, he says, "Frightful, if you were anything but an American I'd know what to do with you. We have instructions about Australians, and Sikhs, and Imperials, and Canadians. But Americans don't exist for us. I suppose I could call Troop Movement Control or Base Depot."

As he picks up the phone, I hold my breath and keep my fingers crossed. If he gets Troop Movement Control on the phone, I know I won't get away. They have papers concerning me and there would be cabling to Cairo and a million other things before I could possibly get released. Troop Movement Control doesn't answer. Then he tries the Base Depot.

"He's an American and I really don't know what to do about him," I hear the OC say to Base Depot. "He has a ship, yes. . . . Well, he got down here to my office under his own steam."

There is another pause. Then the OC says, "And you'll sign the discharge. Right-o." He hangs up.

"You have a ship," he says with a great sigh of relief, "and we see no reason why you shouldn't get on it. Of course, we ought to check with Troop Movement Control but we'll let well enough alone."

Early the next morning an ambulance takes my array of luggage and me to the docks. The ship that is to take me home is gray, dirty looking, and not very big, but from her mast flutters the American flag. A U.S. Army military police soldier rushes down the gangplank. He has a big black automatic strapped to his belt and carries a heavy nightstick.

"May I help you, sir?" he says, picking up some of my kit.

I feel like crying.

WEST AROUND THE CAPE OF GOOD HOPE

The Louisiana lieutenant and the Bronx ship's purser are standing in the main passageway as I limp in from the afterdeck. They introduce me to the ship's OC, Capt. Fred Mayne, and to the ship's doctor, Bill Rogers. Mayne tells me I'll be in the Colonel's suite and that a civilian will be in there with me. Doctor Rogers says he hopes I've got my discharge from the hospital; otherwise he'll be in the soup. He sighs with relief when he thumbs through my papers and finds I've been legally discharged from the hospital. The ship is to sail early in the afternoon. The officers all seem worried and harassed. There is urgency, a get-it-done character about the way they go about their war duties.

Mayne interests me more than the others. From the moment I look into his deep-set, sad eyes I know we are going to be good friends. As I watch the dignity and quiet firmness with which he gives his orders, I feel a pride. I compare him to the British officers I remember. When Mayne gives an order he says silently, "You are a fellow human being, a fellow American, no better or no worse than me. But I happen to wear a captain's bars in the United States Army. We're both in a war trying to get it done and go home. Will you help me do this thing and do it as well as you can?"

Our ship is an empty troopship with a capacity of about two thousand soldiers. It was built for the Delta Line to be used in the Caribbean run. Most of the fine furnishings of the first and second classes have been ripped out and replaced with the steel tiers of bunks just like the *West Point*. My cabin is fore to the starboard just off the promenade deck and is reserved for the highest-ranking officer, generally a colonel, when troops are aboard. There are two comfortable beds with beauty-rest mattresses, no upper berths, and a bath with hot and cold running water.

My roommate for the trip is sitting on his bed sorting out some important-looking papers. His name is George Ross, and he's from Racine, Wisconsin. He has a baby face and a twinkle in his eye. His important-looking papers concern his job as assistant manager of the Shanghai branch of the National City Bank of New York. He tells me he managed to conceal them from the Japs after the fall of Shanghai. He also managed to conceal a few thousand dollars and, after hanging around the town a while after the fall, he bribed his way through Jap-occupied China. He reached Calcutta, wired his bank for more money, went by train to Bombay, and flew to Lourenço Marques. He says he ran into Frank Gervasi of *Collier's* there after he had just flown in from Cairo. Gervasi wanted to ghost a "How I Escaped from Jap Occupied China" kind of piece, but Ross felt that it would endanger the escape of others who might follow the same route.

Ross is cynically amused by the whole show in the East. He can't understand why anyone was surprised at the Japs making such strides with their conquest. The National City Bank cleared its money out of Shanghai in plenty of time. The Jap bank clerks scurried into the bank's building and their takeover was all very polite, business-like, and well planned. The Jap clerks were so damn polite, Ross says, it made you sick to your stomach. An air of respectability surrounded the whole business. But underneath, the Japs said in the quality of their smiles, "I guess you Americans and British know who's top dog in the East now."

Ross and I go down to have lunch in the First Class Dining Room now used by officers of the army, navy, and merchant marine. We are the only strangers in the room and I can see the men whispering to each other as to who we are. The food is wonderful: American coffee, steak, French fried potatoes, real butter, and ice cream. The steward, Moe

Levy, comes over to our table and tells us that we can have anything we want, just ask for it. He also tells me that if I don't feel so good just ask and he'll have my meals sent to my cabin. Nothing too good, he says, for any man that's "seen action." He used to have a half interest in a Brooklyn delicatessen.

After lunch, we go up on deck to take our last look at the receding shores of South Africa. We watch the gaiety of the crew relaxing from the duties of the departure. All at once I realize that I am thoroughly weakened. Ross takes me back to our cabin and helps me undress and removes the steel brace that I'm now wearing instead of the cast.

I sleep the rest of the afternoon. Dinner is brought up on a tray. Ross goes off to play bridge with the navy wireless officers. The ship is tossing and plunging and every few minutes it smacks a wave with an earsplitting crash, making the superstructure tremble and shudder. But every crash is that much nearer to home.

Major Mayne comes in to see me. He pulls up a chair and begins a story about a colonel who had this cabin on a certain trip and had an army nurse in with him most of the time. The boat makes a terrific lurch before he has finished the story and his chair keels sideways on two legs.

"This boat wouldn't be bobbing around the ocean like a cork if I'd been allowed to take aboard the cargo lined up at Durban. And it was stuff needed in America, for the war effort, too. I used to work for the Grace Line and it hurts me to see hulls going empty. I sent several wires to Washington trying to fix it up, but there was nothing in the regulations. It was only the merest chance that we were able to dig up a regulation concerning the repatriation of nationals in foreign ports and make it legal to carry you. But, then, the whole business of war is waste, so a little more or less waste here and there won't matter. But I still wish we'd been able to take on some kind of cargo as ballast. Easier on our stomachs."

I ask to borrow a book I noticed he had when I met him. It is Thomas Wolfe's *You Can't Go Home Again*. I am glad he likes Wolfe and I ask him why.

"Because Wolfe says more to me than any American writer," he replies, "more than any writer of any nationality for that matter. I brought along everything he ever wrote in my cabin. I like to read him and reread him. Funny thing about Wolfe, it's most fun when you meet someone who doesn't do much reading, some seaman or carpenter or fitter, who has just happened to get interested in one of his books. Then you talk about train whistles, and the strange quality of a lunchroom in a small southern town at three in the morning, and the screwy women you've met that were just like the ones Wolfe talks about. It's hopeless talking about Wolfe to an intellectual because they always want to argue with his form or style or self-discipline or some nonsense—forgetting the whole point that he does something to you inside. He articulates things you felt or sensed, but could never quite put your mitts on. Wolfe comes closer to getting at the truth of what America is than the whole kit and caboodle of professors and scribblers who are always shooting their faces off in the public prints."

Our talk drifts along. Just as I understand the shame and sadness he feels at the waste he has seen and been part of, so he understands my resentment at the hundreds of soldiers I have seen—inarticulate, frightened little guys. They had nothing before the war; they suffer during the war, and get nothing after the war. My talk is violent and chaotic. His is quiet and full of deep resentment.

"We carried Tommies from Iceland to England. While we were tied up in Scotland, they charged us $1,000 a day dock fees. I signed papers for supplies we took at outrageous prices. It hurt me to attach my name to things like that. It's somebody's money. They say it all comes out of Lend-Lease but sometimes it seemed, when I signed for things, that they were trying to make the whole debt up on what they charged us."

Gradually, we get around to doing what all men do in war when they have long hours together and know they have met a friend. We tell each other the story of our lives. We remember girls we had forgotten and moments with them and funny little ways they had. Much of Mayne's life has been dominated by dance music. He played the clarinet in the band at Dartmouth. It made life pleasant for him but he really wanted to study symphonic music. Then he fell in love with a girl he wanted to marry and landed a job with the Grace Line so as to make a living. Since he's been in the war, he's often wondered if he were not foolish to have given up his dream of playing in a symphony orchestra. If it had not been for his pride, he could have received help from his family and from hers. When the war is over, he is going to find some way of being a serious clarinet player, whether full or part time.

However, something much more serious than the clarinet troubles him. A year before the war his wife thought she was pregnant. He took her to a fine, expensive obstetrician and had her examined. The verdict of the doctor was that she was not pregnant. His wife, who was very slim and athletic, continued to ride horses. A month later she had a miscarriage. Since then she has not become pregnant again. Mayne says he finds himself continually asking army and navy doctors he meets if a miscarriage makes it impossible for a woman to have a baby again. They all say no. But there is the anxiety in Mayne's mind: a vision of him and his wife ending their days childless and unloved.

After Mayne leaves, I nod off to sleep. A loud crashing sound awakens me. Suddenly, I am back in the desert. Gerry's dropping his stuff again. No use worrying. If it gets you it gets you. I feel the pain in my back and hear the buzz of planes. Now the pain is in my leg. I realize I am not in the desert. Perhaps a torpedo has hit the ship. That wireless operator today kept telling us about those warning messages. A German sub, based off Morocco, is within a radius of eighteen miles. If we're hit, Ross could still help me to a lifeboat. And if I do drown, it doesn't matter much. It's better than being a cripple the rest of my life. No. It was just a wave smashing our cargoless ship. Ross is snoring. I take two codeine tablets and the pain in my leg recedes. I'm going home. I'm going home.

NORTH ACROSS THE EQUATOR

There are no ceremonies at our crossing of the equator. Our crew of seamen and gunners are now veteran world cruisers. Today from the lifeboat deck, I watch a bunch of them, officers and men, squirting each other with a heavy stream of salt water from the fire hose. One of them is supposed to be washing down the deck, but they've all put on bathing suits and are having a wonderful time playing leap frog and pushing each other around as the torrents of cold salt water spray them.

Captain Mayne invites me to his cabin for lunch. He comes from New Orleans and spent some years piloting ships on the Mississippi. We discuss a beautiful old stern-wheeler which I once photographed making a trip from Cincinnati to New Orleans. He impresses me as being nervous, jumpy, and troubled.

Later, Mayne tells me he is continually plagued by the idea that he is a coward. He thinks he's a coward because he is frightened that a submarine will hit the ship and he will die. Mayne says he is continually troubled by the fact that he cannot bring himself to believe in God. He tries hard, but his scientific mind continually throws out the idea as preposterous.

The happiest man aboard, with the least worries, is the little sixteen-year-old cabin boy who brings my meals to me on a tray. His name is Mike McCarthy and he has been repeatedly told of the tradition in his family that the McCarthys of County Limerick never die in war. Besides, his elder sister is a nun in the Ursuline convent in Buffalo. She prays for him every day and has a Holy Mass said for his safety every week. In each mail he receives holy pictures and copies of special prayers to the Holy Mother and the Saints. One of them, which he lets me read, has a foot-note at the bottom of the page: "This prayer has kept from death every soldier, in this war and the last, who repeated it faithfully once a week."

The least concerned man aboard is a sergeant of gunners who spends every minute of his spare waking hours reading detective stories and true romance pulp magazines.

There is little or no discussion of why the war is being fought, no discussion of the postwar world. The news that comes in on the radio is mentioned occasionally, but only in terms of whether we're winning or losing. Soon it will all be over. Occasionally there is an allusion to the "big shots" who run things, or the politicians who muck everything up. Some of the men seem to be growing more mature and philosophical as a result of their experiences in the war. All want to go home as soon as possible. Watching them and knowing them, you want more than ever for God to grant them this wish very soon.

OFF AMBROSE CHANNEL LIGHTSHIP

We have made it. My hunch that something else was yet to befall me was unfounded. It is getting light and we seem to be just coasting along. The waves rock us ever so gently. Ambrose Lightship passes us to the port side. Way out here the waters of the Hudson are mingling with the Atlantic in an undersea current. It is still gray and dark when we pass Sandy Hook. We stop in the Narrows and take on Immigration and Health officers from a cutter.

As we nose our way, with the help of two screeching tugs, alongside a pier on Staten Island, the sun bursts forth from behind the clouds. I have come home and everything looks just the same.

Mayne has arranged for an Army truck to take me, my kit, and all my photographic paraphernalia to Manhattan. When we say good-bye he shows me a letter that was waiting for him at the dock. His wife is six months pregnant. "Things look pretty good," he says, a big grin sweeping his face.

There was mail for everybody but Ross and myself. It brought news, some good and some bad. The cabin boy's sister has gotten married. The engineer's wife passed away. Births and deaths, but for the most part letters all carry the same wail: "When are you coming home? Hurry!"

I hurry to go take the Staten Island Ferry. It is not the same fun it used to be when I would take along a pretty girl for a ride during hot summer evenings—although I hear the same whir of wheels loosening the clanking chains as we are turned free of our moorings.

Standing on the prow, I see again the gleaming magic city. To the east in the Lower Bay are liners. I remember the days when, as a young reporter with a pass in my hatband, I sped down to the Bay in the Immigration and Health cutter and went aboard the great incoming liners to interview celebrities. I was fresh, eager, and a little arrogant.

That was a long time ago. I am a different person now. War has done something to me beyond laming me. I am not sure yet just what. I was bewildered because we were taught one thing in our youth and then asked to completely reverse ourselves when we grew to maturity. War and killing was a sin. Now war is a sign of your virility, and killing is justified if you're ordered to do it.

All this should throw me, but I don't think it has. It seems to me I have learned at least one thing from having gone to war. There are eternal values. There is some thread, some line of continuity other than time, running through our lives, the lives of those who went before us, and the lives of those who will come after us. And it's not war, even though the Middle East pointed out vividly to me how war makes a pattern and swings in rhythm down through the centuries.

I believe I learned that the battle lines are never clearly drawn, with the enemy on one side and us on the other. Now the enemy is everywhere. He is passing us on the street. He is around the corner. He is in our homes and families. He is in us. You don't always know him at once for what he is. He is selfishness and lack of consideration for the other fellow. He is money-lust and wanting to have more and better things than his fellows. He is ignorance and unkindness and anger. How strange we should have to go to war to find out these very obvious things.

Perhaps war jolted me from the routine of my self-centered life. Living with soldiers and having worldly possessions meant little or nothing. Sharing with them and having them share with me made me wonder about my old life. So much of what I had thought important was shown to be very unimportant and petty. Why should I pit my ego against another man's? We can all live and let live—if only we will.

Now the ferry is passing the Statue of Liberty, small and blurry in the morning mist. To the north is the shimmering Hudson River, flowing silently in the sunshine to the sea. How well I know her valley, through which so much of America's history has passed. Yes, and I now feel a new pride in being an American. Living in these other countries and knowing their peoples has given me a new faith in America. Her new conceptions of freedom and her deep-rooted respect for the dignity of man are part of the contribution she is ready to make. We Americans have an opportunity, a fine chance to fulfill this responsibility, to give these things in which we believe to the world.

But our giving must be done with great understanding, tact, and love. Idealism will not be enough. We will, for a certainty, have to return to the problems we had before this war. We will be faced with man's inhumanity to his fellow man as carried on in civilian life—man's tendencies to barbarism. Our young men will still have to unlearn the arts of killing and destruction, in which they have become skilled.

What, then, is the answer?

I believe the answer is in ourselves, in our own inner integrity and in our sense of values, ethics, morals, and religions. It lies in the simple truths that men of good will live by. The answer lies in the good that is in all of us.

We are approaching the ferry slip at the Battery. Water traffic is heavier than I have ever seen it here. Ship and tugboat whistles call out to each other as they always have. One tug is pulling a barge that is carrying a whole section of the steel hull of a ship. That's something new.

Our army truck rolls off the lip of the ferryboat and clatters the wooden planks of the old dock. As we hurry through the Battery, I am aware of the familiar smells of roasting coffee and fried fish. We drive too far up the fast Westside ramp and slow down to look at the big grey-painted ships hugging the docks. We see the hull of the once proud *Normandie* lying on her side in pathetic humility.*

The army driver helps me get my stuff out of the trunk and up the stairs into my old apartment on West Twelfth Street. Just as I am about to climb up the stoop of my brownstone, Joe Andretsky, who used to do my laundry, comes up the street. He stops and looks at me, puzzled.

"Been away, haven't you?" he says. "Where was you?"

"I've been to war," I say proudly.

"Yeah?" he says. "Which war? You mean you was in this one?"

---

* Considered the epitome of the luxury liners of the 1930s, the *Normandie* made its last Atlantic crossing at the outbreak of WWII and was ordered mothballed in New York Harbor. Just as she was to be converted to a troop ship, a fire broke out and her burned-out hull spent the rest of the war listing to port. Sabotage was suspected.

AFTERWORD

As my father was voyaging home, the tide of the North Africa campaign was turning. As he steamed into New York Harbor, Montgomery and the British Eighth Army were defeating Rommel at the Second Battle of El Alamein, ending Axis hopes of controlling access to Suez.

The West Twelfth Street basement apartment he returned to in October of 1942 would be his home for only the next four years, but they would be transformative. His war experience had ignited in him a passion for the cause of the "little guy" and a determination to make meaning out of the suffering he had seen. But first, he had to pay for the medical treatment he would need to regain his ability to walk. He was proud to deliver publicity photographs to Director Stephen Galatti at the AFS New York Headquarters to benefit its operations, but that was not work he could resell. He sold a few other photographs to *Look* and *Harper's Bazaar*, but the serious money came from a story on what he had learned about land mines, which he sold to *Esquire*. He wanted to call it "Practical Jokes for Death," but *Esquire* titled it "Soldiers Learn the Hard Way." He worked on his war book, honing its message of hope for a world without war, a world of democracies in which men could live as brothers, but patriotic fever was at a high pitch and no publisher wanted to buy it. Eventually, he completed the new treatments for his polio-stricken leg—which worked. When he was able to walk less and less with a cane, he got a job monitoring the foreign news at NBC, although he would always walk with a limp.

He had been "in it," and he signed up with the Victory Speaker's Bureau at the Office of War Information. The draft board reclassified him as 2-B. (His registration was deferred because of occupation in a war industry.) He was a popular speaker. In mid-February of 1943, just as the U.S. Army's II Corps and Rommel's Panzers were beginning the first full-fledged confrontation between the Americans and the Germans, he spoke to an audience at the Plaza Hotel alongside Sir Owen Dixon, Australian ambassador to the United States.

By the spring of 1944, my father was married to Marjory Luce Hill, with a child (me) on the way. He put aside his war book and began writing for the crusading liberal newspaper *PM*. He covered the Hyde Park burial of FDR, V-E Day, the dropping of the bomb, Japan's surrender, and the formation of the United Nations. In 1945, with another child on the way, the Bowen family left 144 West Twelfth Street for a small Greenwich Village townhouse nearby. By 1948, my father was carrying the mounting stresses of being associate editor and senior reporter for a newspaper that had been losing money, was rumored about to be sold, and for whom popular support for its left-wing liberal editorial stances appeared to be waning. In 1948, the paper folded and he obtained a position as a *New Yorker* staff reporter.

But soon the failure of the United Nations to prevent hostilities from breaking out along the Korean border, his long commute to Connecticut, where his wife, two girls, and a third child on the way were by then living, and the delayed effects of the trauma of being bombed all culminated in a nervous breakdown. Severely depressed, he lay for long weeks in Payne Whitney Psychiatric Clinic in Manhattan. On his release, he was advised only to take a vacation in Florida and then return to family life. He never completely recovered.

The trajectories of my father's private life and his work as a writer then diverged. In only three decades he created a considerable body of work. The meticulously researched psychological profiles of criminals in *They Went Wrong* (1954) and the groundbreaking documentation of the relationship between the plays and personal history of Eugene O'Neill in *The Curse of the Misbegotten* (1959), a National Book Award finalist, are his finest contributions. He also wrote prolifically for magazines. But his family life suffered, particularly after the tragic death of a toddler son. After his first heart attack in 1961, he returned to New York City to live alone. He pursued a passionate though brief affair after which he conducted a thorough Catholic "examination of conscience." He sought reconciliation with my mother, Marjory, but she would remarry. As mentioned in the foreword, the Vietnam War affected him deeply.

He survived two more heart attacks and went on to enjoy his Connecticut farm; a friendship with the folklorist and nonfiction author Carl Carmer and wife Betty, which began in the 1930s; and his three daughters. His brother Bill, who had divorced after the war and then worked for Radio Free Europe, returned to New York, remarried, and then left the U.S. in 1961 to live in Ireland and Spain. He would return to New York to die of cancer in 1968.

In my father's last years, he undertook a loudly bewailed stint of "writing only for money" in Madison Avenue public relations, which he called "being a paid liar for corporations." Returning to writing on subjects he believed in, he published in the *Atlantic* and the *New York Times*. He began work on a semiautobiographical novel and revived correspondence with Supreme Court Justice Felix Frankfurter, whose mentorship had shaped his ideals about the role of journalism in a democracy. In 1971, at the age of 66, he died of a heart attack in his New York apartment.

APPENDIX A:

An Essay on Photography

My father finished the following essay after returning from the war, although he may have begun it while working as a photojournalist in the late 1930s in New York. Ideas in it inform the photographs and commentary he planned to publish as "Sun, Sand, and Sorrow" in the first section of *Back from Tobruk*. Whereas the second part, the memoir which he called his "Diary," was to contain his subjective feelings and impressions, "Sun, Sand, and Sorrow" was to be objective. Into it, he had put key images around which he had written a "word track" that expanded the stories the images told. Such had been the style of *Great River of the Mountains* (1941), the book of prose and photographs on the Hudson River he published before he left for the war.

The images my father chose for his war book were his favorites among all the many negatives he exposed and developed in the field, probably using the bathtub in Shepheard's Hotel as a developing tray. Back at home, he made some of them into 8.5" x 11" prints and mounted them on paperboard in preparation for the publication of his memoir, which never happened. My sisters and I would come upon them from time to time in the barn of our Connecticut farm. Then the barn was sold, and the photographs, along with the negatives, disappeared.

I remember finding some of the mounted photographs and bringing them out to my father to ask about them. Behind his brief answer was an ocean of feeling. There was pride in having done what it took to create them. There was mild nostalgia, but no great bitterness at having put aside his former calling as a photographer. He was at peace with himself, relieved that he had managed to trade the more physically demanding, travel-intense yet less remunerative work of a photojournalist for that of a writer, reporter, and father. He had simply moved on to another way of "making a contribution." "Making a contribution" was how he defined a life well-lived. What mattered to him was that he was still able to do that.

It has long been a strong conviction with me that a modern reporter should simultaneously make use of the camera and the notebook. They are the newest and oldest instruments for recording impressions.

During the twelve years after I got out of college in 1929, I tried to do many things. I was a newspaper reporter, a salesman, an advertising copywriter, and one of the unemployed. I have used a camera as far back as I can remember, but always as a toy. Then I took a course under a brilliant photographer, Berenice Abbott, and an entire world was opened up for me.* I learned about Eugène Atget, a forgotten French documentary photographer of sixty years ago, whose negatives were rescued from oblivion quite by chance at an auction in Paris. His photographs of French life almost three quarters of a century ago turned out

---

* Berenice Abbott (1898–1991) was an important figure in the development of documentary photography. She championed "straight photography," refusing to manipulate or distort the image in the name of artistry or subjective "truth." She met and championed the work of Parisian photographer Eugène Atget (1857–1927), who documented that city with his camera, and upon returning from Paris to New York in 1933, she taught photography at the New School, where Bowen was her student.

to be historical truths, which inspired later documentary photographers to a full realization of their responsibilities.

After that, I began to see all the world as a location for my photographs and all the people in it as models. Farmers' freshly plowed fields were not rows of promised fertility, but possibilities for pattern shots to be photographed, preferably from a high tower or an airplane. The enjoyment most men experience in staring at a pretty girl was always somewhat spoiled for me because I was apt to look at her face in terms of eye socket shadows, distortions, highlights, skin texture—all the things that tend to make a woman take or not take a good picture. People often laughed when I'd be looking at a beautiful sunset or landscape with them and I'd say, "That would make a good photograph." I never seemed to care. Whenever I saw anything real happening—a street fight or a boy kissing a girl or a cop arresting somebody or an automobile accident—I saw these things telling the story in black and white, or maybe, when that day finally came, in full color.

A good documentary photographer tries to illustrate an idea, not just take nice pictures. If the picture also happens to be an artistic composition, he's in the money. Such a print can serve as a key picture, around which an entire story can be built. A photographer confronted with the problem of presenting, for example, a sociological island where a strange group of people lives may use a good decorative shot of the locality, perhaps framed by a limb of a tree with one of the group standing in the foreground as the key picture. Then he will get a picture showing how these people eat and sleep and pray, earn their bread, spend their leisure, how they dress, and how they move around. The things they say, the stories they tell, and the songs they sing have to be written down. In every picture, however, the idea that these people are different from other people must get across.

Photographers do get a distorted view of life, though. Human beings don't really behave as you'd expect when they're confronted with having their pictures taken. They get touchy, probably because the cameraman is a threat to their vanity. Sometimes, they're touchy for other reasons.

The most fatal thing a photographer can do is to take pictures at eye level. Sometimes, when he's hurried, it's necessary, but when possible he should try to place his camera high up or down on the ground. He must make his subjects rehearse doing what they were doing over and over again before he shoots them doing it entirely without self-consciousness. He may also have to wheedle them, persuade them, and even yell at them.

To get a good picture of an ocean liner docked at Fifty-Fourth Street in Manhattan, I photographed her through a life preserver hanging on one of the other decks. Some linemen were repairing a telephone pole, and I got them through a coil of wire. In New Orleans, grilled iron work on the balconies of the old houses is very characteristic of the old city and makes a superb screen through which to photograph the narrow streets and Creole houses. It's not a good idea to frame pictures for no reason, but if used, a frame ought to be a characteristic part of what is being photographed.

Probably, however, the most successful war picture ever made was a framed picture. All parades are apt to look as they have to look in news pictures: the same. But a photographer covering a routine assignment of an American Legion parade saw a spectator with one leg leaning on his crutch in such a way that his body and the crutch made an inverted V. In the center, a girl drum major was strutting in front of marching veterans. The picture didn't need any caption. It was printed everywhere.

Another technique, which stems from one of the basic rules of composition used in painting and etching, employs a person with the subject, be it landscape, a tragedy, or happy family. One news picture, which has been judged great, was of a woman who'd been hit by a car. She lay down on her back in the street. There are lots of photographs of people lying dead in the street but this one was great because the relative had just come along and, although he had his back turned to the camera, his whole body was limp with terror and grief. It's the same thing with the beautiful landscape or street scene—someone in the foreground responding to what is in the picture makes it better.

A widely reproduced photograph from the present war is one of two Medical Corps orderlies giving a plasma transfusion to a wounded American soldier. The idea of this picture had been done many times in America and overseas, but in this print there were three Italians looking on. An old woman looked at the soldiers with sadness and weariness. A girl of about sixteen diverted her glance to the skies, away from this unpleasant reality. A little girl of less than ten looked on with eager curiosity.

A professional photographer is somebody who can take pictures editors will buy and print. Most anyone can take snapshots, just as most anyone can turn out copy on a typewriter. But a professional must learn certain tricks that will make his pictures stand out among the bales of them piled on an editor's desk. To do this, he must acquire certain knacks: choosing carefully what he photographs, getting angles, making people do things, getting them to look unposed, and all the things that, if they go wrong, spoil his pictures. His skill in using cameras, light meters, films, and color filters must be as much taken for granted as that a reporter can take notes and pick news leads.

He must continually see everything as new and exciting, as if he'd never seen any of it before. He must love life and people with violent enthusiasm. Especially, he must love his work, because the financial rewards are very slim indeed. Even after he finds he has acquired a facility at getting marketable pictures, he is likely to feel frustrated by the confinement imposed by editors who are sure what the public wants and are responsible for the tripe that clutters up so many of the picture magazines.

Like an artist or writer or composer, he must make his way over one of two roads. He can do hackwork, like girls undressing, or people making fools of themselves, or faked up advertising shots. Then he will eat occasionally. Or, he can take pictures with a degree of integrity that satisfies some creative drive in him. Then he is assured to starve. And it's virtually impossible to do both.

APPENDIX B:

AFS Volunteers Who Gave Their Lives in North Africa and the Middle East, 1935–1945

George Rock, *History of the American Field Service*

Thomas Stretton Esten	(Western Desert)	April 29, 1942
George Oscar Tichenor	(Western Desert)	June 11, 1942
Stanley Blazei Kulak	(Western Desert)	June 11, 1942
William Keith McLarty	(Western Desert)	July 21, 1947
Arthur Paisley Foster	(Western Desert)	September 3, 1942
John Fletcher Watson	(At Sea)	December 4, 1942
Randolph Clay Eaton	(Western Desert)	March 25, 1943
John Hopkins Denison Jr.	(Western Desert)	March 27, 1943
August Alexander Rubel	(North Africa)	April 28, 1943
Richard Stirling Stockton	(North Africa)	April 28, 1943
Curtis Charles Rodgers	(Middle East)	May 1, 1943
Caleb Jones Milne IV	(North Africa)	May 11, 1943

ABOUT THE AUTHOR
AND EDITOR

Croswell Bowen wrote extensively for *PM*, the *New Yorker*, *Harper's*, *Town & Country*, and *Cosmopolitan*, among other publications, in the 1940s and 1950s. His books included the National Book Award–nominated *The Curse of the Misbegotten: A Tale of the House of O'Neill* (1959). He died in 1971.

Betsy Connor Bowen is Croswell Bowen's daughter. She has worked as a community organizer, elementary schoolteacher, college instructor and assistant professor, securities analyst, journalist, and filmmaker. She has a PhD in English and comparative literature and an MBA in finance. She has written academic articles, investment reports, short stories, local history, a novella (*Spring Bear*, Maine Literary Award 2010), and is currently writing a biography about her father. Dr. Bowen lives in Maine with her husband, a golden retriever, and a Maine coon cat, and serves on the boards of several organizations involved with filmmaking, the environment, and historic preservation.